BOMBS AND BOUGAINVILLEA

AN EXPAT IN JERUSALEM

L. E. DECKER

(WINNER OF THE SCOTTISH ASSOCIATION OF WRITERS
NON-FICTION BOOK OF THE YEAR 2018)

Published by Newport Press, London, 2020
Copyright © 2020 Linda Decker
Cover image copyright © 2020 Peter Lawrence
First Edition

Production and formatting by AntPress.org

Available in ebook, paperback and large print editions.

ISBN: 978-1-8381203-0-6 Paperback edition
ISBN: 978-1-8381203-1-3 Large Print edition

Some names, locations and identifying details have been changed to protect the privacy of individuals mentioned in the book.

This book is dedicated to my husband, Christian, and our children Liberty, Amber and Morgan. We have travelled the world together in love, with excitement and with too much baggage. And to my parents, May and Neil McCaffer, for encouraging me to believe anything was possible.

CONTENTS

BONUS MATERIAL—JEWISH CUSTOMS

INTRODUCTION

After living for eight wonderful years in Jordan, over ten years in the Arab world and two decades in Muslim countries in the Far and Middle East, in 2010 my family and I were relocated from Amman in Jordan to Jerusalem, a journey of only 80 kilometres.

For the first time in two decades of being a global nomad, I felt alien in my new host country. I did consider calling this book *Being Gentile with the Jews*, but that would place too much of an emphasis on religion. I had the opportunity to meet and get to know Israelis and Palestinians, Jerusalemites and Ramallahns, and to enjoy their food, celebrations, culture and ways of life.

I learnt about all sorts of Jews, the holidays, the matchmakers and the kaleidoscope of people, nationalities and beliefs, all of which make up modern-day Israel.

At a time when the Israelis and Palestinians live in parallel, with virtually no opportunity to experience how the other half lives, it's worth taking time to discover what day-to-day life is like for ordinary Israelis and Palestinians, and exploring the nation of Israel beyond the political rhetoric.

This is a personal account of life lived and observed both in Israel and in Palestine. It is anecdotal and not an academic or historical account. It was a privilege, a pleasure and at times a heartbreak to travel on this journey.

As Albert Einstein said: 'Peace cannot be kept by force. It can only be achieved by understanding.'

Linda Decker

THE CROSSING

We left Jordan on a hot evening in July, on the same night as the entire Jordanian population of Palestinian descent decided to visit their homeland for the summer holiday, or so it seemed. The Jordanian schools had broken up for the long summer vacation, and the border crossing between Jordan and Israel, known as the King Hussein Bridge on the Jordanian side and the Allenby Bridge on the Israeli side, was chaotic.

For a small fee (not that small), you could bypass quite a bit of the bedlam. I had detailed instructions to part with $100 per person, the fee necessary to get a VIP pass, to make the crossing with my son, Morgan. Morgan was made in Jordan and born in Jordan, his birth assisted by the late and truly wonderful Dr Patricia Quoran, otherwise known as the amazing Irish dancing doctor with the incredibly fast legs. 'And we can do Irish dancing in the delivery room too, if it helps!' she declared at our first antenatal appointment.

When you leave the Jordanian side of the crossing, you're segregated by nationality, and so we boarded a minibus with three other 'foreigners'—a charming Jordanian man and his wife, who were holders of Canadian passports, and a Filipino maid (who was travelling with a very glamorous Palestinian Jordanian employer called ma'am and two whining and noisy young children).

My heart stopped when ma'am (which rhymes with ham) was so busy barking out orders to the maid through the open window of the minibus that the children ran uncontrolled in front of an oncoming vehicle and were plucked onto the pavement by a well-meaning stranger. He was ignored and not thanked. Perhaps ma'am was just too preoccupied with the potential difficulties of the border crossing to notice the act of this good Samaritan in the Holy Land.

We'd waited in the Jordanian version of the VIP lounge for almost two hours, with no offer of the famous Jordanian hospitality and with flies buzzing around us. This wasn't the usual ambience or standard of service. There were no seats to be had. It was nearly seven o'clock in the evening and close to border closing time. I was anxious as I'd handed the keys of our rented villa in Amman back to the owner earlier in the afternoon and overseen the departure of our worldly goods onto two open, rickety trucks. No such thing as the secure shipping containers of past international moves. I was assured that all goods would be packed and palleted at the warehouse and that I wasn't to worry. As a very tall stranger with a theatrical Arab headdress (*kaffir*) and beard to match strolled through my house, it may have been slightly tetchy to enquire whether he was a sightseer or crew.

'No!' Our shipping company representative assured me with a relaxed smile on his ever-friendly face. 'He's the lead truck driver.'

After a cast of many had removed the boxes, I felt I could have left our worldly goods on the pavement outside and they would have been just as secure, there were so many boxes and so many people milling around inside and outside the house. At this point, I should make it clear that we'd engaged the services of one of the leading international shippers and movers in Jordan. They came highly recommended.

However at the border crossing, several busy hours later after trying to reclaim massive deposits for utility accounts (unsuccessfully), return our long-term rental car and manage the luggage which was to clothe and entertain us for however long it took the shipment to travel the 80 kilometres from Amman to Jerusalem, the only option was to wait patiently.

It was still as hot as Hades, although the huge orange sun had dipped and disappeared below the horizon which was veiled in a fine gauze of dust from the arid Jordan Valley. Tempers were fraying, and designer high-heeled shoes were being stamped by a certain ma'am who was left in sole charge of her little ones. The maid departed in the air-conditioned minibus, leaving behind two children wailing for her attention, and a shiny-faced employer.

As we prepared to drive off, ma'am yelled through the open window, 'Whatever happens, do NOT let them stamp your passport. You must tell them that you need it to travel to the Gulf.'

So there we have it. The first problem a foreign visitor will face when entering Israel is the prospect of an entry stamp on a shiny and expensive passport, which will make you an unwelcome visitor to many countries. In fact it's impossible to visit some countries at all if you have such a stamp in your collection.

At this point in the journey, I was surprisingly relaxed. When I'd visited Israel earlier in the year to look at schools and hunt for a house, I was given precisely those orders.

'Do not let them stamp your passport; ask them to stamp a piece of paper.'

Well I did, and they did, stamp my passport I mean. So it doesn't matter now. I may need to go to the trouble and expense of getting a new passport if I ever want to visit my old friends and our former home in Dubai. We did still own a house there but had decided to rent it out in the hope that it might recover in value following the global recession and crash in property values.

I couldn't help wondering how the diminutive Filipino would fare. I feared she was in for a hard night.

The Jordanian man-and-wife team were experts at this crossing. Having deftly grabbed the only remaining luggage porter for hire, the husband then very gallantly helped me with our two massive suitcases, while I grappled with chaotically packed hand baggage and tried to fix Morgan's guitar case on his back.

The funny thing is, within ten minutes of getting on the minibus, we knew how long the Jordanian couple had been married, where they lived in Amman and where their kids went to university (it transpired that one of their sons worked with my friend's husband in the Hyatt Hotel in Dubai). This was information they weren't willing to share with the Israeli immigration authorities.

We were shown into the VIP lounge on the Israeli side of the border, which was air conditioned and furnished with comfortable modern red sofas, computers with internet, a coffee machine, chilled water and magazines. A young girl in military uniform, who was about the age of our daughter, Liberty, who was twenty at the time, then asked which of us were travelling together. Our new Jordanian friend and self-appointed spokesman replied, 'None of us is; we are all travelling separately.' I piped up that I was in fact travelling with my nine-year-old son, but as it turned out, perhaps I shouldn't have.

You need a tremendous amount of patience to make that crossing. As we sat in the VIP lounge, we looked at the hundreds of people who were waiting to be interviewed by immigration officials and who were being herded like cattle just outside the door. I wondered whether it was left open deliberately to infuriate those who had no possibility of a comfortable seat and had a very long wait ahead. I recognised some faces in the queue from the VIP lounge on the Jordanian side. And here's the thing. Although you've paid for the service, it seems you can't avoid the long lines on the Israeli side unless you have a foreign (i.e. non-Palestinian) passport. The little Filipino maid squirmed in her comfortable upholstered seat as her boss stood for hours on impossibly high heels, waiting to be granted entry.

The Jordanian couple were cleared for entry and waving their goodbyes relatively quickly. They'd been interviewed separately, as strangers, and this was a strategy which had clearly worked.

I was called back for a second interview with the immigration authorities.

'Yes, I've visited before, and I'm back for another visit.'

'Yes, I do have accommodation to stay in.'

'Yes, I'm staying courtesy of my husband's employers who are providing furnished accommodation.'

'Where?'

'Ramallah.'

So after three hours of waiting, during which time Morgan had performed an impromptu guitar concert due to popular demand, I had my third interview with immigration.

'Yes, my son was born in Amman, Jordan.'

'And your husband is Palestinian?'

I was tired and confused. 'No, he's British.'

'Not Palestinian?' the fresh-faced immigration official probed.

'No, definitely British.'

'Can you prove that?'

Call me naïve but I thought that as a holder of a British passport myself, Her Majesty Queen Elizabeth II had politely asked that I be granted permission to enter the country on my own account. You can hear her scary and slightly stern voice uttering the words which we all have on the first page of our British passports: 'Her Britannic Majesty's Secretary of State requests and requires in the name of Her Majesty all those whom it may concern to allow the bearer to pass freely without let or hindrance, and to afford the bearer such assistance and protection as may be necessary.'

No qualification that all of the above is dependent upon the nationality of her husband. I don't remember ever discussing the nationality of my husband, Chris, on previous sojourns around the globe. However, I sensed that running that argument wouldn't be particularly fruitful, so I invited the young border official to telephone my husband. He was waiting for us in a vehicle at the outer boundary of border control. My mobile phone was of course blocked for security reasons. It was impossible for me to make contact with Chris (or anyone for that matter) to let him know what was going on and why the delay.

We'd been detained for an extra three hours on the basis of a misunderstanding that if a child was born in Amman and was travelling with his British mother, his father must be Palestinian. To be frank I don't think my passport photo helped either. I was sporting a very Jordanian hairdo, my signature style for the previous ten years—a shoulder-length straight bob with a little volume—courtesy of my hairdresser, Mr Ghaleb.

We were asked to resume our seats in the VIP lounge. I've never been so grateful we weren't standing. The queue was still long, and a very old and elegant Arab gentleman, who was wearing an eclectic mix of Savile Row tailoring and *kaffir*, and who must have been 80 years old if he was a day, was being pushed back with the herd which had pressed forwards a foot too far. It was easy to see how tempers might fray and difficult scenes could lead to outbreaks of harsh control.

There was such animosity and suspicion from both sides of the border that night, it was amazing to think that the word peace was on the agenda. Just for the record, there's a peace treaty between Jordan and Israel.

Over five hours after setting out on our 80-kilometre journey, Morgan and I entered Israel and were glad to part with 100 new Israeli shekels (about $25) for the three-minute, hair-raising ride through the moonscape of no man's land from the Customs hall to the perimeter fence of the crossing point. For security reasons only specifically licenced taxis are allowed to provide the very short ride to the outer edge of this strictly controlled area. Needless to say you're not allowed to walk. My British husband was still waiting for us. But the 100-shekel note he'd given us in advance to pay for this set-fare journey (such a rip-off, and the first of many) was firmly rejected as a forgery, a common problem apparently. Another acceptable note was fished out of Chris's wallet. We've since watched a documentary which suggested that some unscrupulous taxi drivers in other parts of the world use this ruse to get forged bank notes into circulation, deftly switching the original bank note for a fake and asking for another real one. I have no idea where the forged note originated from that night.

Thankfully, and by huge coincidence, Chris had been much cheered by the sight of some well-drilling rig equipment finally being cleared through Customs and setting off on the road to the West Bank. It had been held up at that border by the Israeli authorities for months and was needed for an infrastructure project he was working on. This was to be one of the many frustrations in delivering projects on schedule and budget in an Occupied Territory where there would always be circumstances beyond your control. It was a risky business in more ways than one.

We jumped into the Jeep, kindly provided by his employers to facilitate its programme of USAID work in the West Bank, and drove into the night towards Ramallah, our temporary home.

A friend of a friend wrote a poem after reading of the initial difficulties we encountered on the Israeli side of the King Hussein Bridge.

Linda's Moving Saga

The Lord's city is so pretty,
Thought Linda as she drove,
Swapping sand and barren land
For light and olive grove.

Full of smiles, eating the miles
In her air-conned car,
Linda dreamed as Jerusalem gleamed
And welcomed from afar.

Nearing the border, all was in order,
Jordan was nearly past.
Over the ridge of Allenby Bridge,
The Holy Land at last.

Linda thought, *This is like sport.*
I'm really going places.
A word or two, they'll let me through.
I'll even beat my cases!

As Linda slowed, a young guard strode
To where her car was stopped.
'Papers, please.' No charming ease,
And Linda's light heart dropped.

Otherwise, through sapphire skies,
Her luggage made its way.
At the border the guard floored her
When Linda heard him say,

'It seems to me, though from GB,
There is a little quirk.
Your hair's not by Toni & Guy,
More Kemel Atatürk.

'I must confess, though you profess
From Scotland so to be,
Your bouffant lines put me in mind
Of a Jordanian lady.'

It's very hard when a border guard
Questions your coiffure.
AND your cases are going places
They've never been before!

Three long hours with the powers
That patrol that border point
Left Linda reeling; her hair feeling
Most put out of joint.

These great stresses with her tresses
Were at last forgot.
Accelerating, ire abating,
Shouting, 'I'm a SCOT.'

Full steam ahead, our Linda sped,
Testing the car's traction.
While up in space, each well-packed case
Became 'missing in action'.

As dusk's sweet gloam silvered the Dome
In Jerusalem's great city,
Linda arrived, thought, *I've survived.*
Braveheart's got naught on me!

She's sitting pretty, in that city,
With a capsule wardrobe.
This clothing state will not abate
While her luggage roams the globe.

For Linda's part her steadfast heart
Her annoyance will repair,
And we will smile a goodly while
About her bouffant hair!

Annie B

2

THE WALL

The move transpired to be the most challenging we've ever encountered. We were truly, in the words of the British passport, 'without let or hindrance'. No rental property and no furniture.

The idyllic house we'd so luckily found on the moshav (an Israeli village) in the outskirts of Jerusalem slipped from our grasp on more than one occasion. We were led to believe that the landlord's lawyer harboured a deep suspicion of foreigners. I wondered whether he was a real lawyer, which of course he was and is (Israelis can be litigious, so I have to make that clear). We'd just reached the conclusion that we faced the depressing task of revisiting the Jerusalem property market when common sense prevailed.

Chris, who was based in Ramallah, West Bank, at the time, simply refused to deal with the Jerusalem-based lawyer any more. He spoke to the landlord direct, and we had an agreement that same day. Apart from the sound negotiating tactics employed, I'm convinced that Reiki Master Julia's manifesting on our behalf while I was still in Amman didn't hurt either. She'd called me just as the deal had fallen through and detected the dejection in my voice. Julia instructed me to drive out to the International Community School near Amman for the afternoon school run while she got down to the serious business of manifesting on our behalf. I think this involved some heavy-duty meditation. By the time I got home, Chris had telephoned from Ramallah to say the deal was back on. Julia, if you're reading this, I would like to win the lottery.

We'd rented a stone villa on the edge of the Jerusalem Forest for one year, with an option to extend for a second. The villa had a large wooden deck with panoramic views of a lush valley, and green parrots swooping around the garden, but no furniture.

Finding the right school for Morgan within daily commuting distance of Ramallah was a high priority which was why we chose Jerusalem as our base. The only schools which taught a curriculum in English for his age group were there. We had a choice between the Anglican School and the secular Jerusalem American International School (JAIS). We chose the latter because it was small, nurturing and set in the Goldstein Youth Village campus, which was a green and leafy, undulating park, both tranquil and totally walled in from the outside world. The Youth Village was home to several schools, a basketball pitch, a gymnasium and a swimming pool. It wasn't the tales of body parts being collected from the grounds of the Anglican School during the Intifada (Palestinian uprising) of 2000 which swayed our decision.

We all spent a month together in Ramallah while waiting for our house, and latterly our shipment of assorted treasure (other family members call it junk but, believe me, it's all in the category of antiques of the future) to be delivered by road from Amman via the Allenby Bridge. Chris had spent longer in Ramallah as he'd been based in the West Bank since the spring, popping back and forth to Amman for the weekends with family and friends. After the move he would begin a new daily commute to work between Jerusalem and Ramallah.

The first shock in visiting Ramallah was travelling through Qalandia, the site of a massive checkpoint terminal and Palestinian refugee camp. It's without doubt one of the most depressing travel experiences on the planet.

There's a security wall between the West Bank and Israel, and I imagine it looks a bit like the Berlin Wall used to before it was torn down. Looming above a traveller are vast slabs of grey concrete, cast like the giant keys of a xylophone standing on end and laid side by side for kilometres, over 600 kilometres in fact. The wall is eight metres high and grim. Add heavily armed soldiers, razor wire and checkpoints to the depressing cocktail.

'One wall, two prisons,' Chris observed, as we sat in an endless queue to cross back to Ramallah one evening.

Israelis aren't permitted to travel in and out of certain areas of the West Bank, and with few exceptions, Palestinians aren't allowed to travel into Israel. If they do want to go, they need to apply for a permit well in advance. This may or may not be granted and is time restricted. We had dinner with a Palestinian chief executive officer of an international company in Jerusalem. His permit meant that he had to be back on the other side of the wall by ten that evening. As we had a lot of socialising to do, we started dinner at six. This is totally contrary to the Arab culture of eating late and no rushing through proceedings. Arabic meals tend to unfold in layers and over the whole evening. Food isn't to be hurried through with one eye on the clock.

Cars carrying yellow licence plates (Israeli) are allowed to pass between the West Bank and Israel, but green-plated Palestinian-registered vehicles cannot and must stay in the Palestinian Occupied Territory.

'So,' our Israeli relocation agent asked with interest, 'what are things like in Ramallah?'

Well, the short answer is that it's a bustling city with cafés, bakeries, a lively market and family-owned shops and businesses. From handmade silver jewellery to fresh honey, there are always serendipitous finds for the determined shopper.

In order to get to Ramallah, you have to cross the bandit territory of the Qalandia checkpoint, one of the few crossing points. The approach and exit roads are single lane only, but in true Arab style, nobody wants to queue. So what happens is one smart Hassan (a popular boy's name meaning 'horse' in Arabic) will get impatient and overtake, although the queue is solid to the checkpoint. He'll meet a bus or a truck or another car coming in the opposite direction, and suddenly nothing moves until he, and all the other cars which have followed his lead, edge back into the single lane. This can only happen as the cars get through the checkpoint. They would pass through with reasonable efficiency if not for the horrendous traffic jams on the other side, after the checkpoint has been cleared. That's when you truly enter the Wild West Bank. The one-and-a-half-kilometre stretch of road after checkpoint clearance is totally lawless and disorganised. It gets logjammed with people deciding to cut the queue and just drive on the wrong side of the road or around the roundabout the wrong way. Sometimes a Wild West motorist will get creative and make a third lane out of a one-lane carriageway or simply drive across the huge roundabout instead of around it, thereby cutting the wait. When you get through the O.K. Corral, as I've affectionately called it, you then run the gauntlet of cars driving down the dual carriageway the wrong way to save making a U-turn a kilometre up the road. Or better still, in the dark with no headlights. If you survive the other drivers, you need to watch out for the potholes. Small vehicles could disappear in some of them. Junk is strewn everywhere, and it's nothing short of a chaotic mess. A stark contrast to the tree-lined streets and neatness on the other side of the wall.

To be fair, the area around this checkpoint is in effect a no man's land. It's controlled by the Israeli military, and I'm not sure whether the people who live and work around it would be permitted to get it cleared up. It was depressing to drive through on a daily basis, so I can't even imagine what it's like to live your life within sight of it. The refugee camp has been established there since 1949, a lifetime for some of its residents.

In Ramallah we were put up in a beautiful, bright, clean, modern and spacious apartment, well-furnished and equipped. Another advantage was the proximity of our bedroom window to the mullah's loudspeaker at the local mosque; we never missed a prayer time. There are five a day, and the first one of the day, usually at around four in the morning, is particularly useful if you're getting up for work at seven.

Our neighbour upstairs clippity-clopped across marble floors in high heels. What is it with Arab women and stilettos? She never took them off. She clip-clopped around until the small hours every night, which would have been very annoying had her young children not been running and shouting all over the building until two in the morning at the very earliest anyway. The summer days are hot, so most playing around and exercise is taken at night, with families staying up late and sleeping late in the morning. It was this experience which set my mind firmly against having an apartment if our slice of paradise on the moshav fell through again.

Ramallah, home of the Palestine Liberation Organisation (PLO) headquarters and forever associated with the late Yasser Arafat, is an attractive town with hidden treasures. I was surprised, mainly in a good way, by the choice of restaurants and the quality of the food, from the wood-oven pizza restaurant, which overlooked a small city park, to the international restaurant in the mature and leafy garden of the Royal Court Suites Hotel. It was so pleasant and relaxing there, you could be anywhere in the world. There was an abundance of lovely places to eat delicious Arabic food, drink, and smoke a hubbly-bubbly pipe. But be warned, although these water pipes smell like fruit, one hubbly-bubbly session delivers the equivalent in carcinogens of many, many cigarettes. If you ever happen to be passing through Ramallah in need of a good feed, my favourite Arabic restaurant in this town was Darna. My favourite passive smoke was cherry-flavoured tobacco. It's hard to avoid passive smoking in public places in the Arab world.

After you'd passed through the security wall and shaken off the neglect, dust and dirt of the surrounding area, you entered normal life. Families in Ramallah shopped, cooked and went to work and school. They also bought kilos of the most delicious dark-burgundy cherries which were heaped high on wooden street carts and peddled loudly by the cheery cherry vendors. The fruit on sale from mobile cart vendors changed depending on the time of year. In May the watermelons were piled high; in June it was dark-cherry time.

The supermarkets were well stocked, with the usual assortment of heads, tails and anything in between hung in butchers' shop windows. Sweet shops were as tempting as ever, offering thread-dough concoctions which looked like birds' nests, liberally peppered with pistachio nuts and soaked in sugar syrup. *Kanafeh* (hot cheese) was also a popular and delicious dessert, but I've been told by more than one person that the best *kanafeh* comes from the Nablus area, about 50 kilometres north of Jerusalem. I had Nablus *kanafeh* twice, hand-carried to Jerusalem and Bethlehem by natives of Nablus. It was good but quite a distance to drive for the Arab equivalent of a cheesecake dessert.

The café scene was vibrant, and on a Thursday night, the night before the Muslim Friday holiday, the streets were packed with families having a hugely sociable time. There was a lot of strolling, shopping, buying falafels, and eating shawarma sandwiches stuffed with chicken or beef freshly shaved from a rotating spit and stuffed in bread with salad, brightly coloured pickled vegetables and sauces of your choice. There was also a lot of noisy kissing on a busy Arab street, and that was just the men. The kissing was usually followed by a hand-on-the-heart gesture delivered with touching sincerity.

There was no shortage of wine, beer and spirits for sale, and if you were an expatriate on a well-paid posting, it was a great place to spend some time and a lot of money.

Downtown Ramallah reminded me very much of the Rainbow Street conservation area of Amman before it was renovated and restored. It was charming, with traditional pale stone villas and flowering gardens overflowing with bougainvillea, and not at all what I'd expected.

In the Arab world, a great deal of care and attention was given to the sanctuary of the family home and the cultivation of colourful and often beautifully scented gardens. Little or no attention was paid to anything beyond the garden wall. It was a cultural difference we were to notice time and again as we saw the neat sidewalks and communal spaces in our moshav.

We found the West Bank prices shocking. The cost of a very simple meal out was $100 for two adults and one child. (Morgan did have a big appetite but no bigger than most energetic boys of his age.) This level of bill was well out of the budget of most Ramallahns. Even a take-away tacky burger meal cost between 40 and 50 shekels per person and a loaf of bread between 14 and 18 shekels. There were approximately four shekels to the US dollar at the time, and six to British sterling. The currency in the Occupied Territories is the new Israeli shekel (NIS), which I found surprising at first. I'd expected an Arab currency, maybe a dinar or a dirham, but not an Israeli shekel.

There were small supermarkets which offered many of the goods sold on the other side of the wall. My favourite yogurt cost ten shekels in Ramallah but the same yogurt cost twelve in Jerusalem, where the cost of living was even more expensive. I found a jar of pasta sauce in Ramallah which I usually kept for emergencies, but even I put it back as it cost more than 25 shekels! If we were finding it hard to shop at these prices, how did the average Palestinian family manage?

The only major shortages were expensive expatriate needs most locals would have overcome.

I ran out of my usual daily disposable contact lenses and went into an optician's shop to buy any brand at all which was in my prescription.

'There are no disposable contact lenses in Palestine,' the very helpful and friendly optician told me.

Surprising when half an hour's drive away in Jerusalem there was a wide choice of lenses, both local and well-known international brands.

The other problem appeared to be the supply of medication. I needed to fill a prescription for blood pressure medication, which I would definitely be stocking up on if I was going to make the journey through the checkpoint on a regular basis. I went to the 24-hour pharmacy on my way home one night, but it was closed. When I caught the pharmacy open at ten thirty the next morning, the pharmacist had half a box of my regular medication in stock, having split it and sold the other half. I took it, and he ordered more in for the next day. It was expensive, and I guess some patients bought it in two-weekly supplies.

Oh, and just in case you were wondering, I clarified that the 24-hour pharmacy in Ramallah was open from around 9.30 a.m. until closing time, maybe around nine or ten in the evening, *inshallah* (Arabic for by the grace of God, by God's will). When I lived in Jordan, the term *inshallah* was used all the time. If you dropped off a film for developing by speedy twelve-hour service, and if you clarified that if you drove all the way back into town to get your photographs, they would be ready in twelve hours, the predictable response was always, '*Inshallah*.' It was the same story with the dry cleaning, '*Bukra inshallah*,' being the usual response, 'Tomorrow, by the will of God.' It certainly reduces stress levels when the responsibility for all deadlines and opening times is passed up to the highest authority.

So if you were a well-paid expatriate, life in Ramallah was fine. If you were a wealthy Palestinian, life in Ramallah was fine. If, like the majority of Palestinians, you weren't well-paid or wealthy, day-to-day life was challenging to say the least.

There are no airports in the West Bank. Jerusalem airport was closed by the Israeli authorities at the time of the second Palestinian uprising. The Palestinians who are permitted to leave need to travel across the King Hussein Bridge and drive to Amman if they want to fly anywhere. This is assuming they're able to obtain the permits necessary to leave the West Bank and transit through Jordan. Palestinians aren't permitted to fly out of Ben Gurion International Airport in Tel Aviv with a few very rare exceptions. There are no direct flights between Israel and a list of countries in the Middle East, including the United Arab Emirates and Lebanon.

I find it very hard to imagine living in a world in which I can't travel if I want to. I think of all the trips to see Gran, Grandpa and Granny, aunties, uncles and cousins, the summers in Europe, Easters in the USA with Chris's dad and his wife. It's difficult if my car goes in for a service and my travel wings are clipped, so it must be sickening to lose that precious freedom of movement, and of course that's the least of the losses you suffer every day when living under occupation.

Apart from the border and boundary issues, the lack of opportunities and hope, coupled with the cost of living, make life a struggle for most.

After a whole month of camping in our smart, if noisy, apartment, eating out and waiting for the Israeli lawyer to organise a completion meeting at his convenience (we've bought properties which took less time and trouble than this one-year extendable lease), we had a house and a delivery date for our shipment. Our real life in Israel and Palestine was about to begin.

Word of the day: shukran — thank you (Arabic)

3

THE MOVE

Our shipment was fumigated (this is standard procedure apparently and in no way a reflection on my housekeeping abilities). It was also taxed although most of it was tatty and tired like its owners felt after an interesting interview on the fringes of Ben Gurion International Airport with an Israeli Customs officer. This provided a good excuse for a trip to IKEA and collecting a trolley full of life's essentials, not to mention a couple of dozen meatballs between us for lunch. Disappointingly there was no loganberry sauce served with them as it wasn't certified as kosher, we were told.

We had an appointment with a short, lean, tanned, late middle-aged and straight-faced Israeli official who obviously loved his job. How many of you know what make your television set is? Or its dimensions? Do you know the cubic capacity of your refrigerator? I spotted a smallish guy strolling past the office in overalls, and at this point said sensibly to our interrogator, 'The fridge is about his size. I have no idea of the make, but I can, without question, confirm its colour.'

The ice melted a bit, and the stern-faced official launched into a detailed conversation about toasters, mixers, microwaves and more stuff I had no clue about. Functional things you never think about unless they break and you need to replace them.

We then spent a good ten minutes on our bikes, so to speak.

'Do you have any bicycles in the shipment?'

'Yes, we have five of them.'

'What sort of bikes are they?'

'Four adult bikes, second-hand, hybrids, nothing special and one child's bike,' offered Chris. 'Why, are bikes taxable?' he asked, on point as usual.

'No, they aren't. I was just wondering if you had any.'

A virtually imperceptible raising of one eyebrow from my husband, and we were straight onto the fascinating arena of our carpets. I don't know if the chap was efficient or just nosey, but it took a while.

Import tax is very high, so if you're planning to move there, think carefully about what you'll bring. It's worth remembering that the voltage is European, so none of the American voltage appliances will work without transformers. I know from experience that our Yamaha Clavinova piano began to smoke when used without a transformer. As we live in a no-blame culture in our family, I won't name names.

On the day we were to receive our shipment, Chris had to be at work in the West Bank but had kindly agreed to drive me to collect my new hire car from East Jerusalem in the Arab side of town. It had rally stickers all over it, with waving chequered flags. A bit embarrassing really as I don't drive that fast. It also had a whiff of fuel, and I was warned to go straight to a petrol station in French Hill, a residential neighbourhood nearby which I'd never been to before. Why can't car hire firms put just a little fuel in a car, and why does it always have to be so nerve-racking? I took the wheel and drove off into unknown territory to find the petrol station and just made it without running out of petrol. Visions of removers sitting outside in the baking sun at our new house and me causing a traffic jam evaporated away. Petrol, surprise, surprise, was expensive there compared to Jordan which had, until relatively recently, imported heavily subsidised fuel from Iraq.

After paying a considerable number of shekels, literally hundreds, I leapt into the car in a cheerful frame of mind, congratulating myself on my driving, navigation and generally on my bravery. That was when I received the next cold shower. The car wouldn't start. Like most newish cars in Israel, it had an engine immobiliser. I cleverly flipped down the visor, as that was where the code was hidden in Chris's rental car. No luck. I phoned the rental company, but the telephone was constantly engaged. I ignored the queue forming behind me at the petrol pump during rush hour, and then called my other half.

'Try looking behind the visor,' he suggested helpfully.

Morgan pointed out that there were some numbers on the key ring which was dangling from the ignition, and hey presto, we fired up the engine and were on our way to our new house in sunny Beit Zayit, which means House of Olives in Hebrew.

The shipment made it across the Allenby Bridge quite quickly, and we were hopping from foot to foot as it crept into our line of vision and made its way slowly but surely through the Jerusalem Forest and into our moshav.

Our excitement was only slightly dampened when we saw that the massive wooden crates had been spray-painted 'Dicker' everywhere which our nine-year-old thought was a bit rude and hugely funny.

The crew were unbelievably strong. One man carried our piano on his back from the truck, down a flight of stairs to our garden and into the house. The men worked incredibly hard in high heat in the middle of the day. Unfortunately the moving company had allowed one day to unload and unpack a shipment which had taken three days to pack and load on the other side of the Dead Sea, and five days to do a proper job in Dubai on a previous move. The team did what they could but left a shambles and mountains of packed boxes behind.

Boxes were missing, furniture broken and a precious carpet slashed with a Stanley knife when it was unpacked from its paper wrapping with ill feeling at the end of a long hot day. We'd never had a move like it and hoped never to have another one.

The final straw was when the supervisor insisted on turning on the fridge so we could all have cold water. I raised the alarm when it started smoking. The movers had failed to remove the packing paper inside before turning it on. What a crew!

There was nothing for it but to drive back to Ramallah at the end of a long, hot, tiring day and try to move into the house at a later date.

To round off a not-so-perfect day, a motorist ran into the back of my new hire car at a crossroads in the West Bank. He didn't even have the courtesy to get out of his shiny Mercedes. I got out of my car and infuriated him by suggesting a modicum of care would be appropriate in the future. My feeling was that the young Arab stallion wasn't used to being talked to in this way by a woman, far less by a woman in a Kia. Fortunately there was no damage, except to my eardrums after his rude and ungallant reply. I bit my tongue and was relieved to reach home, which is what we called the apartment in Ramallah then.

On day two, following some firm conversations with the movers, they sent us a pair of carpenters in the evening, after they'd done a hard day's graft elsewhere in the heat of the long summer day. We'd hung around all day unpacking dozens of boxes and waiting for a little bit of help. When I say 'we', I mean 'me'. Chris had to go to work. The carpenters were charming and wanted to be helpful. They mended some of the broken stuff, unpacked books and failed to find the legs of several pieces of furniture. On the plus side, they brought two 'work-experience' boys (one of whom was the carpenter's nephew) who were around Morgan's age, and they all played happily in the garden with a football.

I then spent the next several days on my own, unpacking our remaining boxes and sourly reflecting that it was a good job so much stuff had gone missing or I would never have finished.

Words of the day: mazal tov — congratulations (Hebrew)

4

THE MOSHAV

I woke up well rested to a spectacular first morning. This was timed to coincide with the weekend so we could all sleep well, settle in and enjoy the new surroundings.

Houses in Jerusalem are smaller than their Amman counterparts, and our large four-poster bed was asserting its territory in a bedroom where every available space was filled with upended boxes which stood Stonehenge-style and were marked 'clothes'. Thankfully my handbags were in boxes which I'd cleverly labelled 'Chris's tools', or we would never have got through the door. Until the IKEA clothes racks and rails were assembled and installed in our walk-in wardrobe, this logjam would remain.

I'd tried to put together our new IKEA toilet brush sets the day before and was crestfallen to discover that I even needed a screwdriver for that job. First things first, find the tool box (the real one).

Although this was the first sleep in the new house, it was Saturday, the fifth day of unpacking 306 boxes (minus the ones still missing and unaccounted for).

The whole of our valley was covered in a grey mist. The day before had been the hottest day of summer so far and must have been in the high 30s, delivering a brutal, bright and relentless heat. The shutters had remained closed, and even at six in the evening, when all the doors and windows should have been thrown open for cool fresh breezes, the air was still too hot and heavy to let inside.

Our moshav nestled on the lower slopes of the Jerusalem Forest. From the deck at the front of the house, we had panoramic views of green rolling hills, poplar and fir trees and red-tiled roofs. Stunning vistas which reminded me of the views I'd enjoyed on holiday in the South of France. There was an air of Mediterranean affluence in this and the surrounding communities. We were treated to the sound of bird song, both in the wild and from our neighbour's aviary, all day long. This, coupled with the panoramic landscape and gentle smell of warm pine needles, created our little paradise on earth, an oasis of calm after the gruelling commutes to school and work through the traffic of the Wild West Bank and the chock-full roads of Jerusalem. This was to be our personal place of peace in this land of guns and roses.

From the backside the picture was entirely different. My wine merchant in the United Arab Emirates used to describe the rear end of his premises as 'the backside'. He once made the disturbing but thoughtful offer to serve me 'from the backside 24/7', almost but not quite putting me off my preferred New Zealand sauvignon blanc.

At the back of our house, which was the main entrance, there were old, beat-up cars parked on the other side of the road, and higgledy-piggledy steps leading up to what would be described as garden sheds in the more affluent parts of the UK. They were in fact family dwellings. There was even a shipping container which had been converted into a home. Tall, skinny, grumpy-looking young parents, who looked like they needed a decent meal, drove beat-up cars and went barefoot in baggy cotton, faded clothes. They passed in and out and never smiled. We were soon to discover that this was a trait. Israelis, in our experience, weren't great smilers compared to other nationalities. The Balinese get my vote for the most smiley people in the whole wide world, in case you're interested.

Our moshav fell into two distinct parts—the original land where the garden sheds, allotments and chickens lived, and the new section which had been sold off to bring in some money. On the part which had been sold off, large new villas had been built, with varying degrees of extravagance. Ours was bright, simple and modern in design, but we had neighbours who had hand-painted frescos and clouded ceilings crying out for cherubs. Michelangelo would have been proud of their ceilings. We rented the house from a local businessman. His family own a chain of coffee shops across Jerusalem and beyond. I'd counted many outlets, so our rent wasn't their only source of income.

Many residents in the newly built homes worked in Jerusalem and weren't agriculturalists. There were also artists and crafters living in this beautiful little community. What was yet to become clear was how such a diverse mix of people rubbed along together.

I was wary of the true moshavniks as they seemed extremely poor and careworn. There was a considerable discrepancy between what they had and what the average commuter living on and enjoying the benefits of the lifestyle had. The haves and have nots. I was also concerned about our garden furniture—Balinese teakwood items which were at least fifteen years old but had grown into the fashionable description of shabby chic (more shabby than chic), an antique Arabic tile frieze, a lucky duck which was a cast-iron, life-sized image of the real thing, a milestone birthday present and tormentor of the local cat population. Even the cheap plastic chairs sold in all the hardware shops were expensive in Israel, and I'd seen nothing like our collection of well-worn wooden garden chairs and tables which had been bought straight from the carpentry workshop in Ubud, Bali, where the craftsmen had sat cross-legged, creating the most intricate wood carving. But I digress.

Most of our neighbours had dogs, and security signs written in Hebrew hung from their garden gates. I'd asked the estate agent to translate them. I felt very security conscious in this quiet leafy village, but perhaps that was natural when you were uprooted from a familiar patch and transplanted to a strange environment, until the time came when it wasn't so strange.

We sat on our deck as the mist lifted and the bright blue skies of another day were contrasted against the green trees of the beautiful forest. Green parrots flew overhead and landed in our neighbour's jacaranda tree, preening their vibrant feathers.

As this was the Jewish Sabbath, all was quiet. We were still amazed by the phenomenon that is Shabbat, as the Sabbath is called in Israel.

We were shopping one day in one of the busiest shopping centres in the country, the Jerusalem Mall, on a Friday afternoon. It was packed full of people. The sort of full you see in the UK when it's Christmas Eve and everyone's surprised that there's only one day to go, despite the fact that the retail countdown has been going on since October.

Apart from the international chain stores like Mango, Pull&Bear and Zara, there were small stalls everywhere selling handmade jewellery, hats (always very popular in Israel), olive soaps, cakes and sweets, hand-painted ceramics, chocolate goodies and flowers. Flowers are a must-have on the Sabbath and are on sale in every mall and even from pop-up pavement vendors. It was the tradition for a husband to take flowers home for his wife on a Friday. This tradition I liked. The cafés were all full to bursting, and it was hard to get a seat and then to get served. All of the cafés and bakeries sell what we called Shabbat bread. It's called challah in Hebrew, and families carry multiple loaves of the delicious, freshly baked, light and white plaits of the stuff home. The loaves are usually covered with poppy or sesame seeds, and at nine shekels for a huge loaf, were a weekly bargain and a tasty treat.

Traditionally the Shabbat meal begins with the blessing of two loaves of challah. The blessing is called *Kadosh* in Hebrew. I know this because one of the loveliest cafés we found on Jaffa Street, Jerusalem, and which wouldn't be out of place in Paris, was called *Kadosh*, and being curious, I asked what it meant. The religious significance of the two loaves is that when the Jews fled Egypt and spent 40 years wandering in the desert, they received manna from heaven, but not apparently on Shabbat or holidays. So the bread signified the manna from heaven and the double quantity because there would be no manna on Shabbat.

At three o'clock on a Friday afternoon, when the shops were heaving and everyone had been at work all week, the shopping centre closed. All shoppers left, and the Jewish ones went home to make final preparations for the Jewish holy day which starts at sunset on Friday and ends at sunset on Saturday.

In Jerusalem the siren is sounded, indicating the beginning of the Sabbath. It's the same siren which is sounded if there are incoming rockets, so it's wise to remember it's Friday and that the siren will go off at sunset.

As Chris got Friday and Saturday off work, this meant he had approximately half a day of his weekend when anything was actually open. All shops, without fail, closed in Jerusalem, and all public transport stopped. We also learnt, when we were dangerously low on fuel (it's a habit of mine), that the petrol pumps were switched off at 2 p.m. without exception, even if you'd pre-paid for fuel two minutes before and in the rush your other half had stopped beside the wrong petrol pump. Such is the observance of Shabbat there. On the Friday you'll be greeted with *Shabbat shalom* (peaceful Sabbath) until it's time to tote your bags and go home to your own moshav.

Where else in the world would this 24-hour religious observance every week take precedence over commerce and profit?

For a whole day, Shabbat-observant people stay at home, eat Shabbat meals with family, walk to synagogue and pray. It's forbidden to work or operate machinery on the Shabbat. Many Jews won't drive their cars, and in ultra-orthodox areas, whole streets are barricaded off to prevent anyone who may be tempted driving through. When Chris and I were school and house hunting, before moving to Jerusalem, we accidentally drove into the ultra-orthodox area of Mea She'arim on a Saturday. We were trying to judge travelling distances and suitable routes to and from the Anglican International School which is situated on the edge of Mea She'arim. Well, we know that now. Fortunately we were only met with angry shaking fists, and we didn't make that mistake again. We both felt very guilty at the upset we'd caused.

Another expatriate wasn't so fortunate when she was a relatively new arrival. She strayed in Mea She'arim while exploring the city on foot. Unfortunately for her she was wearing jeans, which aren't acceptable in this area. The dress code is very strict, with long skirts to the ankles being the norm. It's also important to have long sleeves and your collarbone covered, either by a scarf or high-necked T-shirt. Sadly this woman was struck by a stone on her forehead. She made her way into a small shop to telephone for help as she was shocked and bleeding. The shopkeeper turned his back on her, literally, and refused her any help. I visited this area of town but would only do so with a guide or as part of a small tour group. It gives a whole new meaning to the phrase Jerusalem Rocks.

During the Sabbath, lift buttons may not be pressed, and that's why you'll find the phenomenon of the 'Shabbat lift' in hotels and apartment blocks. You don't need to operate the lift by pressing a button. It stops automatically at every floor all the way up and all the way back down again. Our kids used to achieve the same effect in towering hotels in the Far East by pressing every button for entertainment and 'giving the lift somewhere to go'. A naughty and short-lived game.

I'm not so sure about the logic of the Shabbat lift. If you aren't permitted to drive around in a car on the Shabbat, what's the difference if you're being hurled up and down vertically in a lift? I suppose you aren't actually operating it if you don't push the button.

Friends of ours lived in an apartment block which had a lift, but not a Shabbat lift. It wasn't unheard of for their Jewish neighbours to throw rocks (small ones) at their glass patio window to attract attention so that the non-Jews could press the lift button for them.

The rules of Shabbat provide that you can't apply heat to things to change them in any way, hence the buying of bread in quantity before Shabbat and the cooking of food in advance. Families gather for Shabbat meals, and food is cooked and warmed or kept warm on the stove top with special warmers. Often cookers are left on a low level of heat for the whole of Shabbat. That can't do much for global warming or the gas bill.

On a Friday morning, food stalls spring up in all the malls selling stuffed vine leaves, filled pastries, inventive salads and other savoury food which can be bought and taken home for scoffing with no preparation needed at all.

You can't switch on or off a light if you're observing the Shabbat, so it's important to be organised and to switch on the lights you want before the Sabbath begins. It's also important not to switch them off accidentally, and this can be particularly challenging in a bathroom environment (I imagine). As we're in the bathroom anyway, I'll share one of the bizarre upshots of observing Shabbat. As it's forbidden to detach any item which is attached for a purpose on the Sabbath, it's crucial to pre-tear your toilet paper before Shabbat begins. I strongly recommend a box of emergency tissues in the bathroom in case you misjudge the 'here's some I made earlier' pile.

Writing and drawing are also to be avoided as they're both work. There's a scary story that in the more religious hospitals in Israel on Shabbat, the doctors write all their notes in special Shabbat ink which disappears or fades away, James Bond-style. I'm told that the notes are transcribed in permanent form after Shabbat, but imagine the problems which could arise if there's an administrative blunder. It would be a fine day in court, litigating medical negligence only to find that the evidence crucial to your case had vanished. I'm hoping this is an urban myth!

Cars are driven in town, but it's essential to avoid certain areas if you don't want to run the risk of damaged paintwork or passengers due to stone throwing. There's nothing open anyway, so most people make the most of relaxing time at home.

Having said all of that, the saving of a life under Jewish law is paramount, so all rules of Shabbat can be set aside in the case of an emergency when cars can be driven, phones used and switches switched.

Things are a bit different in Tel Aviv. While there's no public transport, you can find a restaurant, buy a bottle of water and other basics. Many Jerusalemites leave the city and head for the glorious Mediterranean beaches there.

The beaches are busy with secular Israelis sun worshipping, body worshipping, jet skiing, kite surfing, smoking, drinking, guitar playing and fishing. They fish with long poles from the shore and proudly strut back along the beach in late afternoon with a few tiny flat fish strung from their waists. The size of fish a Scotsman would use as a lure.

We found a beautiful bay at Ashkelon Beach, south of Tel Aviv but disturbingly close to Gaza. Many Russian Jews have immigrated there and made Aliyah (immigrating to Israel) into this seaside town and have influenced its culture. Apart from the natural beauty of the beach and the sea at this spot, it's not as commercialised or busy as the beaches in Tel Aviv. It's still possible to buy a flame-grilled burger or a decent grilled-chicken wrap on Shabbat, so along with flocks of others, we were regular visitors to this town.

I was fascinated by the whole concept of the observance of the Sabbath and how important it was to the people and the kosher production process. For example, Israeli wine is only certified as kosher if it's produced by Shabbat-observant male Jews. Now how would that go down in the politically correct, discrimination law-observant, situations-vacant columns back home? 'Vintner required, only Sabbath-observant practising male Jews need apply.'

Apart from the loud chatter of birds coming from our neighbour's aviary, all was quiet and peaceful on this first day in the new house, until Chris got his electric drill out to fit the hanging rails and racks in our walk-in cupboard which was destined to be a wardrobe. Our doors, windows and shutters were closed, so we hoped that we weren't disturbing the peace of the Shabbat for our neighbours.

It was another roasting hot summer day, and it wasn't until nine o'clock in the evening that we sat out with a well-deserved glass of something cold, the glass beaded with condensation, and watched life around us resume. Our peaceful Shabbat continued until sunset when the roads sprang back to life and trails of car lights were strung like crystals through the forested hills of Jerusalem. The shopping centres re-opened at nine in the evening on a Saturday, although as I sat and admired the twinkling lights of the city of Jerusalem on the hill above us, I couldn't imagine who would want to rush out and shop at that time of night when there was work to go to the next day. Now I was beginning to sound like the person I lived with, and that was a bit worrying.

As I climbed the stairs to our bedroom, weary and desperate for the refreshment of sleep and the comfort of my own familiar bed, I caught my first glimpse of our next-door neighbour. He was sitting in what was presumably his study, gazing at a computer screen. Two very long curled black ringlets framed each side of his face to his shoulders and appeared to be attached to a black skullcap on his head. He was busily tapping away at his computer and dressed in a monochrome ensemble. The lucky boy had an internet connection. *I really must make an effort to learn a bit about what this man might believe in and how his beliefs differ from the man I spotted wearing what looked like a large black fur tyre on his head matched with a black silk dressing gown*, I thought. *How do they see the world of their new neighbours, the Dicker family?*

As I drifted towards a lovely sleep, I made a mental note not to permit any form of drilling on Shabbat again.

Words of the day: layla tov — good night (Hebrew)

5

THE VILLAGE

Day two on the moshav and we woke to another perfect sunrise from our deck. Descriptions of the absolute beauty of the views from this spot on earth may become tiresome, so I'll limit them to special occasions. I now knew why our valley was so green when it was 40 degrees in Jerusalem the previous day. A mist settled over the hills and treetops, and at six o'clock in the morning, everything was damp. Birds cooed, called and generally flapped about, and the sun rose spectacular and beautiful in a brief sepia light around six thirty.

There was still a Stonehenge of upended wardrobe cartons in our bedroom.

Although we were looking for a cheap storage solution, in case this posting turned out like the last one (a three-year assignment was cut to ten months after the Jordan Red-to-Dead Sea project Chris was working on was delayed), we couldn't quite bear to go for the very cheap option—a white, plastic-covered wire, dish rack-style storage solution. No, we'd chosen a medium range, curly, dark ironwork design, six racks for the walls and six for the floor, and as with all items from IKEA, there was a formidable amount of screwing involved. Chris planned to leave this to the end of his working day as he found it a great stress reliever.

On account of there being things to do, the Israeli movers hadn't been back. They hadn't even been in contact. We'd had the worst level of service in over twenty years of being global nomads. After the last move back to Amman, we'd had to let the movers go on day three for being pleasantly useless, but at least they put in an appearance.

There were almost as many dogs as humans on our street, and poop scooping didn't seem to have reached Israel in the way that it had in other parts of the world, where no self-respecting dog owner would leave home without a fragrant nappy sack tied to the lead, on clear display. Many dogs seemed to walk themselves in this neighbourhood and pooped wherever they felt like it. A good number of them lived outdoors; I suppose less as a family pet and more as Gnasher the guard dog.

I walked to the moshav village centre with Morgan and had a general peek through fences and over garden walls. There was still quite a bit of small-scale agricultural activity going on. Even in our manicured and professionally tended patch, we had limes, lemons, small green orangey-looking fruit which weren't nectarines but must have been first cousins, and a huge harvest of ripe passion fruit. They made delicious and healthy desserts, stirred into fresh natural yogurt. I defy even the best cook to rival the flavours of nature in the raw, especially when freshly plucked passion fruit is on offer.

The display of bougainvillea and other flora was outrageously colourful and so rampant and tropical that it really did distract the eye from the dog turds which had been dumped on the pavement. We also had gorgeous green and black olive trees. The organic goat farm down the hill, coupled with a riding stable in the village centre, contributed a strong smell of country air. This and the sound of cockerels crowing all day long simply added to the charm of rural life.

The village had a post office with banks of mailboxes, a synagogue, a clinic, a picturesque village green, outdoor exercise equipment and a little playground. There was a stage, a notice board and a real community feel about the place. Many Israelis aspire to bring their families up in the secure and safe environment a moshav provides, and houses are very rarely available.

This idyllic community also had a small supermarket, with

everything your heart could desire if you were willing to sell your youngest child on eBay. It was expensive but charming in a sort of 'you will wait twenty minutes to have your carefully selected long-life goods processed through the till' way. It had a monopoly and kept very convenient opening hours— for the shopkeepers. Chris was incensed every time he visited as he could only see how he could improve the experience. Fortunately it was closed by the time he got back from the office, so his irritation was kept in check.

In the beginning I was convinced that as a foreigner and newcomer, I was regularly fleeced but not so outrageously that it was worth complaining, especially when all till receipts were printed in Hebrew and I didn't speak a word (except the words I've shared with you). I made a point of only selecting items that were actually priced. After a very short time, I realised that *I* wasn't being fleeced; we *all* were by the outrageous price of groceries in Israel. The limitation of what was on offer, and the wish to have something left in the nest egg for retirement, prompted me to plan to explore life outside the moshav one day soon and head for larger more competitive shops.

On that first day, I learnt my first new word of Hebrew—*todah* (pronounced *toe-da*) which means thank you. I made a point of asking madam shopkeeper because I really didn't want to be the stereotypical Brit who shouted at everyone in English and got frustrated and rude when they didn't understand a word being said.

Our house overlooked a valley which was dry in summer and used by hikers, dirt bikers, quad-bike riders, cyclists and horse riders. We were told it was flooded in winter, as a dam had been built. We lived on Haagam Road, which means Pond Road in Hebrew. (A 'Hot' guy told me that. More of him later.)

I was impressed that there were big metal cages, often decorated with large brightly coloured metal flowers, on our moshav, and in fact all over Jerusalem where you could post plastic bottles for recycling. There were also large paper-recycling skips and an absence of plastic bags. That had to be a good thing. The rest of the world is now catching up as we appreciate the catastrophic impact which single-use plastic has on the environment, but Israel was way ahead of the curve.

The lively community notice board with all sorts of exciting-looking advertisements attracted my attention, but they were all in Hebrew and so remained a mystery for a while.

I'd been told by our relocation agent that there was another British family living on the moshav. They had two boys who both went to the school Morgan would be attending. Like the majority of the expatriate population, they'd left for the summer and weren't expected back for weeks. Fortunately Morgan was so glad to be reunited with his essential electronic play gear, which was now unpacked and plugged in, that no other company was needed for the time being.

Word of the day: todah — thank you (Hebrew)

6

THE OUTSIDE WORLD

After a morning spent trying to fit too many clothes, toys, PlayStation games and books into too small a space in Morgan's new bedroom, and creating a satisfying heap of empty boxes in the garden, we struck out beyond the village and into the wide world.

The limitations of the local shop forced me out of the gentle cocoon of moshav life, which I'd donned like a security blanket. Too many days of not leaving the house had passed, and I knew the time had come when I had to put on my brave knickers and drive up the hill to Mevaseret Zion, our nearest town. It lay just past our village on the main road to Tel Aviv. Morgan and I crossed the valley and wound our way up the hillside switchback road to a very modern shopping centre. Apart from the obvious benefit of having shops, it also had internet access, so I could catch up on my emails and connect with the world.

Security stopped us on our way into the car park and asked, 'Do you have a weapon?'

It was a common question in Israel, but it gave me a jolt the first few times I was asked. If the other grown-up in our family was feeling mischievous, he repeated the question but with a slightly different intonation. 'Do *I* have a weapon?' However, that day it was just Morgan and me, so my glove compartment and boot were checked by the armed security guard, and the security barrier was lifted. We were in.

By way of bribery for getting Morgan out of the house and away from his PlayStation, I allowed him an unhealthy lunch. At the International Community School in Amman, his class had a healthy-eating month, and ever since, he'd been obsessed with getting his fair share of unhealthy food. It was a constant battle.

Here we found a McDonald's, kosher of course and in fact the first kosher McDonald's in the whole world, which opened in Mevaseret Zion in 1995. One of the things you don't ask for after your first week in Jerusalem is a cheeseburger. You may well know that it's not kosher, but certain members of our family hadn't read the guide book. Well the Mevaseret Zion branch of McDonald's has a kosher certificate, but I now know that for more kosher than kosher, I needed to find the McDonald's outlets which had blue and white signs, not the usual red and yellow livery. Only in very few locations around the world have McDonald's conceded changes to the famous logo colours, the Champs Elysées in Paris being one of the others. There the signs have to be in gold. I seem to remember there was gold livery at the Palm Beach McDonald's in the USA too.

Meat doesn't seem to feature that highly in the Israeli diet. The mainstays are salad, vegetables, fruit, bread and cheese. They also produce delicious pastries in many varieties which should be avoided if you're to keep fitting into your clothes. If you want to observe the rules of kosher eating, when meat is eaten, there should be a gap before dairy is eaten. They shouldn't be eaten together, so cheeseburgers are out. I had an interesting chat with the daughter of a rabbi (not 'the' daughter of a rabbi, Reva Mann, but another bright, friendly and interesting lady).

'In my family we always allow a six-hour gap between eating meat and dairy,' Shula shared. 'But some Jewish people prefer to leave a twelve-hour gap, and others are happy with four. It just depends.'

So when your child has wolfed down a Big Mac at the kosher McDonald's and can't live without an ice cream to seal the deal, he has to queue separately in a screened-off ice cream section, and the feeling is just so wicked that he can't leave the restaurant without one.

'Mum, you go up and get it,' he often said, as he knew it wasn't quite the done thing. I found the ambience of our kosher McDonald's pleasant and sociable, but frankly I couldn't have waited six hours for my dessert.

Many Jews keep a kosher kitchen, so different sets of cooking utensils are used for meat and dairy, different crockery and so on. Dishwashers have to be very well organised so there's a rack for dairy and a separate rack for non-dairy items. Alternatively you can wash all your dairy utensils, run the washer empty and then wash all your non-dairy items of cutlery and crockery. In a country where water is a precious and valuable commodity, careful thought should be given as to how you can do kosher washing-up and be environmentally friendly at the same time.

The rules of kosher only apply to hot food, so fridges and their organisation aren't so difficult. I do know that some landlords in Israel won't rent to foreigners who don't keep a kosher kitchen. I thought I was doing really well if I managed to give the work surfaces a cursory wipe over and there was fresh milk in the fridge, so I don't think I'm kosher kitchen-keeping material. It sounds like really hard work.

Almost all food is kosher in Israel. This adds to the expense as it has to be slaughtered in a particular way in accordance with Jewish law, and all the way through the processing from beast to shopping basket there's a kosher certification system, which must cost plenty to administer. My American-brand mayonnaise was, for example, 'kosher parve, under supervision of the Chief Rabbinate of Israel'.

My new daughter-of-a-rabbi friend was hanging out in McDonald's with Koby, her lovely chatty son who was about the same age as Morgan, or maybe a little older. I met her in McDonald's as she was trying to escape the brutal heat of her apartment, which had no air conditioning, not a comfortable scenario if you're able bodied, but this cheerful, talkative lady had impaired mobility and was passing a few hours in the mall to stay cool. She and her son overheard us talking in English and crossed to our table for a chat and a better look at Morgan's portable Nintendo Game Boy machine.

After carefully examining the device, we got onto the subject of kosher food rules.

'Did you know,' Shula asked, 'that if a cow is slaughtered and found to be carrying offspring, that cow can't be eaten under the rules of kosher, and if the offspring survives, that offspring can never be eaten and nor can its offspring?'

I didn't know that, but it must all add to the expense of shopping for meat in Israel.

After the food has been produced, a further layer of expense is added when eating out. All restaurants with kosher certification (most restaurants in Jerusalem) are supposed to be supervised. I read recently that there was inadequate supervision in most restaurants to check that, for example, the salad leaves are washed thoroughly. Some believe that salad leaves should be examined individually and carefully for bugs and insects. If an insect is inadvertently eaten and has a speck of blood in its body, that's not kosher salad and shouldn't be eaten except with meat. There are meat restaurants and dairy restaurants all approved under the kosher certification system, so this potential salad problem is a big issue.

Is it just me, or did anyone else immediately think of the old children's song:

There was an old lady who swallowed a fly.
I don't know why she swallowed a fly.
Perhaps she'll die.

If you want to scare your kosher friends even more, look up the lyrics to this cautionary tale.

In Amman we were able to buy Australian, New Zealand, Argentinian or Brazilian beef, not to mention the locally farmed variety, for five Jordanian dinars (about $6.25) a kilo. The beef available in the shops where we now were, 80 kilometres to the west of Amman, was about five times more expensive and the beef fillet ten times more.

It wasn't hard to see that shopping for and feeding a family could be a struggle and this, along with security fears and atrocities of the past, could more than account for the grumpy faces which seemed to be the default expression in this town.

We 'enjoyed' two McDonald's meals which cost me a shocking 85 shekels and took a stroll past one of many cafés. The pastries and food looked so good, I was tempted to take some home for later, but resisted.

One of the many reasons for visiting the shopping centre was to procure more screws and rawl plugs for the evening's entertainment and a very long Phillips head screwdriver. I was also hoping to get a list of the documents needed by the bank to open an account. I imagined it would be quite a list, based on my brushes with bureaucracy so far. We were told we needed a bank account to organise our internet, phone and satellite TV connection. The bank was of course closed as it was after one o'clock by the time we'd had lunch and made new friendships, and I was too used to opening hours which suited the customer.

Morgan spotted a small toy shop tucked away in a corner and found a piece of must-have miniature skating park plastic for a mere 70 shekels, and twice what we would pay in the UK.

'Can I have it, please?' he begged, and on this occasion I buckled and part with the shekels.

I was just about accepting that the cost of living was extremely high there so will no longer bore you too often with price checks. You get the picture.

To cheer myself up, we visited the book shop, which was large, bright and well stocked. Apart from one small shelf, approximately 60 centimetres wide, all books were in Hebrew (not surprisingly) and like Arabic books, are read from back to front. My brand-new friend had warned us about translations into Hebrew from English.

'They are mostly appalling!' Shula cautioned us. 'We mainly read books translated into Hebrew for a laugh.'

Koby read them in English too, for enjoyment. I was looking forward to the day when I could judge whether a translation into Hebrew was good or bad.

Morgan spent an agonising half hour identifying *Diary of a Wimpy Kid* (a series to which he was addicted), but it was in Hebrew, and a fold-out dinosaur book in Hebrew, but he was unable to locate his latest target, *My First 1,000 words in Hebrew*, in English of course.

I'd just unpacked approximately 30 boxes of books, and I was in no mood to acquire any more in this lifetime. However, amazingly, in the limited collection of English books, there was one title which caught my eye and which I had to have. *The Help* by Katheryn Stockett had been recommended by a very dear friend as a great read. A very dear friend who had only weeks to live, having been diagnosed very recently with a brain tumour. I was stunned that there was one copy of this book I'd barely heard of before among so few books in English. I picked it up and was unwilling to part with it physically. I held onto it as if it had created a connection across the airwaves to my brave and beautiful Elaine. I couldn't let it go. When Morgan bounced across with his find, a large coffee-table book, *Top Ten of Everything*, in English, with an interactive CD game, I was beyond uttering the usual 'put it back'. I paid for our books and carried my friend in my head and in my heart, as I had done for weeks. That tangible connection was my small miracle of the day.

One of the components of all our previous postings had in fact been 'the help'. We'd been very fortunate to have wonderful housemaids, and only a few not-so-wonderful ones, in all our postings around the world. This wasn't to be a feature of our life in Israel. Chris was working in the West Bank and had no work visa in Israel, so we couldn't legally employ any help at all. This was set to be a new and possibly energetic posting.

Morgan and I made a point of not forgetting the DIY stuff, did a speedy supermarket sweep and headed back to the car. I was suddenly feeling drained and in need of some privacy.

Surprisingly we found the car again in the labyrinth of a carpark and were then faced with a dilemma. There were exit and entrance signs but all in Hebrew, and I didn't know which was which. The parking spaces were full and tight, as were the access ways. I didn't want to be caught head-on with another car if I accessed the ramp the wrong way.

'Which sign should I follow, Morgan?' I deliberated out loud.

'Go for the shorter word, Mum.'

This had an element of logic, so I complied, until we were faced with really large, shiny, spikey tyre shredders which were installed for security reasons in all the malls there. I had no idea whether I was going to drive across them in the right direction in the new hire car. So I did what any cautious person would do. I decided to reverse back, tuck in and wait until someone else drove across them successfully. In a Mr Bean sort of a way. Well there's only so long you can wait when you want to get home. Morgan bravely offered to go out and test them himself by jumping on them, but I was unwilling for him to acquire tyre marks on his forehead if a car suddenly rounded the bend on the ramp to our level at speed. So we drove around until we spotted a busy exit on a different level in the distance. To reach it I had to drive between a couple of concrete bollards which had been carefully placed there to prevent motorists crossing the car park that way, but frankly by then I'd had enough and was on the verge of simply risking shredding the tyres and starting again.

We reached home, and after a restorative cup of tea, I decided to rearrange the furniture for the umpteenth time, and finally I got it right. We could now walk across the open-plan ground floor without bumping into sofas. We could also see the heavenly view of our valley from the quiet sofa, which had been placed in a large bay window, facing outwards with a view of the vineyards. This was destined to become a refuge for grown-ups of an evening. All the other furniture had been successfully fitted in between five random pillars which graced our open-plan lounge.

I prepared our first dinner in the new house. It was the quickest, easiest and yummiest meal and very versatile. I would recommend it as a 'date dinner', or if you're further along life's motorway, a dinner for impressing the in-laws. I served it once in Jordan to two lovely colleagues from the United States. One, a lawyer, joined me in the kitchen and helped cook the honey mustard salmon. She was so enthusiastic about the cooking that it had obviously been a while since she'd had the luxury of a weekend off. The other visitor, who spent ages on the phone reporting the business of the day to head office in Denver, Colorado, missed the cooking but asked for the recipe to cook for his family when he got home. It's kosher and totally irresistible. I will share it with you at the end of the chapter.

This meal takes a maximum of fifteen minutes to prepare and cook and was great for the first night of catering in a new house with a brand-new oven which still contained the instruction manual and bits of Styrofoam. I particularly recommend that you wash the meal down with one or two glasses of chilled white wine.

The review I received from my resident food critic was as follows: 'I'm just a bit worried. I don't know how you're going to better this tomorrow night.'

I intended to. I'd think of something that took ten minutes to make, or maybe we would light the barbeque and have some testosterone-fuelled cooking.

After a perfectly relaxing evening in our new home, we climbed the wooden hill to bed. Chris opened the windows to the night air. I expressed my deep-rooted fear that a pigeon might come in (I have a debilitating fear of birds), so we compromised. That's what marriage is about, after all. We left the windows open but brought the electronic shutters down so that there was no space for a pigeon to pop in uninvited. We settled comfortably in our wonderful super king-sized, four-poster bed, and after less than a minute of calm, Chris was bitten by an insect, then another, and the howling of the dogs in the valley was just scary. We closed the windows, put on the noisy air conditioning and fell into a state of unconsciousness. Bliss.

Word of the day: kosher — (literally) legitimate (Hebrew)

HONEY MUSTARD SALMON

Ingredients
1 piece of salmon per person (steak or fillet)
Wholegrain mustard
Runny, clear honey

Method
Wash and pat salmon dry with kitchen paper.
Before cooking it, you may remove any bones with long-nosed pliers.
(I keep some in the kitchen drawer just for this job.)
Leave the skin on and place fillets skin side down in a hot oiled frying
pan or skillet.
Put one teaspoonful of grain mustard on top of each fillet and a
generous squeeze of runny honey.
Spread both together over fish with a teaspoon.
Cook until you can see from the side view that the salmon is almost
half cooked through. The cooked part of the fish will be opaque and
paler.
Flick over and remove the cooked skin carefully with the pliers. It
should peel off in one piece.
Put one teaspoonful of grain mustard and a generous squeeze of honey
on this side of the fish.
After side one has been nicely caramelised, flick back to this side so the
marinade can be cooked.
The fish is delicious served hot, or even more delicious if allowed to
cool and served with salad.

Serving suggestion
Empty bag of ready-made salad on plates.
Bake sweet potatoes wrapped in kitchen towel in microwave. If I
hadn't just moved house, I might have made Dauphinoise potatoes
with roasted vegetables, but not that day.

7

DANGER MONEY (OR ANOTHER DAY IN PARADISE)

The sun was struggling to break through a thick, pale grey covering of clouds in the sky. After the oppressive heat of the previous few days, the cool morning air was a welcome relief, a relief which lasted until eight o'clock that morning.

To sit in this green valley, with its close-knit community and pretty, tranquil and leafy village, we were paid danger money on top of the normal expatriate pay package. Danger money which wasn't an insignificant amount at 25% of salary.

When you got used to the wall, the soldiers, the huge weapons on display and slung across shoulders in shopping malls, and the constant security which was apparent in every shop and restaurant in Jerusalem, you could settle into a feeling of relative calm and safety. You could even think to yourself on such a spectacularly beautiful morning, *Danger money? Why?*

The previous evening, Chris's commute from Ramallah to Jerusalem, which usually took around 40 minutes, took one and a half hours. All gates through the security wall, which allow passage from Ramallah to Jerusalem, were closed. Chaotic and busy at the best of times, they quickly become very congested if there's a problem. We were informed that an Israeli soldier had been stabbed while on duty at one of the gates. As a result the wall was locked down. The situation was tense. There is Palestinian housing around the Qalandia gate. Chris and a colleague decided to bail out of the wait at the gate as they were both travelling in new shiny vehicles and didn't feel they wanted to sit around for the stone throwing to begin. They drove on to the next gate in case of trouble. This can erupt at any time, and the rocks and missiles are hurled at the soldiers who are heavily and well kitted out with full military protective gear.

I drove through the wall and the gates many times during our month-long stay in Ramallah. My favourite gate was the Pisgat. I shuddered when I first formed this opinion. It seemed obscene to have a favourite gate, but it was true. The Pisgat was more civilised. The first night I was held up in Jerusalem and travelled back later than usual, I had a call from Chris to check where I was and that I was okay. 'Oh, I'm at the Pisgat. I'll be home in half an hour.' The words uttered with all the casualness of someone held up in a queue at a supermarket checkout.

Initially when we lived in Ramallah, there was a requirement to log all journeys with central security in Chris's office. I'm not used to telling anyone where I'm going or for how long, so it was a strange feeling to leave our Ramallah apartment and to notify the office staff of our departure. The neat trick was to remember to tell them when we'd reached our destination. This was essential for every journey at that time but wasn't required when living through the wall on the Jerusalem side. Once we were living in our house on the moshav, this was a fact of life I no longer contended with on a daily basis. Sadly, other people did, Chris and his staff included. Kidnapping was one concern; working as Westerners as a contractor of the US government was perceived as dangerous too. USAID staff weren't permitted to enter the West Bank without security protocol, armoured vehicles and escorts.

The Pisgat was brighter, cleaner, more orderly and less busy than the other gate, but you still had to drive through the O.K. Corral to get to Ramallah. You just managed to miss the worst of the queue jumping and undertaking (which is what we call overtaking by the inside lane). Yes, that was a favourite motoring strategy, to drive up the inside metre of road and squeeze through with no room to spare, just to pop back into the official and only lane when an abandoned tyre, large rock or litter too large to squash with a fifteen-year-old beaten-up car was encountered.

The Pisgat became my regular point of crossing, and the Israeli soldiers were a surprise, and not a horrible one. This is because I'm not Palestinian, so I could cross with relative ease. I was nervous the first few times I passed through the checkpoint and don't think our experience at the Allenby Bridge helped.

The soldiers manning each lane of the checkpoint were all around the same age as Liberty. They were young, fit, tanned, polite people, most of the time. I always made a point of being polite and courteous to them.

I had to restrain myself from saying motherly things to them like, 'Did you remember to put sunscreen on?' or, 'Are you drinking enough water, because it's hot today, and that gun must be very heavy to lug around all the time? You don't want a headache due to dehydration.'

Most Israeli families live in fear of their children's lives when they're doing compulsory service in the army. The cost of this never-ending occupation is very high in human lives and peace of mind on both sides.

That day, one of these young people was stabbed. Someone's daughter or someone's son. As I had no satellite TV, internet connection or contact with the outside world, I wasn't sure what the outcome for the soldier would be. Nor was I sure what would become of the attacker, who was assumed to be Palestinian, correctly on this occasion.

To round off a tense day on the border with our new host country, we heard that rockets had been fired from the Sinai Desert into Eilat, an Israeli Red Sea tourist spot popular with Israelis and foreign tourists alike. Apparently some of the rockets fell in the Red Sea, and at least one fell on the front courtyard of the Intercontinental Hotel in Aqaba, Jordan. We'd been lucky enough to be invited to the soft opening of that beautiful resort. This development was very unsettling.

You can see Aqaba from Eilat, which is just along the beach but separated by an international border. It's also possible to cross from one country into the other at this border, but only on foot, although border crossing rules and requirements change frequently, so do double check before travelling. You can then hire a taxi to take you into Aqaba or Eilat when you reach the other side of the crossing. As with all crossing points in this neighbourhood, patience is needed. The runway of Aqaba and Eilat airports are in very close proximity, and I was amused to hear that one unlucky pilot landed in the wrong country by mistake.

So as I walked across my bedroom, now clear of boxes of clothes, and tumbled into my bed, I knew with certainty why we were paid danger money.

The only time I felt that my life was in danger there was when Chris decided to use the diplomatic security gate near Beit El on the outskirts of Ramallah for variety. As a holder of a USAID identity card, Chris was entitled to use this much quieter gate, but it was a long way round to Jerusalem. So one weekend, to take in fresh scenery and a different route, we tried it out. By this time we were well used to just slowing down at the Pisgat and being waved through with a cursory glance. As we approached the dippy gate, or diplomatic gate as it's officially called, we slowed down. There were no other vehicles at all, just a handful of heavily armed young male soldiers. They appeared totally disinterested in our car which had Chris and Morgan upfront while I lounged in the back. Morgan was wearing his usual cheery smile and a Chelsea football strip. This had been generously given to him by one of my friends from Amman, a Palestinian Jordanian, who now has her heart's desire, a British passport. She's one of the kindest, most friendly and hospitable people a person could ever hope to meet.

Our happy families outing to Jerusalem was rocked when all hell broke loose. One of the soldiers became agitated, prepared his weapon and started shouting at us, in Hebrew of course. Chris lowered his window and asked if there was a problem.

'You did not stop,' yelled the soldier.

'We don't usually stop unless we're stopped,' replied Chris.

'You always stop,' yelled the soldier, still cocking his weapon.

'Okay, we will do next time,' soothed Chris.

At this point the soldier poked his head into the car and said to Morgan, 'You support Chelsea?'

'Yes,' beamed Morgan. 'They're my favourite football team. Do you?'

'No,' came the curt and grumpy reply. Then after a second's hesitation, 'I support Manchester United,' said soldier boy.

'Me too,' agreed Chris, and this was no act of diplomacy at the dippy gate; he always has. Sir Alex Ferguson is greatly respected in our house as one of the best football managers ever and has been since his days at Aberdeen Football Club. So our support has continued although the club management has changed.

It was later, as I re-lived the tension at that crossing, that I realised how our failing to completely stop and our taking for granted previous experiences at other gates could have led to our family being shot in the back of beyond at the checkpoint between Palestine and Israel.

Note to diary—must make a will

8

MEGA SHOP

The day arrived when I had to venture into Jerusalem proper, so Morgan and I climbed the hill from the moshav towards the Jerusalem String Bridge (which we'd been calling the harp bridge in our ignorance, but it does look like a harp). We then took the Ben Gurion Highway in a southerly direction towards JAIS, where Morgan would study when school resumed. It was always better to do a 'dry school run' than to get hopelessly lost on the first day of the new school year, when nerves are tightly strung and butterflies are fluttering in tummies. In any case I was keen to get to Jerusalem Mall and an internet café to connect with the outside world for the first time in days.

There were absolutely no spaces available in the Jerusalem Mall multi-storey car park, and cars had been perched on kerbs and parked against concrete walls in highly dubious places. It was alarming to realise that if the carpark got much busier, it would be difficult to negotiate our way back out through the limited space left for moving vehicles. Maybe that's why most cars are so bashed and scratched in that part of the world. Being unwilling to leave without my internet and Facebook fix, I abandoned my car in a naughty spot, but not without a degree of concern and worry. On the plus side, I was parking like a local already.

'D'you think the car will be alright parked there?' I asked Morgan, knowing full well that in Glasgow it could be clamped or towed if I parked in such a haphazard way.

'Sure, Mum, don't worry,' said the boy who didn't want to lose out on his café visit and the possibility of some chocolate cake as a treat.

We settled into comfortable seats in one of our favourite cafés so far and were soon sipping and surfing in a very efficient way.

According to my MSN homepage, there was likely to be a war between Israel and Lebanon following the rocket attacks. Looking on the bright side, there were still 6 or 7 of the 306 boxes now accounted for that I hadn't unpacked.

The possibility of conflict was one which weighed heavily on the older generation of our respective families. I reassured my mum in Scotland that all was peaceful on the moshav, apart from the loud, cross-valley canine conversations which reverberated back and forth every night. They sounded disturbingly like the opening scene of a scary episode of *The Hound of the Baskervilles*. I later found out that the howling was of packs of jackals which inhabited the forest and the valley near our house.

Liberty, who was in her final year at Glasgow University reading law with economics at the time, was due to arrive at the weekend for a short holiday. She'd worked all summer and was keen to see our new home before two stints of legal work experience in Glasgow and London. I wondered if she'd actually booked her flight yet and if it was wise to do so.

Other tasks designated for this day were to get my iPhone checked out so that it worked in Israel. I'd bought the phone at vast expense in Jordan, but it seemed that without a costly 230-shekel de-chipping process (but putting it in perspective, it was only five meals at McDonald's), it was useless in Israel. I left my phone with the iPhone fixer man, after skilfully negotiating a discount to 150 shekels (only three McDonald's meals). 'It will take me half an hour, with the latest programme installed on your phone. You should come back later.' Good advice from Mr Fixer.

Morgan and I filled in the time with a visit to a toy shop, which was frankly another disappointment. It was hard to believe it was part of a famous international chain. The store was dingy, poorly laid out and so expensive ($100 for a Nintendo DS game).

'Put it back, Morgan,' I heard myself say repeatedly.

I was in no mood for acquiring yet more toys as we were having problems fitting the ones he had into his much smaller bedroom.

'Ah,' said Morgan. 'I've found stuff I don't mind clearing out of my room.'

I wished he'd been as motivated six weeks before when we were packing up his must-have junk in Jordan. Mercifully we left empty handed with vague promises of amazon.com fulfilling his gaming needs, provided of course they were delivered to and hand-carried by the next visitor. I really wasn't up for another interview with an inquisitive Customs official and a huge import tax bill.

We also found a better supermarket called Mega (it's not that big), stocked with everything your heart could desire except bright orange cheddar cheese, a necessary commodity for most Scots. How else would we keep our place as the top heart-bypass country in Europe, if not the world?

Disconcertingly, people who hadn't found a trolley, and there were none in obvious view, were stuffing goods into their shoulder bags. It was like shopping with a convention of kleptomaniacs. I waited for security guards to pounce, but nothing happened. Everyone was doing it. I stalked a grey-haired matron to the checkout till and watched her unpack all of her stuff from her canvas shoulder bag and repack it back into the same bag when paid for. Barely any plastic bags were used at all. I'd never lived in a country which was so conscious of saving the environment.

Unlike the customer service received on the Jordan side, I was required to unpack my shopping, repack it and carry it to my car. So uncivilised. The checkout girls in this shop were a stern warning against ever colouring your hair at home while abroad. The colours ranged from Irn Bru orange (Scotland's other national drink) to coalpit black, and there were several tartan heads on display. The staff all looked worn out, tired and unhappy and seemed to disappear regularly to the customer service desk to negotiate receipts, small change and other essential deals. By the time you got through this sort of queue and waited for the assistant to shuffle back to the till, eat a handful of Twiglets and resume ringing your goods through, the contraband ice cream had melted.

I noted that the wine we paid 43 shekels a bottle for in our charming moshav shop was on offer for two bottles for 55 shekels. My suspicions were confirmed. It's always better to buy more wine than less. *I must find my way back to this mall.*

After two whole hours, I made my way back to Mr iPhone Fixer's turf at the bottom of the escalator to reclaim my iPhone. I was disappointed to note that my phone was so old (ten months) that it needed an even older version of the de-chipping software that he could put his hands on at two hours' notice. I reclaimed the antique and undertook to return it soon for the installation of the antiquated software it seemed to require. Cheekily I asked if the old software might be cheaper, but no luck.

On the plus side, I'd assembled three IKEA breakfast bar stools by the time Chris got back from Ramallah. I thought I might have to invest in the world of flat-pack furniture.

Word of the day: ken—yes (Hebrew)

I'm getting the hang of this, I thought when I heard the word. *They say 'ken' in Aberdeen and it means much the same thing—'Aye, ah ken.' (Yes, I know.) They also sell kippers in Aberdeen, but they bear no resemblance to the kippahs, or skullcaps, which are sold in Israel (small round headgear worn by Jewish males). The variety of head gear for men is astounding. Black velvet kippahs, colourful crotchet kippahs, black fedora hats, black fur tyres worn as hats. I really must find out the significance of the head gear.*

9

DO IT YOURSELF (DIY)

Next day I aimed to move beyond the realms of unpacking and planned to restore order. I couldn't take any more living with this level of disorganisation. It's one of the disadvantages of being a global nomad. You move four times in three years, and you can't find a pair of scissors. That's why I now own at least six pairs.

I'd reached an impasse due to the absence of brawn and assembled storage shelves. As Chris had long days in his new role and communications across difficult time zones with late conference calls booked to the USA and back, and with work impinging on yet another weekend, it looked like it was DIY in the true sense.

I managed to assemble two full sets of floor-to-ceiling shelves for the laundry and linen room. My boudoir was cleared and beautiful.

I was hot and sweaty after this energetic endeavour. The top floor of the house was like an oven in the daytime. Insulation must have been minimal, and I wasn't looking forward to how cold it could get in winter. It does snow in Jerusalem.

Liberty's planned trip was looking increasingly doubtful as the return flight had gone up in price to $1,200. You just can't afford to dither when booking flights.

I went for a lovely walk in the evening and was accosted by a middle-aged woman who spoke to me in Hebrew, thankfully smiling. She'd mistaken me for another lady she knew, so I must have been fitting in. There seemed to be two quite distinct camps on the moshav. There was the long skirt and headscarf brigade, usually wearing training shoes, or the gorgeous gym gear, long glossy hair and iPod brigade, all taking their evening exercise. The calming views of rolling hills, vineyards and olive trees all made this a relaxing way to burn off a few calories and spy on the neighbours. More of spying later. Morgan quite rightly pointed out that the view was like a mixture of Scotland and Italy, two of my favourite places.

Word of the day: shalom—hello or goodbye, but literally means peace
(Hebrew)

10

THE BANK

Morgan and I drove up the hill to Mevaseret once more in an attempt to open our local bank account which I was told would lead to us getting connected to the internet, phone and television cable service.

We got up, showered and out of the house early to avoid the frustrations of early afternoon branch closures. I walked into the first bank I saw, and all signs were in Hebrew, not just the helpful Hebrew words written in English that I've shared with you. No, they were all in Hebrew script (e.g. שָׁלוֹם (*shalom*)).

I asked about opening a new account and was directed to the manager's office. I hung about outside for a while. There was no manager in evidence, or many other people for that matter.

After gormlessly waiting for any sort of customer service or sign of life, I gave up and decided to walk to the next bank, which was only a few metres away in the same shopping centre. I had no idea what either of these banks was called, but they were within a ten-minute drive of home and had ATM machines throughout Jerusalem. I recognised them by the colour schemes inside.

I accosted an official-looking lady with a badge in the next bank, and I was efficiently directed to the correct booth. Two forms of photo

ID were required to open a bank account. My passport would suffice although due to an error on the part of the Foreign and Commonwealth Office, I was stated to be male. Our Scottish lawyer had skirted around the issue very delicately when she noticed the discrepancy.

The only other forms of photo ID I had were my Abu Dhabi and Jordanian driver's licences. As you can't visit the United Arab Emirates with an Israeli passport, I guessed that the former wouldn't be welcome. There's a peace treaty between Israel and Jordan, but as we knew from the horrible border-crossing experience, each side harbours a distrust of the other, so I wasn't keen on handing over my Jordanian driver's licence either.

I had a further forage in my purse and, eureka, my British Embassy Club Amman membership club card had photo ID, but it was such an awful photo, I really wasn't keen to show it.

'The process of opening a bank account will take half an hour,' the customer service adviser explained.

Where had I heard that before? On a roll, I asked, 'Is there a satellite or internet provider office in the shopping centre?'

I had faith that when I had my local bank account, the missing pieces of normal life would slip into place and there would be a phone, a mobile phone, internet and TV, maybe even in English.

It felt quite other worldly having no telephone, Skype, television, news, radio, newspaper or magazines in English, and I quite liked it, apart from the worry that war may break out and I mightn't know about it.

I was missing my very real family and friends, albeit in our virtual world of Facebook, Skype and email communication. I was missing the chats, jokes, new photos on Facebook and the essential news and gossip. I was missing my daily read of newspapers online too, local and international.

The bank clerk helpfully replied, 'You could phone the Hot company and set up an internet as long as you have a valid credit card. There are no offices to visit personally.'

Like a lot of things, this did change in Israel over time, and sales booths sprang up all over town, but not in the era we were trying to get connected with the world.

I did have doubts as to whether my HSBC credit card would be acceptable. I hadn't seen any branches in Israel, although there was a branch in Ramallah which I used.

Word of the day: patuach—open (Hebrew)

11

THE HOT GUY

A Hot guy called me eventually. When I say Hot, I mean it with a capital 'H'. He was from the Hot Cable Company and was organising a triple mega package of TV channels, movie channels and my personal favourite, 'how to move abroad without losing your mind' channels.

The information we were given about needing a local bank account to open a Hot account was clearly wrong, and the Hot company accepted my HSBC credit card, although there were no branches of HSBC in Israel.

Apart from the excitement of the TV, the second element was access to the internet. On balance I hadn't enjoyed being an internet refugee. Until then, in order to check my email account, I'd had to drive to Jerusalem Mall, crossing light railway tracks for the new system which was under construction. It was a requirement which had forced me out of my relative comfort zone and helped me to get orientated.

But the need to be checking my emails regularly for all sorts of pressing reasons had made this extravagant contract a necessity. We were entering into a 360-shekel a month contract for a minimum commitment of eighteen months. It should have been three years but we negotiated this time limit down for the payment of an extra 30 shekels a month.

The third element of the triple mega package was redundant at the time—1,000 minutes of chat time to other landlines in Israel or unlimited calls to any mobile for 35 agorot a minute (each Israeli shekel is divided into 100 agorot).

'I don't know anyone in Israel,' I admitted to the Hot guy, slightly reluctantly. No one wants to be cast in the role of Nancy-no-mates.

'Be optimistic,' he cheerfully counselled. 'You will, and then you'll be phoning all your new friends, and your husband at work.'

Chris wasn't a chatting-on-the-phone-while-at-work sort of a guy, but I let that pass. So we had a mega deal. Dropping the prospect of keeping in close contact with my imaginary friends was just too churlish, so I agreed to this element.

After completing a detailed analysis of my viewing needs and preferences, to the point where Natan, the Hot guy, and I could have entered a veteran's edition of Mr and Mrs, we had a contract.

Now all I needed to do was sign up with a separate Internet Service Provider, and we would be in business. Natan managed to get a person who spoke English to call me straight away, and I quickly added Hot guy and his friend to my speed dial, as finding someone to speak to you in English on the phone is like finding a house on a moshav—a rare but treasured delight.

We had to contain our excitement until next day when the Hot installation guy should arrive. We lived in hope.

On our evening stroll around the moshav, the sky became so grey and thick with cloud it resembled a summer's day in Scotland, except it was dry and warm. I was convinced we would get rain. The temperature dropped to a lovely cool sixteen degrees overnight.

Word of the day: machar—tomorrow (Hebrew)

12

THE 18TH BIRTHDAY

We woke up to the 11th August knowing that it was a special day on our family calendar. It's the day on which our daughter Amber Louise Decker was born, and that year she would have been eighteen years old had she lived.

It's always hard when you're living overseas and apart from loved ones during the happiest and the saddest of times. Liberty hadn't managed to get on a flight to be with us on this day, but the occasion was being marked by friends and family all over the world.

Apart from our move, we'd been supporting Liberty in a charity cycle ride venture she'd organised in memory of Amber. The plan was to cycle from London to Paris over five days and to raise a glass or two of champagne there in her memory on 5th September, the third anniversary of her death. We all knew Amber would have approved of the route, being a girl who loved fashion, family, friends and shopping. All would be embraced on this special trip.

I can't believe that eighteen years ago today, almost to the minute, you
came into the world! You were a very, very beautiful baby, my
gorgeous, and stayed beautiful inside and out the whole of your long-

legged life. I'm so glad that I can write you this FB message today. We have internet in the new house at last. The HOT guy—I'm serious, the company is called 'Hot'—arrived three hours ago, and he didn't disappoint. You and Libby would have been in fits. It was a real two-bras moment (ha, remember that flight!) Anyway, he turned on the TV, and you'll never guess what was on—The O.C.! Your fav. I nearly fell over. You know that you're always with us; we talk about you all the time and miss you more the longer time passes. We're going to make a mega batch of choc chip cookies Spinneys style in your honour today, the first baking in the new oven. Love you all the way to the moon and back and still love you more. Your mummikins xxxxxxxxxxxxxxxxxxx

11ᵗʰ August 16.05 Facebook entry made after the successful installation of our Hot cable system.

After work we drove to Jerusalem and found a trendy restaurant just off a lovely little pedestrian street where we ate a delicious dinner and raised a large glass of wine to our beautiful girl on her birthday. Liberty met with her grandmother, aunt and cousins in Glasgow, and they drank champagne, released a balloon with special handwritten messages and ate dinner together.

That night, after realising that all the basic essentials of the move were at last in place, I knew I had to fly to the UK to help Libby with the final arrangements for the cycle ride. Morgan and I would fly from Tel Aviv to London at the weekend then on to Glasgow, London, Paris, London and back to Tel Aviv. And that, as they say, is another story.

Words of the day: derech tzlecha—bon voyage (Hebrew)

13

IS THAT A GUN IN YOUR POCKET?

I managed to pick up a really yucky head cold. I felt achy and grim with a badly swollen throat and runny nose, and I found it hard to sleep. So I lay awake and worried about all the things I needed to do before I got on the plane to London. I stressed about the finer details of the London to Paris cycle ride in memory of Amber. I thought about all the pieces of paperwork I hadn't done yet (such as our insurance claim for items missing or damaged in the move, the first in nearly twenty years of such moves). This couldn't wait three weeks until I got back, and Chris was simply too busy at work, so I wouldn't add to his workload.

After hours of lying awake, turning quietly, sipping water quietly and trying not to sneeze, I bailed out of the marital bed and headed downstairs to the guest bedroom.

I settled and relaxed into a much-needed drift towards sleep. Just at the moment when I'd almost reached my destination, and in the middle of the pitch dark, the doorbell rang loudly. I was immediately alert with cold fear but decided to ignore it. I didn't fancy answering the front door in the middle of the night. It rang again, more persistently. This time I heard Chris's steps on the stairs and called out to him, 'Don't open the front door.'

'Why?' he asked me, clearly puzzled. This is the man who'll drive to Lebanon via Syria for a skiing holiday, and I do normally love the adventurous side of his character.

'It's the middle of the night, and it could be armed robbers,' I said firmly.

Everywhere I went in Israel, I was asked if I was carrying a weapon. It didn't seem so ridiculous when you saw the rifles slung casually across the shoulders of young people in the mall, pushing baby buggies. Nor did it seem ridiculous when you pictured in your mind's eye the whoppers carried by police, security guards and soldiers who were everywhere.

'Look out of the window first,' I called from my sick bed. I was seriously scared and had no inclination to get up. I don't scare easily. I was known as the snake lady of Brunei during a previous posting. I was forced to get rid of one which was relaxing on my front door mat and blocking my access to the house and the fridge. As I had a car full of groceries, which wouldn't have survived the heat and humidity, it left me no choice. RIP snake.

Chris climbed back upstairs and looked out of the study window where he had a clear view of an apparently unarmed middle-aged man who was shouting frantically, '*Maya, maya,*' which means 'water, water' in Arabic. Our neighbour was Jewish, but it was apparent that our lack of language skills in Hebrew had reached him on the moshav grapevine. As our removal cartons (the last few empties were still in the garden) said 'Jordan Jinx Removers' on the side, he'd reached the conclusion we must be Arabic speakers. If he was hoping for a chat, he was destined for disappointment. (Arabic at that time was the second language of Israel and remained so until 2018 when Hebrew was declared the sole official language.)

I dressed hurriedly and said my *shalom*s to our new neighbour at five o'clock in the morning.

Chris was wearing his trademark Beckham-style sarong, which he wore with flair long before Beckham followed in his footsteps. Sarong wearing at every available opportunity is a relic of his childhood spent barefoot in Kenya, although it wasn't actually an African *kikoy* or sarong he was wearing on this occasion but one I bought in Bali fifteen years before which was so soft and worn, it ranked with the favourites.

'We've obviously got a malfunction in the irrigation system,' Chris observed.

I said a silent thank you that he was a water engineer and had the ability to solve most crises in a cool and calm way.

'The irrigation control panel is over here,' he said over his shoulder as he rushed on ahead.

I followed him to the far side of the house, dodging a geyser which was gushing with formidable force, metres into the air, and dancing like a water display in the wind.

Chris deftly opened the cover of the control panel. We thought of resetting the irrigation timer, but the irrigation instruction manual was written entirely in Hebrew.

'It should go off in a minute, after this section has run its course,' said my calm water engineer of a husband. Well it did—eventually. Now we lived in fear of the bill.

By the time the problem was isolated and resolved, with phone calls to be made to workmen later in the day, it was time to get up and get on with the jobs I'd been thinking about all night. But I just couldn't. I tucked up in bed for another several hours' sleep. I would tackle the lot when I got up. *Mañana, mañana.*

Word of the day: maya—water (Arabic)

14

JEWISH HIGH HOLIDAYS

After the cycle ride, Morgan and I flew back on the 8th September on Rosh Hashanah, or Jewish New Year. I was seated next to a friendly but intense Jewish man, probably in his early 30s, overweight and very chatty. He, like many Israelis, wasn't afraid to resign his job and set up his own business. After asking to borrow the *Financial Times* newspaper I was bringing back for Chris, he explained to me that he'd been in London attending meetings to grow his fledging computer software business focusing on internet security. Despite his technical knowledge, business acumen and extensive experience of which frequent flyer programmes were worth joining, he was clearly nervous and superstitious about travelling on a Jewish High Holiday.

He disclosed this after our flight sat on the tarmac at Heathrow airport with engines running for a while. Apparently there was a minor technical defect in the pushback vehicle, and my fellow passenger saw this as a bad omen. He was quite right. We missed our precious take-off slot at one of the world's busiest airports, and after the engines had been idling for over an hour, we needed to wait to refuel before we could leave. After sitting on the tarmac for two hours, we finally took off. By now my neighbour was twitchy as apparently it was very bad form to arrive home after the sunset which would mark the start of Rosh Hashanah. All Jewish holidays are observed from sunset to sunset.

'I'm sure your family will be pleased to see you home safely,' I offered, 'even if you are a bit late for the special family gathering tonight.'

Rosh Hashanah is the first of the Jewish High Holidays and is regarded as the day of judgement in the Jewish calendar. Three books of account are opened on Rosh Hashanah when all your deeds are weighed up by God. If you're good, you get entered in the book of life for another year. 'May you be entered in the book for another year,' your religious Jewish friends will tell you, while your secular Israeli friends will make do with a cheery 'Happy New Year' sort of a greeting.

On the other hand, if you're considered even slightly dodgy, you have ten days until Yom Kippur (the Day of Atonement) to repent your sins and become good.

Now repenting your sins doesn't mean a private confession and heartfelt sorrow for wrongdoing in the Jewish religion. You're supposed to right wrongs you've done and approach the person you've done wrong by face to face to make things better. I've watched enough CSI episodes to know that this sort of personal interaction, where one person has been seriously wronged by another, doesn't always have a positive outcome.

The third book is for those who are thought to be a lost cause and needn't bother with the atonement process as they're beyond any sort of redemption and deleted from the book of the living forever.

This High Holiday marks the start of weeks and weeks of holidays in the Jewish calendar. There are also special prayers at the synagogue, and if Rosh Hashanah doesn't fall on Shabbat, the ram's horn is sounded.

When Chris saw the price of a decent ram's horn during a Friday stroll around the Old City of Jerusalem, he decided he might retire and start breeding the beasts. A fine specimen will set you back hundreds of dollars, and remember there are two per ram. This could be the retirement plan we'd been waiting for.

Everything shuts down for three days at Rosh Hashanah, and it's like a three-day Shabbat. Groceries, water and other essentials need to be stocked up as absolutely nothing will be available in Jerusalem.

After we landed in Ben Gurion Airport a couple of hours late, the sun was just setting in a spectacular bright orange light show. I was interested to eavesdrop on a late middle-aged tour group with American accents, introducing themselves to each other. All were dressed in comfortable 'I had a reasonable job and am now retired' clothes, expensive leisure shoes and groomed hairstyles (men and women).

'Should we exchange currency here at the airport?' one asked.

Another of the fledgling gang was clued up and told the others, 'It's a public holiday, so it mightn't be possible to exchange cash in Jerusalem.'

He was right, but I couldn't help wondering what they would spend the shekels on if nothing was open, or indeed how they would spend their days and nights.

I now know that Arab East Jerusalem will be open during the holiday, and that tourists can enjoy non-Jewish parts of the Old City, Nazareth, Bethlehem and many other destinations in Israel and the West Bank.

We enjoyed the three days, settling back into our new home, preparing for school which would open intermittently over the next month or so of holidays, and getting to know Chris's newly adopted kitten.

While Morgan and I had been away, Chris had been introducing a tiny wild kitten to the human race and the joys of regular kitty food. She was a real cutie, although very nervous of us. I wondered whether Chris, who had become anti-pets, befriended her while the balance of his mind was disturbed.

'Not the case,' he assured me. 'I needed someone to talk to while you were away.'

In our previous lifetime as parents, when our daughters were very young and we were living in Brunei Darussalam (Abode of Peace) as it's officially known (though shortened to Brunei for the rest of the world), we had a dog, cats, free-range guinea pigs, hamsters and turtles. When we moved to Jordan in 1999, we inherited Christina the tortoise and Tweety the duck. We'd had three international moves in the past three years, so it wasn't easy travelling with a small zoo. I'd coveted a friendly dog for Morgan, who needed a playmate now that his big sister was living almost full-time in the UK. I wouldn't have minded having a little friendly tailwagger either, but Chris was forever practical. Until we knew what the future held on the job front, there could be no tailwagger for us.

Our non-existent Hebrew was a huge problem for us. In previous postings we relied on other people speaking English too much. Hebrew was spoken everywhere as the main language. Israeli Arabs spoke Arabic, but despite living more than ten years in the Arab world and the kids studying it at school, none of us was confident or fluent enough to get by beyond a trip to the shops. Some people in Israel speak English very well, but the majority don't, or don't want to.

I came back from my trip with the children's book *My First 1,000 words in Hebrew*, a great starting point when learning any new language. So if you're planning to come to Israel to live as an expat or to make Aliyah, start learning a few words of Hebrew. You won't regret it. I'm told you need to write a test on Hebrew, maybe even in Hebrew, if you're making Aliyah.

Morgan started at the JAIS and settled right in. There was a huge white rabbit called Sugar, and he lived in the classroom (Sugar not Morgan). I was sure this helped Morgan. He was one of nine pupils in the fourth grade (American system) which translates to primary five in the British system. His teacher was fresh from the USA and was bright, energetic, enthusiastic, focused, driven and well organised.

The atmosphere of the school was relaxed, friendly and nurturing but with a strong expectation of academic achievement and professionalism. I was convinced we'd chosen the right school for Morgan. The principal was a whacky dresser and owned a fascinating collection of Doc Marten-style boots. My personal favourites were the pale blue Doc Martens with delicate pink flowers in a Laura Ashley-like print. The principal's nose piercing was another thing I hadn't come across in any of the principals of the many international schools our children had had the privilege to attend, although the lovely Mr B, head teacher of the International Community School in Amman, was regularly seen in a long satin dress and full make-up during pantomime season. Somehow there was room for everyone at JAIS; individuality was celebrated, but failure to turn in assignments cracked down on severely. It was a very ruly school, if the opposite of unruly is ruly.

After a few days of school, it was time for the most serious of all the Jewish holidays, Yom Kippur. The time between Rosh Hashanah and Yom Kippur is a time of prayer, reflection and repentance. This time is known as the Days of Awe. The most significant day is Yom Kippur. Even Jews who don't normally attend synagogue on any other day of the year will attend on Yom Kippur. In fact some will spend most of the day there, where public confessions are made and prayers said. There are five prayers at synagogue instead of the usual three, and a 25-hour fast is observed from one hour before sundown until sundown the next day.

On the Day of Atonement, it's forbidden to eat, drink, bathe, put on any sort of oil, put on a sandal or engage in sexual relations. On this day at the end of Yom Kippur, the judgement on the book of life is sealed, the Days of Awe are almost over and it's too late to try to change behaviour, if this is thought necessary, and seek forgiveness for wrongs done.

On a lighter note, there are no traffic jams. In fact on Yom Kippur, there's no traffic at all. Driving is absolutely forbidden. If you do drive, you risk having rocks thrown at your car. You'll see people jogging or cycling in groups along Highway 1, the main motorway from Jerusalem to Tel Aviv. This is also the time when bicycle sales in Israel soar as kids get new bikes and can cycle around in traffic-free streets. It's difficult to make the connection between a day of religious reflection and soaring bicycle sales with frantic pedalling, but there we are. For many secular Israelis, Yom Kippur means fresh air and exercise.

I was suffering from suspected appendicitis on the eve of Yom Kippur, and so my doctor in Jerusalem told me that in the case of a medical emergency, you're allowed to drive to hospital provided you didn't live in an orthodox area. But he cautioned that we must drive very slowly because of the pedestrian traffic and kids on the road. If you live in an orthodox area, you really need to call an ambulance. It's either that or risk a new injury if the rock, which is likely to be thrown at your car, hits you on the head.

There was a wonderful photograph in the *Jerusalem Post* by photographer Marc Israel Sellem. It showed a man performing *kapparot* in the ultra-orthodox neighbourhood of Mea She'arim. The atonement ritual showed him holding a live chicken aloft by its feet and symbolically transferring his sins to the chicken ahead of Yom Kippur. He was closely observed by three children whose expressions ranged from amusement to bemusement.

Apart from the religious angst of confession and purification, there were the usual worries over food and drink.

'Jacob, I don't know how many I should buy. Yossi will eat two, and everyone else will eat one, so that's six. But what if somebody is hungrier than usual? I'll get seven. See you later, honey.' The American Jewish matriarch, with her shopping challenge finalised, kissed her septuagenarian husband on the cheek and hustled off to locate the perfect seven pieces of something to be consumed before the 25-hour fast began. Jacob didn't need to say a word during the whole exchange. He sat in a café in the German Colony, a leafy, affluent area of Jerusalem, with his newspaper and coffee but was clearly a crucial sounding board for problem resolution in his wife's world.

Wines were reviewed in the press for their entitlement to grace any holiday dinner table. One particular variety, which has never appealed to me purely on the design of its label, was very favourably reviewed. It had won four international awards and was a 'very reasonable 180 shekels'. Now I had another reason never to buy it. I pushed the boat out if I spent 60 shekels on a Carmel winery bottle, also award-winning and my favourite local wine.

Shortly after the Yom Kippur holiday, the Jewish holiday of Sukkot began. This is also known as the Festival of the Tabernacles and lasts for seven days in Israel in accordance with scripture and eight days in the diaspora (the rest of the world where Jews live their lives and celebrate High Holidays). This festival marks the 40 years that the Israelites wandered in the desert before entering the Promised Land.

A few days before Sukkot, we saw many tent-like structures

springing up in gardens, balconies and communal residential car parks, or in fact anywhere there was space for a tent or two in a crowded urban environment. They're intended to replicate the fragile homes in which the Israelites lived during the 40 years after their exodus from Egypt. While sitting in our doctor's waiting room, I overheard a tragic story of a man falling from his third-floor balcony while erecting his Sukkot tent, so you do have to be a bit careful where and how you set up.

Every restaurant and café will have a tent or packing case-style temporary abode in the garden, or if there's no garden, the tents will be erected side by side along the pavement so that all Jews can dine in the tabernacles for the whole festival. The temporary dwelling can only have three sides, and stars must be visible through the roof at night. Some Orthodox Jews even sleep in the temporary dwellings although the weather is usually turning quite chilly at night by September as Jerusalem is at an altitude of over 750 metres above sea level.

The tents (by far the most popular, in my limited experience) are rectangular, metal-framed structures covered with predominantly white fabric with pictures of wheat, fruit and vegetables printed on the sides. Some are brand new and shiny, while others have seen a fair few Sukkots and are a little tired and faded with age.

The alternative to the rather flimsy tent is an erection which resembles a large wooden packing case. This is a more substantial outdoor dining space which I'm sure is less draughty, but not as aesthetically pleasing.

The next strange sight is the gathering and delivery of large palm fronds and other foliage on a major scale. The leaves are placed on the roof of the tent or wooden box, having been transported across town often on the top of small well-used cars. I've witnessed people hacking large branches from trees at the foot of the Jerusalem Forest.

> 'God told Moses, "On the first day, you shall take
> the product of Hadar trees, branches of palm
> trees, boughs of leafy trees, and willows of the
> brook."'

> LEV.23:40

I thought it was extremely bad luck that on the first day the tents were up and the people were ready to eat outdoors, there was a definite turn in the weather and some large ploppy raindrops fell from above. That was until I was enlightened and informed that during this time, there are prayers for rain to allow Israel to plant, be fruitful and feed the people. So the rain was a blessing and much asked for. It just goes to show.

Celebrants of the festival walked to synagogue, many wearing lovely new hats, and carried unopened palm fronds in long protective plastic sheaths. They also brought citrus fruit (*etrog*) which looked like a big knobbly lemon. The men of Mea She'arim search through heaps of fruit to find the perfect citron for their purposes. In the days before the holidays, makeshift tables appeared all over town selling the fruit, some in gift boxes, some loose, and the kite-like packets of closed palm leaves. That explained the dire but puzzling warning I read in the newspaper: 'US Customs warns Sukkot travellers their *etrogim* face inspection.'

The second to seventh days of Sukkot are known as festival weekdays. So for us, school and shopping resumed after the first day as Morgan's international school only observed the first day of this holiday. For Jewish people, shopping and food preparation continued as this is a time when family and friends gather for delicious meals prepared specially to mark the holiday. Food preparation and gathering is allowed, as is travel to and from each other's houses, and family outings in celebration of the holiday. The Jerusalem Forest was packed with large families picnicking and enjoying the outdoors.

Activities which interfered with the enjoyment and relaxation of the holiday, such as laundry, aren't allowed under Jewish law. I was baffled that house cleaning in honour of the holiday was permitted. It would definitely have interfered with my relaxation and enjoyment of this special time.

During the holiday, our neighbours who had recently moved in across the valley hosted a loud party, where every generation was represented and most encouraged to join in the singing and the dancing. The music was live and loud, with much fiddling and percussion in a hillbilly style and tempo. It was good old foot-stomping, barn-dancing stuff, and as we sat sipping our vino, I was delighted to see so much fun and general hilarity. In time the music veered towards Yiddish folk music which made me think of *Fiddler on the Roof* for the first time in decades. We saw a great stage production of it years ago in Glasgow, not realising how much attention we should have paid at the time.

We then got a squeaky, fiddled version of 'Day Tripper' by the Beatles followed by 'Hey Jude'. The spectacle was mesmerizing, and the jollity and frivolity carried on well into the night. As usual, and as in most cultures, the noise from the junior faction of the family was the loudest.

The guests ate outside in the Sukkot tent, and the smell of roasting meat made our teeth water. Thank goodness it wasn't vegetarian night in our house or there would have been a riot. I made a mental note to get to Abu Ghosh, an Arab Christian village nearby, for some lamb before my family revolted.

The Old City of Jerusalem was the hub of frantic activity as many thousands of tourists had flocked to Jerusalem to celebrate the Feast of the Tabernacles. There was Sukkot entertainment for the whole family, and in Sacher Park near the Knesset (Israeli Parliament), tents, rides and attractions to bring people together in body and spirit.

The centre of town was buzzing with life, tourists and trade. Women of all ages wore white clothes to make the pilgrimage to the Old City, and there was a fantastic festival atmosphere, if a lack of tables and seats at my favourite cafés. It was so busy that I was forced to have a coffee near my usual supermarket stop by Mount Herzl, instead of on Jaffa Street in the centre. I'd stopped at the supermarket earlier in the day to pick up some groceries after the school run, but before going on my fun jaunt into town proper.

As I was leaving the supermarket first time around, I observed a grumpy face through my rear-view mirror, obviously fed up with the delays and the traffic. *My goodness*, I thought. *What a fierce expression at this joyous time.* I realised with shock that it was my own face reflected in the rear-view mirror. My default expression. Once again I fitted right in.

I was also amazed that when I got back to the supermarket area, which was packed with cars stocking up for more feasting, the security guard said to me as I waited to have the boot of my car checked out, 'This is your second visit today.' These security guys really were on the ball.

He also admired our binoculars enquiring, 'Are they for birding?'

'No, just for spying,' was my cheeky reply, out of earshot.

There was also a considerable amount of fractious crying during this holiday as every generation meets up for food in the tents, night after night for a week, and the kids stay up way past their normal bedtimes as the local schools are all on holiday. The kids are out of sorts and out of routine. I made a mental note to remember to stock up on earplugs for the following year.

Even the grown-ups got a bit jaded with the excesses of food and drink by the end of the week, not to mention the same stories which were apparently recycled again and again. Oh, the joys of a multi-generation gathering.

The holiday which follows Sukkot is known as the Shemini Atzeret (the eighth day of assembly). It's regarded as a totally separate holiday, and on the eighth day, the Sukkah (singular of Sukkot—literally 'booth' or 'tabernacle' in Hebrew) is left, and meals are eaten inside the house once more. Of course it warranted another day off school.

For us the weather and evenings were so beautiful that we'd taken our meals outside on every night of Sukkot, without a tent. In fact we hadn't eaten inside once since moving to the moshav in July. However, it was comforting to note that if there was rain during Sukkot, there was an exemption from eating in the tent. It was also reassuring to note just how many public holidays there were in Israel.

Despite the holidays we managed to get Morgan's school medical completed and more or less got the hang of the homework regime. He was unfazed by his new school, its rules and regimes, and this new environment. He was his usual cheerful self. I was a little sceptical when told that most fourth graders were reading *Harry Potter* for fun and writing eight-page essays. My scepticism mainly stemmed from advice we'd been given by very experienced British educators that the American education system wouldn't be as academically challenging as the British. So on day one, Morgan laid his cards on the table with his new principal.

'I do three-page essays, maximum,' he admitted, with no shame.

The principal didn't react. I think she knew he would conform under her guidance, which he did.

We had yet to see where this journey into recess (playtime), pants (trousers) and my personal favourite, tighty-whities (underpants), would take us. Yet another new language to master.

Words of the day: Shana Tova—Happy New Year (Hebrew)

15

THE ROBBERY

I really needed to sort out our post office box so that I could inform the world of our new whereabouts. Well, not the whole world, because the Arab world would be given the office address in Ramallah or we would never get any mail. The PO box number the landlord had provided us with didn't exist, and the key was useless.

So on a beautiful, bright, sunny day, I strolled to the post office in the village centre to try and sort out the confusion. Passing the usual assortment of impossibly colourful displays of flowers, and listening to the birds singing their hearts out, I could have been on a Disney set. 'How many shades of green are there in the Jerusalem Forest?' I asked myself. 'Lots,' was the answer. If talking to yourself was the first sign of madness, I was alarmed that I was now answering myself back.

I arrived at the village square and breathed in the strong smell of horses and hay coming from the riding stables. The cocks were cock-a-doodle-doo-ing, and the village green was totally deserted.

I walked into the post office, and it too was deserted. I amused myself while waiting for the post mistress to return to her counter, and attempted to make sense of the brochures on display—all in Hebrew.

Then a bear of a man, who looked like he could lift weights professionally for Russia, stormed in and shouted at me, 'You must leave! You must leave!' Now I knew very well that the Israelis aren't the most patient at queuing, but this was ridiculous.

Of course I now know that this titan was our full-time security guard who manned the entrance barrier to our village (lowered after dark), kept a night-time vigil and a wary eye out for us all during the day.

I stepped outside into a small gathering of people, newly arrived. They chattered away in Hebrew, and a slim grey-haired gentleman asked me what I wanted.

'I just want to talk to the woman in the post office,' I explained, thinking this must have been pretty obvious.

'Can you come back later? There's been a robbery,' the very calm and quiet man who spoke good English informed me.

'Sure, but was anyone hurt?'

Just as I asked the question, the police arrived, and madam post mistress was led from our mini market carrying a small plastic cup of water. She was taken back to the scene of the crime. A robbery, on our moshav. I was astonished.

I returned to the post office later that day to enquire about the post mistress and whether she was okay. Surprisingly she was sitting behind her desk attending to her normal duties. She did appreciate my concern. She also issued me with the correct box number and a new key so we could receive mail. Progress. Not to mention the fact that she was pleasant, spoke excellent English and offered to help us in any way she could.

Later that evening I was busy with domestic goddess-like activities in my new shiny kitchen when I heard Chris and Morgan chatting and laughing with someone outside. I really hoped that they wouldn't bring anyone inside as I was just catching up with breakfast dishes, although it was almost dark. Plan A was not to turn the lights on if they came inside. I adopted plan B and went out to see what was going on in order to block any possible visit.

I met the treat who was Talia, my across-the-road-and-up-the-hill neighbour, but not a skinny grumpy one. I hadn't seen her before. She was an earth mother with five-month-old twins and a two-year-old in tow. The toddler ran up and down the road with two other children not much older who belonged to a visitor. Both Talia and her visitor spoke very good English.

'Do you repair cars?' Talia was asking Chris as I joined the conversation.

She was clearly confused about what sort of engineer Chris was. We were to discover over the coming months that her ancient people-mover needed regular coaxing into service.

'Sadly not.'

'How many children do you have?' She pressed on with the impromptu interrogation.

'Well, we have Morgan, who lives here with us,' I said. 'Say hello, Morgan.' I nudged him. 'And we have his sister Liberty who's studying at university in the UK.'

I wasn't ready to discuss Amber, on the pavement at a first meeting, although my usual approach is to explain that our middle child died suddenly at the age of fifteen in Dubai. I'm not sure why I held back. Maybe because I was in a new environment among people I wasn't yet familiar with.

'I have six kids and a dog,' Talia continued. 'Where does Morgan go to school?'

'The Jerusalem American International School in San Simon, in the Goldstein Youth Village.'

'I home school mine,' offered Talia with confidence. Where did she find the time? 'Why does the Coca Cola can Morgan's holding have Arabic writing on it?'

This required a bit of a sidestep. I wasn't sure the fact that Chris was working to improve infrastructure in the Occupied West Bank would go down well with our new Israeli neighbours.

'Oh, someone brought some for him…' I answered vaguely.

'What's your work, Chris?'

'I'm providing consultancy services to the US government.' True, if a little sparse on detail.

I also told her about the post office robbery, and her howls of laughter were comforting.

'You're joking of course,' she said, while juggling a baby and tending to a twin who wasn't happy to be stuck in the buggy, missing out on cuddles. I took the happy baby from her arms, freeing her up to pick up the other twin.

'I promise you; I'm not!' I smiled back, pleased by her disbelief that this could happen on our moshav.

'We never lock our house,' she confessed, 'but we have nothing to steal.'

She found the whole scenario ridiculous. 'There's never been a robbery before on the moshav,' she told me. 'The post office is often left open if the post mistress pops out to the shop.'

'I'm comforted to know that robbery hasn't been a problem, at least until now. D'you still grow things on your plot in the moshav?'

'Only children,' was her reply.

I was reluctant to hand back the baby I'd been cuddling. He was just too lovely. I reminded myself that he was just across the road and I'd been given an open invitation to visit anytime, with offers of help if I had any problems at all. This was real generosity of time and spirit from a woman with so many children and a dog, and who was home schooling her family. I never saw Talia after that without getting a cheery smile and a wave. Hers was clearly a lifestyle to be recommended.

It seemed to Chris and me that every female of childbearing age was either with child or had just given birth. I was convinced it must be a lucrative business, all this going forth and multiplying. Arab families tend to be big as well, and I read somewhere that it's anticipated that within the next several years, the Arab population in Israel will outnumber the Israelis.

I wonder whether it's government strategy to hot-house Israeli population growth. Anyone opening a branch of Mothercare here would do very well indeed.

Word of the day: hatzilu — help (Hebrew)

16

THE NEIGHBOURS

During the warm summer evenings, children and parents congregated on the village green and enjoyed each other's company or running around. Toddlers waddled after large dogs, often larger than them. Pre-schoolers enjoyed drippy ice creams, and the older kids cycled or skateboarded in and out of view as they broke out of the cute and into the cool phase of life.

I placed Morgan in the emerging cool category. While I was waiting in a short but tediously slow queue (all checkouts in Israel were like this, I discovered), Morgan made firm friends with Shlomo, a gorgeous golden Labrador retriever. I was still in the queue when he came inside with Debra, the owner of Shlomo. Debra knew all about us as Morgan was quite the chatty one.

'Hi, I'm Debra. I've been chatting to Morgan. He tells me you're new here.'

'Yes, we moved to the village a few weeks ago,' I told her. 'I'm Linda, by the way.'

'How are you settling in?'

'We love the moshav but haven't met many people yet.'

'We came back from the USA three years ago to our family home, and we found the transition hard. Especially Noah, our son, who's

Morgan's age. Morgan says he loves soccer, and the boys in the village are planning a regular soccer game on Sunday evenings. Would he like to join them?'

'He would love that, but his Hebrew is non-existent.'

'Noah speaks English and will look after him. It will be good for him to practise his English too.'

Her beautiful, dark-eyed toddler, Lior, clung to her leg silently.

'I work full-time,' Debra continued, 'but Shimon, my husband, is at home looking after both boys. Lior is two, so things are a bit easier than in the beginning.'

After all this chatting and making arrangements, I was still in the queue at the moshav shop.

Unfortunately the football was cancelled because not enough kids were interested, but the boys arranged to meet on Sunday afternoons when Morgan had no school and therefore no homework. Although Noah had school on Sundays, Debra confessed that there wasn't much homework, so it wasn't a problem.

The first day I dropped Morgan at Noah's house, I was nervous. I didn't know the family. Debra was out at work, but Shimon, Lior and Noah's grandma were at home. I left Morgan with people he'd never met (he hadn't even met Noah) in an environment which, from the front door, seemed devoid of television, computers and electronic games. I asked Shimon to call me if there was any problem, and with some trepidation, I went home for a quiet worry.

That was a wasted two hours. By the time I returned, it was dark, and the whole family was in the garden where the boys were baking potatoes on a fire and playing with Shlomo. Morgan had had a lovely time; both boys were avid fans of the *Diary of a Wimpy Kid* series, and the next play day, chez Morgan, was arranged.

Words of the day: naim lehakir otcha (m) othach (f) — pleased to meet you
(Hebrew)

17

THE JOY OF SHOPPING

Just as Morgan's social life began to take off, so did mine.

At around noon on a Monday, there was a ring at the front gate, and Penny entered our lives. I didn't know it was Penny at the time of course as we'd never met, but I'd heard of her from our relocation agent who also found Penny and her family their house which was a few hundred metres along the road from ours. Our other British family on the moshav.

Penny had popped in to say hello and to offer a shopping tour of the area. While we had been surviving, and there hadn't been many complaints (we were missing decent tasty cheese), it would be good to expand my shopping horizons and forage for more exciting fare.

Just up the hill and obscured by piles of earth and stones was the amazing supermarket Rami Levi (interesting to note that Rami Levi featured on the *Haaretz* newspaper's New Year list of most influential Israelis, assuming it's the same Rami Levi). It was much bigger and better than any other supermarket I'd visited in Israel. There was even room for two trolleys to pass by if they met in an aisle, and space for checking out. Oh the joy. Better still, we applied for our Rami Levi customer loyalty cards and this entitled us to selected items at a very low price. Penny admitted that although she'd lived there for four years, she hadn't applied for her card, but that day we both bit the bullet, and we didn't regret it. After approximately ten phone calls each from the Rami Levi customer service department clarifying our nationalities, addresses and our mother's maiden names (well, I'm not sure about that one, but there were a lot of questions of that ilk), two months later we received our plastic cards. Things just got better and better on the Rami Levi front. They then introduced two checkout lanes for card holders only, and they offered helpers who packed up groceries. Life was slowly getting back to normal.

However, if you were new to the area and didn't read Hebrew, it would be hard to find the shop. Not a single hint that there was a huge well-stocked supermarket was evident from the main road.

After the joys of the supermarket sweep in Castel, we drove back towards Mevaseret Zion and took a right, down towards what looked like industrial units. They couldn't be seen from the road, but I was shown into a lovely shop which stocked dried fruit and nuts, interesting sauces and marinades, cooking and baking ingredients and equipment. Chris and I both enjoy cooking, so this was a real find.

The Avi Ben wine shop was also a couple of doors down and stocked a great variety of quality wines and spirits. We looked forward to trying pomegranate liqueur, a local specialty.

There was also a butcher, a fishmonger, a toy shop and a large well-stocked craft shop with work rooms and art and craft supplies floor to ceiling. Yes, life was really getting back to normal.

We swung past a deli and shared an irresistible special offer—four bottles of Spanish cava for 100 shekels. We split the bill and the bottles. I absolutely recommend the cava in fresh Israeli orange juice for a Buck's Fizz experience.

We noted that there was a sushi restaurant next to the deli and practically on our doorstep, and they delivered too. When you're an expat in a foreign land, the discovery of treats, treasure and leisure activities in your host country can be very uplifting in a way that's hard to convey.

We rounded off a delightful morning out in good company with a delicious latte taken in the shade in a newly discovered café just five minutes' drive from home.

I felt well looked after and much more at home in my wider environment. Thank you, Penny.

Word of the day: yofi—good (Hebrew)

18

ISLAMIC HOLIDAY

I was surprised to learn that around twenty per cent of the population in Israel is Arab. Some of the community is Christian Arab, but the majority are Muslim and live in East Jerusalem in Silwan, Sheik Jarrah, Beit Hanina and Shufat. The United Nations and many foreign consulates are based in East Jerusalem. I know that many employers insist that staff live there because it's considered safer as it's less likely that any planned attack against Israel would target the Arab east side of town. I prefer to think that as Jerusalem is such a significant place for Jews, Christians and Muslims alike, that it may not be targeted at all.

Just as there was a risk that the students of JAIS be required to attend school for a whole week, the Islamic holiday of Eid al-Adha rolled around, and we had yet another holiday.

I was particularly fond of Islamic holidays as it meant that Chris got a well-deserved day off work too. Because he worked in Ramallah, in the Occupied Territory of Palestine, he didn't get the many Jewish holidays Morgan and I enjoyed on the other side of the security wall. So when the school did recognise an Islamic holiday, it was a treat in our world. Chris got Friday and Saturday as his weekend. Morgan got Saturday and Sunday.

When, twice a year, it was time to change the clocks—spring forward, fall back—the Palestinians changed at a different time from the Israelis. So for a couple of weeks or more, twice a year we would have a time difference between Ramallah and Jerusalem. Sometimes I hankered after a simpler life.

For the first time in over sixteen years, I wasn't living in the Islamic world during Ramadan.

Ramadan is a holy month in the Islamic faith during which all Muslims are required to observe a fast, every day from sunrise to sunset. During the fasting month, all eating, drinking, smoking and love making must be refrained from during the day. Even if you aren't Muslim, in some countries there's no eating, drinking or smoking in public, or you can be severely punished, depending on where you are.

When we lived in Jordan, most cafés and restaurants were closed in the daytime. Some hotel cafés catered for visitors (the Intercontinental café was always a favourite of ours), and one or two fast-food outlets served take-away burgers.

We have a lovely memory of our Christian Jordanian Arab finance director coming back to the office with his hidden contraband of lunchtime take-away burgers during Ramadan, depositing them on the window ledge outside his ground-floor office, strolling through the office, closing his door and retrieving his lunch from outside. One day he very generously offered Chris one of the four burgers he'd bought. The director was thin as a pin, so he must have had a good metabolism. Chris declined his kind offer. Our answer to the conundrum was that while we were out, we didn't eat or drink for the whole month, and it often led to a surprising slackening of the trouser waistband by the end of the fasting month.

In Dubai things were much stricter than Jordan, and it would have been impossible to buy even a take-away meal during Ramadan. Anyone caught smoking was taken to court, and every year the unlucky ones were reported in the tabloid press. Kissing publicly in Dubai can lead to a jail term, so it's inadvisable to even consider the making of whoopee during daylight during Ramadan in that Emirate.

At the end of a long day of fasting, there is the phenomenon known as Iftar, the breaking of the fast meal. At the beginning of the month, people and their digestive systems aren't used to the sudden change. So the fast is usually broken with a high energy-release date (the fruit) before the excesses of the Iftar buffet are piled high on your plate. Apart from the risks of serious overeating at an Iftar meal, the risk of dying from passive smoking is high. Deprived of their cigarettes for the equivalent of a non-smoking transatlantic flight, people eat and smoke at the same time. I was unfortunate enough to sit next to a woman in Jordan who smoked non-stop for the whole evening, just to make up for lost puffing time. Fork in one hand, fag in the other.

Iftar celebrations often have entertainment (musical, comedy or both), and the month is a month of early-finish work days (usually 2 p.m.), early-finish school days and evenings out.

On the meaningful side of this special month, the fasting is supposed to make you think of people less fortunate than you who don't have enough to eat much of the time. In theory it's a time of no eating during daylight hours with a celebration meal after sunset. It's also a time for prayer and play, spending and giving.

In some countries the fasting day can be very long and very hot. When we moved to Brunei during Ramadan, our removers arrived with our shipment of household goods in the middle of the day, in 33°C degrees of heat and close to 100% humidity. They pleasantly and with great energy unloaded the shipment and accepted no drinks or rest. The sun sets early in Brunei every night of the year. Muslims in Britain, however, can have a very long summer fasting day. It's not unusual for it to be light at ten thirty at night in Scotland on a summer night, although temperatures of 30°C degrees are a rare treat north of the English border.

My first year outside a Ramadan-observant community in over sixteen years was easier. No closed shops, bare shelves, closed cafés, closed offices, and yet I missed the sense of excitement as sunset approached. I missed the hairy driving if you were on the roads too close to sunset when everybody was screaming home on two tyres so as not to be a minute late for the meal. I also missed the pancake stands which were set up all over Amman, often outside, where you could buy and carry home a tray of steaming, warm, freshly flipped pancakes to have with a delicious cup of fresh mint tea at home.

The holiday of Eid al–Fitr is celebrated at the end of the fasting month. When the new moon is spotted (the Muslim and the Jewish calendars are calculated on the lunar month), Eid is declared. The next day there's no fasting. Actually, quite the reverse. Journeys are made home to visit parents and grandparents, and everyone wears their best clothes. Children are usually decked out in new outfits for the occasion and are given gifts of toys or money. It's usual to see a small Arab boy toting a plastic machine gun or revolver, toy guns appearing to be the preferred holiday gift. There's a lot of eating and drinking together as a family. My family call this holiday Big Eid.

Eid al-Adha is the holiday we call Little Eid or Wee Eid, fairly close to the end of the Jewish High Holidays.

So on this Little Eid holiday, Chris and Morgan both had a day off, and we decided to visit the Jerusalem Biblical Zoo, which was very green, open and well set out around a large lake with pretty pink flamingos and other waterfowl.

We had such a happy stroll around the extensive parklands, taking in the usual reptile house, polar bear pool and lion enclosure. The Animal Ark area was particularly picturesque, and zebra, giraffe and camels with many other creatures hung around conveniently in twos for photographs; at least, they did that day.

The zoo was well kept, and there was a lot of open space for the animals to roam. They were certainly in less cramped conditions than the humans. If you ever decide to visit this lovely facility with a picnic for your family and friends, take my advice and don't do it on Wee Eid.

There was a sea of Israeli Arab holidaymakers all enjoying the facilities and the sunshine. We only saw two obviously Jewish families the whole day we were there (headgear and peyot gave them away), which was almost unheard of in Jerusalem. The majority of the visitors to the zoo were Israeli Arabs having a great day out with extended family and friends.

The downside was that it was impossible to buy a coffee or an ice cream. The queues were just outrageous. It wasn't until we decided to move on and eat elsewhere that we found a good outdoor café near the exit, where we had a well-earned, unhealthy lunch with holiday ice cream.

The upside was that there was a wedding party at the zoo. I have the most surreal picture of an Arab bride in her huge white satin meringue-shaped wedding dress, with her handsome groom, posing by the lake for photographs with the elegant pink flamingos. Unfortunately, in shot, and also posing just above their heads, were a couple of hilarious baboons, swinging their way across overhead lines, in celebration of the marriage.

Word of the day: mabruk—congratulations (Arabic)

19

ALL SORTS OF JEWS

The State of Israel was founded on 14th May 1948. The Declaration of Independence read: 'The State of Israel will be open to the immigration of Jews from all the countries of their dispersion.' That was a direct reference to the Holocaust which caused many Jews to flee their homelands to avoid persecution. Of the ones who didn't flee, some six million are estimated to have perished in the Holocaust during the Second World War. It's a horror on an unimaginable scale which happened as quickly as Hitler's men spread across Europe like a virulent rash.

The melting pot of the State of Israel is home to Jews from the world over. There are Russians, Germans, Eastern Europeans, Dutch, British, Ethiopians and many more. Today there are a lot of American Jews either in residence or in semi-permanent residence, and Jews continue to make Aliyah (immigrate to Israel) in numbers every year. I lost count of the number of times I was asked when I'd made Aliyah. Clearly my new hairdresser, Ariel, was doing an excellent job of integrating me into the local community.

When we first arrived in Jerusalem, I was frustrated by the extensive use of Hebrew, which in my previous life had only links with the Bible and dusty tomes housed in museums. Hebrew has been revived as a living working language which is spoken extensively throughout Israel. The most learned scholars in the land will converse in Hebrew, as will the lad who hands out free newspapers each morning at the traffic lights. The revival of this language has meant that some new words have had to be introduced as there was, for example, no such thing as a laptop computer back in the day. Israeli writers have also written great novels and other works in this adapted biblical language. Thankfully they've been translated into English so that we can share and understand a little better.

On the basis that thousands of people from all over the world come to live and make a home in Israel, it's a bond to speak a common language, like joining a comfortable social group. All Aliyah-makers must learn Hebrew at an *ulpan* (language school) and pass an exam before they're officially admitted to the Jewish family in Israel. I'm glad that I formed this positive outlook on the speaking of this mystery tongue over time. Initially I thought using Hebrew was a security measure, just so that no outsider knew what was happening here. Ditto all road signs. Maybe it's a bit of both.

There are Jews who intend to make Aliyah at some point in the future and have bought real estate which they keep vacant for the day they do. This causes some friction, especially in Jerusalem where property holding of this sort is seen as pushing up real estate prices, which are already high, and contributing to the shortage of available properties. On the plus side, the absentee landowners do pay their taxes and so contribute to the maintenance of the city, without actually using any services. It seems reasonable to suppose that if such generous benefactors didn't exist, we would all be paying a higher rate of municipal tax. So, absentee, wannabee Aliyah-makers, I thank you. Although I fear I might be in the minority in extending gratitude.

Families make Aliyah from all over the world, and there's help available in integrating them into the community. They also enjoy tax incentives when buying cars. Motor cars are scarily expensive, and I saw a Land Rover dealership advertisement on a billboard in Tel Aviv offering a fairly standard model for the equivalent of $150,000. Tax represented a considerable portion of that cost, so some of the benefits and breaks of Aliyah were really worthwhile.

If I were to make Aliyah, I would need to prove that I was Jewish through the maternal line of my family. My mother told me recently that she had a Jewish boyfriend before she met and married my father, but that's just too tenuous a connection to save the tax on a car. The other way is to engage in full-time religious study for two years; another non-starter for me.

So in the melting pot, there are Jews who have been there since the State of Israel was proclaimed more than 70 years ago, those who have been there even longer than that, those who have immigrated in a steady stream following the Second World War (it's amazing to think that due to immigration, the population of Israel doubled in the four years after the State was founded), and those who have been making Aliyah ever since. The population is currently around eight and a half million (2018) and rising every year.

With such a diverse pot of ingredients, it's not surprising that there are many different sorts of Jews, Jewish lifestyles and moral codes.

At one extreme there is the three-times-a-year Jew who goes to synagogue during the High Holidays. A bit like the Christmas-Eve Christians, who love to sing carols and go to church once a year when it's jolly and festive.

At the other extreme is the ultra-Orthodox Jew. There have been objections to this group of Jews being labelled as 'ultra'. Some people have difficulties with the term due to its extremist connotations. For that reason certain American publications have agreed to drop the term ultra-orthodox altogether.

We saw examples of Orthodox Jews as we drove up the hill towards Jerusalem and the central bus station. There were droves of men in black who looked like film-set extras scurrying along the pavement and across the busy road. All wore black fedora-style hats, baggy black suits (often shiny and well-worn with trouser legs bunched around their ankles). Many were rushing with small suitcases on wheels in tow, and I often wondered what they carried in them. They were probably weighed down with scriptures and study material.

If we were lucky, we might spot a man wearing what looked like a large furry car tyre perched on his head. He would also be wearing a shiny silk frock coat, with short mid-calf-length black trousers and hose. This outfit looked like it was caught in a time warp and was lagging at least 100 years behind the rest of the world. I've been told that these *shtreimel* hats are worn on High Holidays and for other special religious days and celebrations. They're worn mainly by married Haredi men (Haredi is a sect of the ultra-orthodox community) and usually made from mink. There's now a debate on whether the religious High Holiday headgear complies with the Torah, and it's been hinted that anti real-fur measures may lie ahead.

By far the normal head gear for men in Jerusalem is the kippah, which comes in different sizes. The plain black velvet ones are larger and fit around the top of the skull. They also tend to be accompanied by long peyot (two long curly ringlets framing each side of the face, although the rest of the hair is short). The other sort of kippah is much smaller and looks about the size of a moulded drinks coaster. It's woven or crocheted from cotton thread, often in some jazzy pattern and colour scheme. It's usually worn on the crown of the head and is regularly seen rolling along the pavement in a high wind if not secured by a couple of hair grips. I think there must be a market for kippah Velcro with one side of a slim Velcro strip attached to the kippah itself and the other side to a hair grip. You just can't keep an enthusiastic entrepreneur down! As a lot of Israeli men like to shave their heads, there's probably a sizeable market for double-sided sticky tape as well, although the shaved-head brigade don't tend to wear kippahs. Maybe if they had access to good double-sided sticky tape, they would.

I was taken aback when shopping in Jerusalem with Morgan. I was admiring some beautiful handmade jewellery in a store, debating whether Liberty might like a specific necklace for her 21st birthday present, when Morgan leapt from behind a pillar wearing a Bart Simpson kippah.

'Can I have it…please?' he begged.

How could I explain without causing offence in front of the shopkeeper that I thought it insensitive for a non-Jew to wear a Bart Simpson kippah in the Holy City just for the love of the Simpsons?

'I don't think it's a good idea,' I told him.

'Okay then, I'll take the Chelsea Football Club one,' was his enthusiastic reply.

We left the shop empty handed, but I pondered why it was that I couldn't let him walk the streets of Jerusalem in a kippah for fun when he'd been allowed to buy and wear full Arab dress in Dubai for fun, much to the delight and indulgence of the Emiratis in the souk who admired his blue eyes and tweaked his cheeks playfully. I suppose there are more religious connotations with the kippah than with the Arab headdress which is more a practical protection from the fierce sun.

This scene was also played out in the days before I came to realise that Israelis just speak their minds in a very forthright and clear way. In the UK we're all used to pussyfooting around issues. An Israeli mother in a kilt shop in Glasgow, faced with the same scenario, would just say, 'No, Yitzhak, put it back. Men don't wear skirts in our country.' End off.

I was reliably informed that apart from the Jewish head covering being a mark of respect to God, whom the Jews believe is above us at all times, it was also a clear signal of beliefs and of who pays their taxes. The ultra-orthodox are apparently exempt from paying taxes while the crocheted kippah-wearing Jewish brothers have no such luck.

The large black velvet kippahs are often topped off with a fedora hat. So there's a double layer of head covering. From what I saw, the fedora comes off indoors, and the black velvet kippah remains in place. This double layer of head covering becomes a triple layer when it rains in Jerusalem. Then the precious fedora is protected from the rain by a large clear plastic shower cap, or if the rain has caught the gentleman by surprise, by a plastic supermarket bag neatly tied over the whole hat and secured under the rim. Quite a sight, I can tell you.

I've mentioned the head coverings of the men folks of Jerusalem, so what about the women? According to the Bible, they must be 'covered or shorn'.

Only a tiny sect of ultra-orthodox women shave their hair off, most covering up with a snood or a wig. So in a very small number of cases, there is double compliance—covered and shorn.

I do find it a little puzzling as to how putting on a wig fulfils the criteria. I believe some rabbis have similar misgivings about wig wearing. I would wager that donning a beautiful, dark, long, glossy real hair wig wasn't what the scriptures intended, but I'm not a religious scholar and couldn't give an authoritative opinion. In fact Jewish law says 'a woman's hair is lust-provoking'. It doesn't say a woman's wig is lust-provoking.

Having canvassed a few opinions from Jewish women, I understand that the whole idea of wig wearing is to create privacy and a barrier between the woman and the world after marriage. It's a sign that she's unavailable. Her hair is reserved for her husband and mustn't attract other men.

I wondered about the poor quality of a lot of the wigs, and about the fact that they almost always looked a bit askew, but I now know that Jewish women want their wigs to look like wigs, a clear sign that they're celebrating their religion and traditions and that they're part of their community.

Just as some suits look better than others, the same can be said for wigs. Some look so artificial, they must pose a fire hazard if placed too close to a naked flame. Keep in mind that there's a lot of ritual candle lighting in the city, and you'll appreciate the risk. Other wigs are long and glossy, made from real hair. I witnessed a discussion between my hairdresser and one of his clients, during which she fetched a spare wig out of her handbag. It was quite surreal to see. She had a replica of the wig on her head—shoulder-length strawberry blonde bob turned slightly under at the ends.

'Would you like a curl?' asked Yossi, my newest hairdresser and the third since I arrived there.

'No, just blow it straight, turned under,' his client instructed.

I'd always assumed that wig wearers had an easier time than the rest of us, so I hadn't focused on the maintenance issues such as a regular wash and blow dry. A time was arranged for the wig to be picked up, and off she went, for shopping or whatever while her hair (or someone else's hair, to be pedantic) was being styled.

Yossi told me that a decent real hair wig cost a fortune, over $1,000, so if you needed to have a spare, it was a major investment.

The more moderate Jewish woman will wear a modest headscarf with hair tucked in, or a hat. Many religious Jewish women don't wear anything on their heads. Even Orthodox Jewish women only need to cover up when they join the ranks of the married woman. Very religious women cover all their hair with a snood, rather than a glossy wig. Morgan's maths teacher wore a snood, so perhaps I would find out. She also refused to shake Chris's hand on account of him being male. She happily shook mine but had no idea that I'm male for passport purposes.

The ultra-Orthodox Jewish man is often a full-time religious scholar. Roughly one half of the ultra-orthodox community are in full-time employment.

Ben Gurion, the first prime minister of Israel, passed laws to allow the Haredi population to re-group and re-form their communities after their terrible losses in the wake of the Holocaust. At the time there were some 500 Haredim. There are now over a million Haredi in Israel out of a population of around eight and a half million (2018).

Many men are engaged in religious studies full-time and without a paid job. They receive numerous subsidies from the government, including subsidised housing, municipal tax relief and an exemption from the military service required of all Israelis (except Israeli Arabs because of the Palestinian occupation). The policy on subsidies was changed, and this led to more ultra-orthodox men engaging in work. However, the coalition government in Israel has to be mindful of the views of the Haredi population and the power they wield, so subsidies had been increased again and the number of Haredi men in employment had fallen.

The exemption from military service causes a lot of ill feeling as most families in Israel wave goodbye to their children for a compulsory spell in the army. The boys are required to serve three years on reaching the age of eighteen, and the girls serve 21 months. It's planned for, just as parents in other parts of the world would plan for university or a college education. The period of 'going to the army' is fitted into young lives.

There's even a social hierarchy within the army, and the unit you serve in can determine your future and contacts in the civilian world of work and business post military service. So the kids may aspire to join the Golani (elite forces). The army and kids in uniform are just a part of everyday life in Israel. I found it odd to see teenage girls in full military uniform wearing sandals with bare feet, swinging waist-length long glossy hair and wearing jewellery. Or to see a group of youngsters in uniform laughing, drinking a fruit juice and batting well made-up eyelids at each other. I suppose I'd never got that close to serving personnel on a daily basis before.

I spoke to several worried mothers of military-service teenagers, and for them, it's a deeply worrying and traumatic time. It's seen as unfair that one section of the population must serve, while another is exempt.

Until I moved there, I thought that all Jewish people were a homogeneous group, another naïve notion which has been dispelled. There's clear discrimination on the grounds of race, degrees of religiousness, orthodox and reform Jews and against women.

Many Israelis are highly educated and enjoy literature, music and the arts. One such Israeli friend dismissed a businessman we both knew as 'a peasant' because he wasn't an intellectual. His family were Sephardic Jews by origin. My theatre-loving bookworm of a friend was an Ashkenazi Jew of European descent.

When I was on a flight back to the UK, a large family of Orthodox Jews boarded the plane. The Israeli man sitting next to me muttered, 'Vermin, they're all vermin,' as his fellow Israelis started asking us all to move seats so they could sit together.

There's further discrimination against non-Jews and Arabs, of whom there's a deep-rooted ingrained mistrust.

One of my many friendly Israeli neighbours on the moshav, who liked to keep a watchful eye out for us, gave me quite the talk one day as I was rushing along the road to meet a friend for lunch.

'You look very nice today,' he volunteered.

I was glad to receive the compliment on my new dress, although I'd misheard him initially and thought that he'd said it was a nice day. He put me right.

Then the conversation took an unexpected and shocking turn, getting right to the heart of the situation here.

'Linda, you mustn't trust Arabs. You might think they're good people, but they aren't. You might think that they're your friends, but they aren't.'

I just listened, knowing differently. Our neighbour wouldn't have understood our friendships with Arabs and working in the West Bank.

There's distrust, and in some cases slight fear, but with very little opportunity to interact due to travel restriction on both sides, and no hope of seeing how the other half live at first hand, there's little to no hope of ever dispelling that distrust and moving forward.

Our fellow resident wouldn't have enjoyed the news that I travelled to Beit Hanina in East Jerusalem every week with Morgan for his guitar lessons with the hugely talented Mr Sami.

Random attacks on synagogues, queues of passengers at tram stops and kidnappings all feed the feelings of deep distrust.

We've made long-lasting friendships with many people as we've travelled the world as corporate gypsies, many of them Arabs, and I had no fear of driving to the West Bank and spending an evening in a family home, or at a wedding or engagement party of one of our many Arab friends.

So there's distrust, which is understandable to an extent, but we had friends on both sides and found the routine and regular discrimination hard to take at times.

Haredi women marry very young, have large families and many struggle to make ends meet.

The girls are taught different subjects in school than boys and are expected to be homemakers and look after children. They aren't permitted to engage in religious studies. With such large families, limited income, a home and sometimes a job to go to, it's little wonder that the Haredi women often look washed out. Is this the origin of the word 'harried', I wonder?

Marriages are arranged in the old-fashioned way, by a matchmaker. Girls are of marriageable age any time after their seventeenth birthday. Boys are usually a little older.

The men often stay in full-time religious studies until they're 42, when they can safely get a job as they're too old to be conscripted into the army.

The Haredim (literally 'one who trembles in awe of God') are insular and live and breathe religion. They have a strict moral code of conduct and dress, adhering to a traditional way of life.

I was interested to read that this code requires sex on a Friday (with your spouse, of course), but no sex if the wife is menstruating. Then she is regarded as off limits and cannot be touched by her husband, not even holding hands or a cuddle on the couch. One of my friends told me that her husband was asked by an orthodox man to move seats on a flight from Tel Aviv to London so that he would sit between the man and his wife who was menstruating. As if travel wasn't complicated enough.

When the wife starts her period, the marital twin beds are pushed apart, and the wife must have seven totally clear days after her period stops before she can take a *mikveh*, a ritual bath. The clear days are checked by inserting a piece of white cloth and doing a quick swab around. If there's any doubt about stains or discharge on the fabric, it must be taken to a rabbi for inspection and a declaration as to whether the cloth is clean or unclean.

After the ritual bath, during which every part of the body must be submerged in the ritual bathing waters, normal marital relations can resume until the beginning of the next cycle when the twin beds are pushed apart again.

The Haredi code also requires food to be even more kosher than kosher. Some rabbinate kosher licences are more kosher than others, so you may have to make excuses if you're unsure about your neighbours' standards of kosherness and you're invited to eat.

Our British neighbours hosted their very religious family friend to share a landmark birthday tea at their home. This involved food and drink, both of which were refused by the guest.

'I know it's just her religious beliefs, and nothing personal, but I can't help but feel insulted when she won't eat or drink anything in our house,' remarked my amiable, normally very laid-back and culturally aware friend.

I was amazed to learn that a child may not be kosher, and that can affect his or her marriage prospects enormously. We aren't talking about cannibalism. Apparently if a child is conceived and the mother hasn't undergone a ritual cleansing bath after the last menstruation, that child isn't kosher. So a child born into a less orthodox family, where the mother didn't engage in ritual bathing, wouldn't meet the marriage expectations of the family of a more orthodox child, born of a ritually cleansed and bathed mother.

The Haredim don't watch television or films, nor do they read secular newspapers. The internet is viewed with suspicion and can only be used if there are filters in place which block pornography. There's even a section on El Al aircraft (Israel's national airline) which is reserved for Haredim where no film or television are shown on the flight.

Haredim have very large families following the 'be fruitful and multiply' direction from Genesis 1:28. How they keep all those children in their seats on a flight with no television or films would be interesting to see.

In the middle of the extremes are many different Jews practising their religion publicly or privately to a greater or lesser extent. Secular Jews, who are in the majority, may or may not wear kippahs and may or may not eat kosher food or 'keep kosher', as it's termed.

I came across this issue when Debra invited us to her house on our moshav. After a couple of play dates for the boys, we were all invited to dinner. It was our little bit of luck that Debra's husband was a chef, and he cooked up a storm. But my dilemma was this. I'd glibly said I would bring a dessert.

'Great,' she replied enthusiastically.

We knew Shimon was barbequing steaks, among other delicious delights. Our predicament was the meat/dairy kosher issue. How do you make a pudding which is dairy-free? You usually need butter for cakes, and milk or cream for ice cream. Apart from fruit salad, I was stumped. I did rather resourcefully find a product known as Rich's kosher cream substitute. But the words of wisdom from the lovely Penny, who had lived here for four years, seemed sensible.

'Just ask them if they only eat kosher,' she advised.

I thought this was tantamount to asking a Muslim if he was fasting during the holy month of Ramadan. That's just not done. The assumption is that all Muslims will be fasting during Ramadan, and it would be rude to ask if they are or aren't. Not the case with kosher. It's not a problem and doesn't cause offence because some Israelis Jews do keep kosher and others don't.

Practicality reigned, and I asked whether the dessert should be kosher. In short, we had a homemade, very buttery, cinnamon and apple crumble with lashings of vanilla ice cream. I was so glad I'd asked. I've shared my easy homemade ice cream recipe at the end of this chapter in case you're tempted.

The Bible also provides that a woman shall not dress as a man. So there are a lot of long skirts to the ground, but orthodox women won't wear trousers, literally or metaphorically, although they'll bring home the chicken schnitzel (bacon being strictly forbidden).

There's no diktat on wearing trainers or extremely ugly shoes with long baggy skirts, but a huge proportion of the population wear really unattractive footwear. It's very holy and spiritual not to take great interest in your appearance as the time should be spent developing inner spirituality and beauty. That explains a lot.

On the other hand, there can hardly be a more glamourous sight than Israeli youth at play on the beaches of Tel Aviv. Just imagine the Israeli supermodel Bar Refaeli and multiply. In a nation of fitness fanatics, they have a higher proportion of potential swimwear models, both male and female, than most countries. Secular Israelis love the outdoors, and I saw droves of them cycling the hills of the Jerusalem Forest in Lycra. If they weren't cycling, they were pounding the roads, hiking the countryside and generally keeping in good shape. Maybe it's the military service which lays down those lifelong fitness habits.

I saw some religious couples and youngsters walking in the forest, but in the main they seemed preoccupied with pushing baby buggies laden with children along the streets of Jerusalem and shopping for provisions. Maybe the habit hasn't been formed, or there's just little time or energy for regular outdoor leisure pursuits and priorities are different.

The occasional ice cream treat never hurt anyone, so here's an easy recipe (no need for an ice cream maker) with optional flavours:

My Easy Homemade Ice Cream

Ingredients
1 litre long-life cream (fresh double cream is better, but rarely available in our postings)
100 g granulated or caster sugar (or to taste)
Vanilla extract (to taste-usually around 5 ml)
Extra ingredient or two before freezing:
100 ml Baileys Irish Cream liqueur to taste *or*
50 ml Tia Maria liqueur to taste *or*
Homemade cherry jam and dark chocolate chips to taste

Method
Whizz the sugar in a food processor if it's granulated.
Add the cream. Whizz but not so that cream becomes stiff.
Add vanilla extract and any extra ingredients you'd like.
Decant into a plastic container and freeze. After a couple of hours, remove from the freezer and give it a whisk to break up ice crystals.
Return to the freezer.
Eat, enjoy!
(I've forgotten to beat the ice cream mid-freeze on some occasions and haven't had a complaint yet, so don't worry if you do.)

Chris's Homemade Ice Cream

Chris makes another ice cream which needs no additional whisking and is absolutely delicious.

Ingredients
600 ml fresh double cream
397 ml tin condensed milk

Method

Beat the cream and condensed milk together until the mixture has the consistency of heavy cream (clotted cream).

Place in plastic container and freeze.

Before the freezing stage, Chris has previously added leftover Christmas pudding, chopped millionaire's shortbread (caramel shortcake slices) or homemade whisky tablet. Not all at once.

Freeze and enjoy!

20

JERUSALEM MARKET

I've visited many markets in our travels, from the huge market in Nairobi, Kenya, where beautiful, hand-woven and colourful shopping baskets were piled high and sold for shillings, to the spectacularly wet and slippery fish market in Brunei where one of the Decker girls in a beautifully hand-smocked dress fell her full length on the stone floor into an inch of fishy juice. She refused to go back ever again, understandable really, but a great pity because fresh red snapper newly harvested from the South China Sea, stuffed and baked with fresh coriander and ginger, is totally scrummy.

Jerusalem Market, or *Mahane Yehuda* as it's known locally, is mainly covered. Originally a network of cobbled alleyways between buildings, it's been roofed in glass supported by black metal beams. There are also main thoroughfares with shops on either side open to the elements, and they also form part of the opportunities for bargains, but the glass-covered alleyways are, in my opinion, the real heart and soul of the place. I was so glad that Penny had now brought me on this voyage of discovery.

The stones are worn shiny and smooth by the passing of the feet of thousands of Jerusalemites daily. This is a place where people come to buy meat, fresh fish, cheese, olive oil, olives, fruit (both fresh and dried), spices, nuts, pastries, freshly squeezed orange and pomegranate juices, in fact anything you could need. Like the Old City, the market alleyways are undulating. The array of dried fruit at one stall was so colourfully displayed that we stopped for closer inspection and the buying of lurid green dried kiwi fruit, slithers of deep-orange, sweet dried mango and the most delicious dark-red dried cranberries.

It was challenging to buy fresh fish in supermarkets in Jerusalem, so we stocked up on several red snapper fish each, all descaled and cleaned as part of the service, and double quantities of meaty pink salmon which was way cheaper than the pale frozen offerings available in the shops. All this after a long wait to buy our fresh produce.

Even after buying, the cleaning of our fish was destined to take ages, and it joined a line of slippery, silvery scales waiting to be removed with a clever sort of electric shaving device. We were advised to come back later. The head cleaner, who must have been 65 if he was a day, was the usual wiry, athletic-looking, well-tanned Israeli. I was surprised that this food handler had a cigarette permanently stuck to the side of his mouth as he worked. Normally I would have boycotted his pitch for this reason alone.

'This is the best fish stall in the market,' we were advised by another customer waiting patiently. 'That's why there's always such a long queue.'

Reassured we wandered and chatted some more, tasting peppery olive oil and purchasing pine nuts—delicious when gently toasted and tossed on salads, and a bargain in the Middle East.

Jerusalem salads are the tastiest, most imaginative salads I've ever eaten. As well as the standard ingredients, the average bowl will contain delicious nuts, toasted pine nuts, seeds, dried fruit, cubes of cheese, herbs and if you're lucky, will be bejewelled with crunchy ruby-red pomegranate seeds. The combinations are endless and led me to discover the cookbook written by the famous London-based chef Yotam Ottolenghi and his friend Sami Tamimi. Both chefs were brought up in Jerusalem, Yotam in Jewish West Jerusalem, and Sami in Arab East Jerusalem. They'd crossed cultural barriers and travelled back to childhood to give us this gem of a cookbook, simply entitled

Jerusalem. It's bursting not only with scrumptious salads but with recipes for falafel, baba ghanoush, latkes and hummus, and brought to life and social meaning with anecdotes and photographs of the city, just as it is, without filter or fiction. There's a heart-warming feeling to this unusual joint venture which bridges the gap between Jewish and Arab culture and cooking. 'Make hummus, not walls' was a slogan I spotted on a canvas shopping bag. I bought it—the philosophy and the bag.

At the market there were also several small galleries displaying pottery and sculptured pieces by local artists. The work was imaginative and funky but very pricey compared to pieces we've collected elsewhere in the world, and less to my taste.

After collecting our fish, we decided on a coffee break. I got to try the Aroma chain of coffee shops for the first time and was very impressed by the quality of the coffee and the service. The waitress didn't smile exactly, but nor was she out-and-out grumpy.

Penny and I got back to the car with one minute 59 seconds left of our allotted two hours permitted paid parking in this zone.

It wasn't until much later in the year that I realised that suicide bombings were associated with this place which Jerusalemites use for daily shopping. Ignorance can be bliss.

I often visited the market, and despite the dark and tragic shadows lurking around some corners, in the main it's a vibrant, human place to visit, to connect with familiar faces, stroll with the locals and forage for fresh and interesting food and spices.

It's also a place where there's a risk of being arrested by the fashion police as it's impossible to make the most of the range of goods available without having the tartan wheelie shopping trolley much favoured by the matriarchs of Jerusalem. I hadn't got around to buying one, but it would go on my Santa wish list that year.

Words of the day: kama ze ole? —how much is it? (Hebrew)

21

THE OLD CITY OF JERUSALEM

The Old City of Jerusalem is a magical place surrounded by thick, golden crusader stone walls, slits in the stonework for bows and arrows, ancient fortified gates and the most spectacular collection of religious sites you'll find in a lifetime of pilgrimages.

It's the Holy City to the Jewish faith, Christianity and Islam, although the first Holy City to the Muslim faith is Mecca. At its centre are the Dome of the Rock, the Al-Aqsa Mosque and the Temple Mount, as well as the Wailing Wall (or Western Wall as it's now called). The city is divided into quarters—the Arab Quarter, Armenian Quarter, the Christian Quarter and the Jewish Quarter. I also discovered that there's a Syrian Quarter too. The Old City isn't evenly divided. It's a warren of narrow cobbled streets, shiny and worn with the passing of many a shopper's sandals and traders' carts. Flights of steps lead up and down to the many streets and levels of this hilly place, so the best way to explore it is to walk, in sensible shoes.

There are layers of history lying beneath the Old City of today, and it's being excavated slowly. Just as there are layers of time beneath the Old City, there are layers of people on top as it's a living, working habitat.

Tensions inside and outside the walls were immediately obvious with an assortment of soldiers, armed police and airport-style security as we entered the Jewish Quarter and the Western Wall. However, there was one constant. On a Friday the children ran, played, squabbled and behaved like children all over the world whether they were Jewish, Christian or Muslim.

It was also easy to walk from one side of the city to the other. It was amazing to think that the entire walled Old City was so small, but so significant in religion, history and politics. If you're reasonably fit, you can walk around the outer circumference of its walls in an hour or so. It wasn't always easy to stroll through the Old City. While under Jordanian rule, only clergy, diplomats, UN personnel and a few privileged tourists were permitted to go from one side to the other. The Jordanians required most tourists to produce certificates of baptism to prove they weren't Jewish.

One of the most spectacular gates, with wide views of the ancient city walls, is the Jaffa Gate. It's entered from the new Mamilla Avenue shopping experience which links the Jaffa Street shopping area with the Old City. I liked it because there was easy parking in a modern, multi-storey car park. Parking could be a nightmare in Jerusalem. There were too many cars and not enough spaces in this city. We once returned to a paid car park by the Zion Gate of the Old City in plenty of time to pick Morgan up from school, only to discover that someone had parked his car perpendicular to the back of ours, completely hemming us in and delaying us to the point of lateness. Not very thoughtful behaviour, but sadly not unusual. So the multi-storeys of Mamilla make for a more relaxing outing, although parking is double the cost of street parking, but for peace of mind, it's worth it.

The shopping centre is also home to several upmarket cafés and restaurants which serve delicious Israeli breakfasts. When we ordered an Israeli breakfast for the first time, we were, in the words of Mark Twain, innocents abroad. The traditional breakfast is a feast of eggs, salad, freshly baked breads and pastries, cheeses, avocado dip, cream cheese, homemade jam, spreads, baked aubergines, freshly squeezed Israeli orange juice and great coffee. There are smaller feasts available, but when in Israel on a Friday, do as the Israelis do. We learnt to order one Israeli breakfast to share with a few extra treats to avoid being immobile for most of the morning. I usually skipped lunch too.

Fortified with some calories, a few more than would be recommended, it was our habit to stroll past the modern art exhibited throughout this wonderful outdoor shopping mall which is constructed with warm honey-coloured stone and blended sympathetically with the backdrop of the Old City. There's even a mini amphitheatre of steps where performers entertain the passing crowds.

My personal favourite is the building which houses the Steimatzky bookstore. I have to confess a weakness for bookshops, but this one is very attractive from outside as well as inside. All the stones were numbered to ensure that the original old building was reinstated exactly as it was before as part of the new shopping experience. All the numbers are still visible from the outside.

The atmosphere in this modern shopping oasis is relaxed and trendy with some arty-farty aspects. We saw secular Israelis at play there, shopping for Abercrombie & Fitch or for those with a smaller budget, Mango and Castro. There's even a Body Shop. It isn't part of the international chain founded by the late Anita Roddick, but I'm sure the namesake doesn't hurt business. I loved the sculptures which were displayed along the avenue of shops, all for sale. There were long-legged, multi-coloured, salsa-dancing figures; African mamas with droopy boobies, and frogs with giant webbed feet. Bronze pigeons sat on benches beside real people resting their feet and their wallets. *If I get very extravagant or come into some money,* I thought, *I'll buy a garden sculpture for the garden of our imaginary retirement villa before we leave Jerusalem.*

A walk past the Avishag Maternity Wear shop never failed to raise a smile from the older members of our family. In fact, 'aving a shag on a Friday is compulsory if you're up to it. *Shabbat shalom!*

And then we ascended the wide stone steps out of Mamilla Avenue and the modern world towards the Jaffa Gate. It was a nerve-wracking experience, watching cars and vans drive through these old gates which were often designed in an 'L' shape for ancient security reasons, and were a tight turn for any chariot. I often had to breathe in as a car squeezed past into the Old City, parts of which can be accessed by car if you're a resident.

The walls were built by Suleiman the Magnificent from 1537-1541. I wonder why we've dropped the superlatives in modern-day parlance. Mandela the Magnificent has a certain ring to it. This was the most important gate in the nineteenth century because the road from Jaffa Port came to this entrance of the Old City. Essential supplies were imported by ship from all over the world and brought 60 kilometres by road from Jaffa to the capital, Jerusalem.

From here you can climb onto the ramparts and walk on top of the city walls all the way around to the Jewish Quarter.

My day out in the city was almost always a Friday, a day of extreme busyness. On a typical Friday, a huge proportion of the Jewish community come to the Western Wall, pressing their foreheads against it and swaying backwards and forwards in prayer. The wall is the last remnant of the second temple destroyed by the Romans in the year 70 of the Common Era (CE), or as Christians would say, 'in the year of the Lord' (AD).

By lunchtime most Muslim traders have closed up their shops in the Arab Quarter, normally by placing a broom handle across an open doorway or an old *kaffir* headscarf over the merchandise, and can be seen hurrying off to Friday prayers at the mosque of their choice. Also around midday you'll hear church bells ringing in a cacophony of percussion. It always fascinates me that the mosques in this part of the world on a Friday are overflowing with worshippers. It's not unusual to see rows and rows of people lined up outside in side streets on prayer mats, listening to the call to prayer of the mullah and dipping foreheads to prayer mats facing in the direction of Mecca. A sea of praying Muslims often blocks whole thoroughfares because the mosques are full.

Add to this confluence of religious observance several tour parties walking in Jesus' footsteps, following a leader with a large wooden cross in the Christian Quarter along the Via Dolorosa, and you have people jams, jostling and severe overcrowding on a normal Friday. Some Fridays aren't that normal, with demonstrations, clashes and heavily armed police officers deployed in droves. On the worst days, we were warned to stay away from the Old City for security reasons.

When you see this melting pot of religion and cultures and the black fedora hats or mink-trimmed car-wheel hats of the Haredi Jewish community, it's hard to imagine that until 1967, Jews had no right of access to the Old City. It was under Jordanian rule until then. Israeli children used to go to see the large model of the city of Jerusalem which was housed at the Holyland Hotel in the Malha district of town. That was how they were introduced to the important sites in the Jewish faith. The hotel was demolished to make way for a very ugly housing development known as the Holyland Development, the subject of a bribery scandal and court case against officials and a leading politician, but the model village can still be seen in the grounds of the Israeli Museum, which is well worth a visit.

The Armenian Quarter is relatively quiet and sedate in comparison, with a good selection of small studios housing artists painting and selling Armenian pottery. This is decorated with intricate, traditional, colourful, hand-painted patterns of flowers and birds. They also paint beautiful tiles which are skilfully inlaid in olive wood tea trays, wall friezes and tables. You can wander through quiet passageways, flanked on either side by walled entrances to private homes in the Armenian Quarter, which always seemed so much more peaceful and less commercialised than the other quarters of the city.

Peeking through wrought-iron gateways, we saw quiet courtyards with pots of flowers, and beautifully painted tile nameplates laid into the old stone walls fronting the pedestrian streets. I was walking around the Old City one sunny morning with two of our visitors and a tour guide. He led us under stone archways and into a part of the Armenian Quarter I hadn't visited before.

'All of the painted nameplates declare names ending in "ian", a sign that they're Armenian households,' he told us. 'The most famous Armenians in the world today are the Kardashians.'

'Well, who knew?' I said.

The tourists from South Korea who formed part of our jolly group looked puzzled and had no idea who the Kardashians were. I knew the name but not much more than that.

The Arab Quarter is very loud, colourful and full of exotic fabrics, jewellery, spices, inlaid furniture and lurid-coloured sweets individually wrapped in cellophane paper. You can also enter the quarter from the Damascus Gate which is spectacular and a totally different experience from the Jaffa Gate entry point. Unlike the redeveloped and modernised Jaffa Gate, it hasn't changed much over the centuries apart from being sand blasted and cleaned up. The Arab Quarter always seems busier and more chaotic with people buying their meat, chicken, falafels and spices together with floor mops, long-john underwear and carpet slippers. There are traditional bakeries which sell warm rounds of sesame-seeded bread and stacks of crispy round discs which look like poppadoms but are sprinkled with sesame seeds and ideal for sharing and dipping. Most of the shopping in other quarters caters to the tourists' need for souvenirs, carpets, jewellery and less basic commodities than food and plastic storage boxes. In the Arab Quarter, they also sell piles of bars of seed and nut cakes of the sort my gran used to feed her budgie Joey, and he lived to a good old age. They're delicious, nutritious and cheap.

For seekers of arts and crafts, a trawl around the Arab and Christian Quarters will throw up an Aladdin's cave of treasures. The bead shops, for making and designing your own jewellery, are usually found in long cave-like shops and hung from floor to ceiling with every kind of semi-precious stone imaginable. Richly woven and embroidered crewel-work fabrics are hung like legion standards alongside twinkly patchwork covers in gaudy colours from India. Sheep-leather handbags, sandals, rucksacks and luggage hang on hooks outside the shops and smell like they've only recently stood still. I often knew I was approaching a sheep-leather shop long before I saw it as they tended to smell a bit of wet sheep.

It's really fun to explore the Old City, and if you find your particular brand of treasure, you negotiate an acceptable price. Bargaining here is expected, and good banter nearly always accompanies a cup of sweet tea or cardamom-flavoured coffee. It's a civilised way to shop.

We were buying some beautifully hand-painted pasta bowls as a gift, and Chris innocently remarked that he could buy the same thing cheaper in Ramallah, his response to all my suggested buys in the Old City of Jerusalem. It saved him a fortune because he hardly ever had time to go shopping in Ramallah. On this occasion, what can only be described as pure pantomime followed.

'Sir, you cannot find such quality in Ramallah, and at this price,' challenged the smartly dressed shopkeeper, standing his ground. 'If you do happen to find bowls such as this at a lower price, bring them to me. If you cannot find them, I will take your wife to dinner!'

'Wrap them up,' said my gallant husband, knowing when he was defeated.

Backs were patted, and all were happy by the charade which is shopping in the Old City. We always smiled and waved as we passed that shop and have entertained many a visitor with the quality banter and the merchandise.

In another shop in the Christian Quarter, Liberty, my mum and I were invited to the back of the shop (quite some distance away from the main entrance and thoroughfare) to see the shopkeeper's ancient stone water well. There's safety in numbers, so we all traipsed through the rooms of amazing antiques and artefacts to the back of the shop. Sure enough there was an ancient stone well which was lit up so that we could admire it, and it led down to the original Old City. It was so well preserved that I was sad Chris wasn't with us as he would have enjoyed seeing it. I absolutely loved this shop. It was like a mini museum, and I'd walked past it so many times. From the front it just looks like any other with its selection of pashminas and scarves, Druze woven bags and cushion covers, but inside it was food for the collector's soul with antique furniture such as Syrian inlaid bridal chests, chairs, chests of drawers, tables and porcelain. I vowed to return with my other half for some serious shopping. On the way out, and after a lot of chat and laughter, the shopkeeper and his brother then showed us at least ten new ways to tie an ordinary 10 shekel scarf so it looked amazing. This is what I call shopping!

Chris got chatting to a real old-timer one morning near the Church of the Holy Sepulchre. The man was sitting on a folding chair in the sun, minding his merchandise which was half inside and half outside his shop. He shared the fact that he was 92 and the wisdom that all that mattered in life were your family and your health. We were both astonished that he was still putting in a day's work at that age, but I suspected he did a lot more philosophising and chatting than selling. He seemed very happy with his lot in life. There's no way this old gentleman would be bored and lonely, the fate of many old people in the Western world who retire from work decades earlier than he had the opportunity to do.

The Church of the Holy Sepulchre is perhaps the holiest site in Christianity. It's believed by some to be the place where Jesus was crucified and buried. The marble slab where it's said his body was anointed is situated near the entrance to the church, and we regularly saw pilgrims touching the stone and placing amulets and tokens upon it, often in a state of high emotion.

This site is shared by many Christian denominations from around the world, which are said to be proprietorial and suspicious of each other. Actual punch-ups between priests have been recorded. Not very Christian. In fact when we looked at the front of the building, we saw a step ladder propped up against an upper window. It's reportedly been there for over 100 years following a property dispute between the various Christian denominations. It's interesting that a Muslim family keeps the keys to the holiest Christian site, as there's a worry (allegedly) there might be a power struggle if any one Christian faction held them.

We also visited the site where the Last Supper was held, and there was a group of singing priests on a pilgrimage from an Eastern European country. The singing was so beautiful, I was moved to tears. Sometimes the significance and enormity of a place can be conveyed by the simplest of human voices. At other times special moments are lost in the rush and the crush.

It used to be the case that no non-Muslims were allowed to visit the site of the Dome of the Rock or the Al-Aqsa on the Muslim holy day, which is Friday. There seemed to be restricted access for non-Muslim visitors even if not on a Friday. We tried to visit a few times, but it was always closed to us when we got there.

One day when Chris and Morgan had days off work and school which coincided, we got up especially early and headed down to the Old City before breakfast. We joined a long queue waiting to get access to the Temple Mount area. Yes, you do indeed have to be there early in the morning, and we were advised that we would have to leave again later in the morning before prayer time. As we were only a small party of three and independent of the official tour groups, we were told we could walk to the front of the line. We felt awkward doing so but secure in the knowledge we'd been instructed by officialdom. The queue was several tour buses long, and there was stringent, airport-style security for access.

The sky was bright blue and in stark contrast with the twinkling golden Dome of the Rock. This houses a rock which is said to show the hoof print of the prophet Muhammad's horse. The iconic blue Islamic tiles which face the walls of this shrine are detailed and stunning, even on a dull day. The Dome is covered with 80 kilogrammes of gold, paid for and donated by the late King Hussein of Jordan.

I was surprised to see a small version of the Dome, with a silver-grey dome, sitting alongside the Dome of the Rock. This miniature version served as a model of the real thing for construction purposes. We accepted the offer of a guide who filled in the huge gaps in our knowledge about the buildings, history and religious rituals, and entertained us with many anecdotes.

I was enchanted to watch three young boys play an energetic game of football in the forecourt of the Dome. People seemed to use this vast open space of the Noble Sanctuary (Muslim) or Temple Mount (Jewish) area for strolls, chats, to relax and to picnic. It's a meeting place for the community and a welcome open space after the tight alleyways of the Old City. Like a municipal park, without the usual litter.

The aspect of the Dome itself was blighted for photos as there was a tile space of the Dome which appeared to have been removed for maintenance work, or perhaps ventilation, and a ladder was propped alongside the gap. This made me think about the ladder on permanent display at the front of the Church of the Holy Sepulchre. I hoped this was a temporary feature and angled my camera to exclude it from photographs.

We also walked the length of the Al-Aqsa Mosque, past a long row of shiny stainless-steel taps where the observant wash before each of the five prayer times daily. The Al-Aqsa is topped by a dome which is more ridged and gun-metal grey in colour. Al-Aqsa means the furthest in Arabic and is named as such as it's supposed to be the furthest point Muhammed reached in his spread of Islam. It's amazing what you learn when you hire a guide.

Although it was possible to gain access to this area during specified times, and from the main access point if you aren't a Muslim, you can't enter the buildings.

If you aren't able to get up close because of the restricted opening times, the view from afar of the golden Dome and Al-Aqsa are truly beautiful sights. There's a particularly good vantage point for photographs as you walk from the Jaffa Gate, through the Armenian Quarter towards the Western Wall, via the perimeter road just inside the wall. It's possible to climb the ramparts just before rounding the corner to the Western Wall and to get a magnificent photograph. The late Ariel Sharon is said to have sparked off the Palestinian uprising in 2000 (the Second Intifada) when he visited the Al-Aqsa Mosque, the third holiest site in Islam after Mecca and Medina.

Having taken hundreds of photos of Jerusalem and the Old City from various vantage points, my personal favourite is the view of the deep golden Dome of the Rock from the elevation of the Mount of Olives, where the majesty of the Old City is starkly contrasted with the high-rise buildings of modern Jerusalem in the background. It's particularly lovely when there has been rain and the dust of the long hot summer has been washed off.

If, like me, you enjoy rooftop views, the view from the top of the Austrian Hospice Hotel in the Old City is hard to beat. The collage of domes, steeples, minarets, crosses and crescents is a panorama not to be missed. I also enjoyed the fact that washing lines of clean clothes could be seen flapping right next to the famous domes, undergarments being dried in the sun for all to see.

One of our favourite viewing spots at night was from the rooftop restaurant of Notre Dame. It also had a delicious selection of imported cheeses which we enjoyed. It took us a while to track down this cheese fix. Most Israeli cheese is quite tasteless because rennet isn't kosher so omitted from the cheese-making process. Even if you're too pushed for time to stop and eat, it's worth visiting the rooftop of Notre Dame for the spectacular view and a refreshing drink.

The security at the Western Wall is always high, but it's particularly vigilant on a Friday. Bags are passed through airport-style X-ray equipment, as are humans. Sometimes the guards will joke around asking, 'Do you have a bomb?'

My usual reply was, 'Not today.'

The Western Wall is the holiest site in the world for Jews. It marks the outer perimeter wall of the Second Temple which was destroyed by the Romans in AD 70, four years after the Jews rebelled against the Romans in 66 AD. When we reached the Western Wall, men and women were segregated. The shoulders of women have to be covered, and the women are given a much smaller section of the wall to pray against than their men folks, although the women aren't permitted to wear a prayer shawl at the wall or read from the holy Torah scriptures. In the male section, which is partitioned off but visible if you perch on a plastic chair, and many do, there are tables set up, and it looks as if mini synagogue gatherings are held at each table. Chris and Morgan donned complimentary white nylon kippahs and visited the male side together. Men and women are permitted to pray at the Western Wall and to touch it. When we got close up, we saw that every crevice was stuffed full of folded pieces of paper. The papers contain prayers left by the faithful. Twice a year the crevices and cracks are cleared of the holy missives which are taken and stored elsewhere.

When we embarked on a Western Wall tunnels tour (it's not possible to enter without a guide), we were taken down to another subterranean world of buildings and pillars from Roman times, with rudimentary games carved into stone slabs. This tour under the Old City to the very Old City was certainly worth taking. When we exited the wall, we headed out through the Dung Gate, named for obvious, but thankfully historical, reasons, to the fascinating City of David.

Prepared to get wet, we carried our torches and waded through the tunnel which connects the Gihon Spring to the Siloam Pool. After the excitement and the intrigue of the experience and the coolness of the water against our bare legs, we basked outside in the warm sunshine on ancient stones. It felt like not much had changed since King David constructed the city 3,000 years ago to unify the tribes of Israel. It was what I call a Gardens of Gethsemane moment.When I visited the gardens for the first time, I was struck by the fact that this peaceful place, with its gnarled and ancient olive trees, was mentioned in the Bible and that in essence, if you were lucky enough to visit on a quiet day, you could feel the significance of it. There are of course many Gardens of Gethsemane moments to be experienced when exploring Jerusalem and beyond, and the need to wade thigh deep through flooded tunnels with torches just added to the excitement and intrigue of it all.

I was always fascinated by the intensity of prayer of ultra-Orthodox Jews. They could be waiting for a lift at the side of the road and while waiting, they'd be reading from a small, obviously religious, book and rocking back and forth with great intensity. I'd been surrounded by women on a train, all reading from miniature well-thumbed volumes, mouthing words and rocking slightly. Even on a packed commuter train, I got the feeling that those women, on their way to work as shopkeepers and receptionists, had transported themselves to another world entirely. So you can imagine how much more intense the power of prayer gets at the Western Wall.

I once travelled back to Tel Aviv from London on an EasyJet flight. At prayer time (there are three prayer times a day for Jews), the front of the airplane was given over to those who wanted to pray, and it was an odd sight to see this group of grown men and boys, rocking back and forth, squeezed shoulder to shoulder in the forward gantry. There was a variety of dress from fringed prayer shawls and monochrome outfits to sneakers and jeans with sweaters and grubby prayer shawl fringes dangling from each side. The power of the devotion to prayer and ritual was impressive. The repetitive rhythmic rocking forward of all praying may have concerned some of our more nervous fellow passengers as it seemed it could just have tipped the whole plane forward into an alarming nose-dive at any moment.

Over time it became clear to me that the whole Jewish way of life has a different rhythm. The calendar, like the Muslim calendar, is lunar based, and so every year is eleven days shorter than the Gregorian calendar Christians and others adopt. The week is different. There are five and a half days of work and then the near total shutdown for one day from sunset on Friday to sunset on Saturday, although more and more Israelis are taking a two-day weekend, usually Friday and Saturday. The holidays are different and celebrated with an intensity of purpose and often remembrance of difficult times, except at Purim which is a whole lot of fun.

The centre of life for all Jews is family, family and family. There are celebrations, births, bar or bat mitzvahs, marriages and deaths. All are observed along with the deep-rooted traditions associated with each milestone event, to a greater or lesser extent, depending on the beliefs of the celebrant and where they lie on the spectrum of the Jewish religion.

While there is a great respect for life, its phases and for the celebration of family life in particular, there's also a great respect for death. Yahrzeit is the annual remembrance of a loved one on the date they've passed. I suppose it's a bit like the in-memoriam notices some families place in newspapers annually elsewhere in the world, remembering the anniversary of the passing of a loved one and expressing continued loss. But in Israel it reaches a whole new level of memorial. I was astounded but heart-warmed to read that on the 26th of December, the yahrzeit of a Jerusalemite was to take place. This was advertised in the *Jerusalem Post*. It was the chap's twelfth yahrzeit, and the buses for family and friends were to leave Jerusalem at a specified hour. Twelve years on and his family were still being taken with friends by busload to his graveside. A comforting thought.

22

OLIVE PICKING ON THE MOUNT OF OLIVES

If you're planning to pick olives, there's no better place to serve your apprenticeship than on the Mount of Olives. I'd never been on an olive pick, despite being the proud joint owner of more than 200 old olive trees spread over nineteen terraces, constructed of thick dry-stone walls retaining fertile soil in Puglia, a region known as Italy's bread basket. We planned to farm there one day and to build a house. At the moment we have two ruined trulli and a selection of wonderful olive, fruit and nut trees. While our farming and house plans are still imaginary, we do know some real characters there. We have a huge emotional attachment to the place as our last family holiday with Amber was spent in a villa nearby while we planned the build. After we lost her, we put the Italy dream and designs on hold.

I'd read about the effort of harvesting olives. Many expatriate writers have described the back-breaking, muscle-straining, heat-induced, headache-producing task of bringing the olives in.

However, it's an activity I would highly recommend. As my mum always says, 'Many hands make light work.' The secret is to do it with a group of friends, enjoy the camaraderie and do it for a great cause.

I joined a group from the Jerusalem Expat Network in the autumn sunshine for just one day of picking. We were a mixed group of expats from the UK, Ireland, Australia, Canada, Finland, Denmark, Italy, Holland and many other countries. Most of us were trailing spouses and had given up careers to support our other halves in the diplomatic service, the United Nations and various governmental and non-governmental aid agencies, or in the employment of international corporations.

We were greeted by a volunteer with Mercy Corps and induced into the skill of picking an olive tree bare. I also had a mini lesson in pruning a tree as I expressed an interest in our mentor's pruning skills. She tidied and snipped while we picked and chatted. Mercy Corps harvests the olives in East Jerusalem, and the oil produced is sold for the benefit of needy Palestinian families.

To spend a day with good friends in the autumn sunshine on the Mount of Olives, picking the fruit with a timeless view of the Dome of the Rock, is perhaps the most spectacularly meaningful and beautiful first olive-picking experience a person can have.

We spread the vast, dusty, tattered tarpaulins under the trees and descended like small groups of locusts. Some of our party finger-picked the olives, letting them fall below onto the tarpaulin. We were careful not to step on the precious fruit of our labours. I was lucky enough to be put in charge of a long-handled olive rake. I stretched to the sky and pulled the teeth of the narrow rake through the dusty, silvered leaves above my head. The fat black olives fell to the ground with a satisfying pitter patter. It rained olives. Some of my more nimble friends climbed to the top of the ancient trees to ensure that not an olive was left behind. After several hours of thirsty, dusty work, we pulled in the corners of our tarps and poured the piles picked into large jute sacks. Each sack held around twenty kilogrammes, and we picked somewhere in the region of one hundred kilogrammes in one morning.

As we chatted companionably in the warm yellow autumn sunshine under clear blue skies, it was hard to think of a more pleasant or satisfying way to spend a morning.

It was also hard to explain just how dirty a person can get when olive picking in an arid climate. We often didn't get rain from May until October, so by the time the olives were picked in late October or early November, the trees were silvered with dust. By the end of our picking session, we all looked like coal miners. Our faces were smeared with sweat and grey with dust. Our hands, some usually carefully manicured, others not, looked like we'd been heavy-duty gardening, which in a way we had.

We all scrubbed up as best we could in the Mercy Corps bathroom, forming a long grubby line. We'd booked a table for lunch in the garden of the imposing Augusta Victoria Hospital grounds just across the road. We didn't want to alarm our fellow diners or be turned away as we were ravenous and thirsty.

Before leaving, most of us snapped up the large recycled plastic water bottles of olive oil that Mercy Corps sold. This olive oil, while not from the actual olives we picked that day, had been pressed from olives of the same grove. It was a beautiful golden-green hue and too good to cook with. I use special oil like this to make simple salad dressings and for dipping crusty bread with a splash of balsamic vinegar to invigorate the taste buds.

Apart from salad dressings, olive oil is used to make mild and moisturising olive soap. I loved the large tactile blocks of green olive soap which are sold unwrapped and can be slightly pockmarked and scarred. There are also beautifully presented gift-wrapped versions available to take home which are infused with honey, oatmeal, rosemary and other aromatic delights. They're widely available in Jerusalem.

Did you know that if you take a tablespoon of warm olive oil, grind in some sea salt and massage your hands and feet for a few minutes (or even better, get someone to do it for you), you'll feel like you've had the best manicure and pedicure ever? Your skin will feel miraculously soft. That's a promise! But I would never use Extra Virgin Olive Oil (EVOO) for this purpose and definitely none of my special East Jerusalem Mercy Corps olive oil. You can take the girl out of Scotland, but you canny take Scotland out of the girl!

To our relief we were welcomed warmly across the road and fed and watered in the shady garden of the old Augusta Victoria Hospital. None of us turned down the three-course set lunch on offer. I for one was hoping that my first olive pick in Jerusalem wasn't my last.

I know that this experience was a privileged one. Many Palestinian farmers in the West Bank have very restricted, or no, access at all to their olive groves at harvest time. They and their families have lived with the constant threat of personal violence and destruction of olive trees rooted in land which has been in their families for generations. Apart from the substantial emotional and physical toll living under this pressure takes on West Bank families, the financial toll is devastating. For many families it's their only source of income.

I take happiness and contentment from the areas in which I can get happiness and contentment. This is a survival technique I was acquiring, slowly.

Olive Oil Salad Dressings

Here are two of our favourites which can be whizzed up in less than the time it would take for you to open the fridge and retrieve a shop-bought bottle of less tasty dressing.

Lemon Dressing

Ingredients
Juice of ½ a fresh lemon
Generous glug of good quality EVOO
Sea salt and black pepper to taste

Method
Mix the juice and EVOO.
Grind in some sea salt and black pepper to taste.
Shake vigorously in a sealed jar. I save small jam jars for this job. Any leftover dressing can be stored in the fridge for a couple of days.

Honey Mustard Dressing

Ingredients
1 tbsp grain mustard
1 tbsp EVOO
1 tsp clear runny honey (or a bit more if you like your dressing sweeter)
1 tsp balsamic vinegar

Method
Put the grain mustard in a small ramekin dish and add the EVOO. Stir. Add the honey and vinegar. Stir until well mixed.

23

THE DEAD SEA

The Dead Sea is the lowest point on earth at 430 metres below sea level, and on the last day of the last millennium, I had fun sending friends and relatives happy new millennium greetings from there. We were living in Amman at the time, waiting for catastrophe to hit all computer systems at midnight on the 31st December. Thankfully planes didn't fall out of the sky, and the world kept turning into the year 2000 and beyond.

On the Jordan side, there are some pretty swanky resort hotels to enjoy, Mövenpick being the oldest of the international chains, then Marriott followed by Kempinski. Mövenpick was my personal favourite and was built in the style of a traditional Arab village set in beautiful tropical gardens with ducks and other bird life. It also has a fine spa and an amazing infinity pool with views across the Dead Sea to Israel. Chris and I started the tradition of celebrating our wedding anniversary at the spa, which was so relaxing that I could swear I levitated clean off the treatment bed.

From the hotels on the Jordan side, you can walk down to the sea, although alarmingly the sea was further away each time we visited, so it was more of a trek than it used to be. The Dead Sea is shrinking. The water level is falling by about a metre a year. So just in case you're ever on *Who Wants to Be a Millionaire,* on the last question, with no lifelines, and this subject comes up, I think I've given you a few pointers.

There are a couple of hotels for the more budget-conscious traveller, one owned by a local family and one by an international chain, but quite a distance away from the Dead Sea. At the Dead Sea, and quite often in life, you get what you pay for.

On the Israeli side, the hotels are old, tired and expensive. You don't get what you pay for. I don't think they're nearly as attractive or as aesthetically pleasing as hotels on the Jordanian side. The other problem is that because they were built long before the Jordanian hotels were, they're much further away from the Dead Sea than they were 20 or 30 years ago. So if I had the time and the choice, I would pop across the Allenby Bridge for the Dead Sea experience. The Jordanian service is just so smiley, pleasant and helpful, there really is no contest. But that's just my personal opinion.

However, on the 7th November, in the first year of this posting, when our lovely daughter Liberty turned 21, we had plans to go out to Dolphin Yam, our favourite fish restaurant in Jerusalem, for dinner, and based on previous experience at the Allenby Bridge, we knew we could spend a large chunk of the special day stuck at immigration. We also had my mum staying, along with Easton, the boyfriend (Libby's not my mum's). So that would have amounted to about $250 in exit tax at the bridge and $600 on the VIP service to have any hope of getting back home in time for dinner.

So instead we had a wonderful champagne breakfast in our pyjamas on the deck at the house on the moshav, lit candles and ate homemade birthday carrot cake after breakfast. We then squeezed into the car and headed off for Mineral Beach on the Israeli side of the Dead Sea.

The sea wasn't too far away, so after paying the entrance fees, we strolled down to the beach. Although it was November, the sea was a lovely temperature for a float. The water was so salty, it was well-nigh impossible not to bob into a floating position. It did get a little cold when the sun disappeared behind the looming, lunar, rocky mountains, which then cast us into deep shadow.

After writing the number 21 on Liberty's tummy in Dead Sea mud, we all covered ourselves in the mineral-enriched health and beauty mud so favoured by spas and treatment centres the world over. It was available free of charge in huge pools. Some of us went too far and covered our faces as well. Not a good idea, take heed. I ended up with a face like a well-skelpt arse[1], which wasn't the look I was after for the birthday dinner outing to the city that evening. You can buy Dead Sea facial mud packs, which I've done many times, but I now know that it's unwise to slap the mud straight from the beach on your face, especially if you also hope to participate in the holiday photos.

As usual we were over ambitious and drove to Masada, a World Heritage Site, after leaving Mineral Beach but got there in time for closing. Its claim to fame is that it's a fortified palace built on a plateau high above and with views over the Dead Sea. It's one of Israel's most popular visitor attractions and is famous for the siege which took place there. Almost 1,000 Jews and their families were held under siege by Roman troops during the time of the Roman Empire. Rather than surrender, all the Jews committed suicide in preference to being captured. The leading account of this significant historical event by Flavius Josephus suggests that two women and three children survived the massacre by hiding in a drain. The women reported that the Jews under siege had drawn lots to kill each other as suicide was against their religous beliefs.

When we visited later that year, we caught the cable car up and elected to walk back down. The walk down is tiring, especially when the weather gets warmer. There's absolutely no shade in the harsh and barren desert environment.

---

1. Colloquial Scottish for a bottom that's been hit with a hand or object.

24

THE RAMON CRATER AND BEN GURION'S HOUSE

After the excitement of hosting Liberty's 21ˢᵗ birthday celebrations in Jerusalem, and the fun of having three generations of women under the same roof, we decided to get over the tranquillity by inviting Morgan's friend Noah around for a play date. The boys scoffed treats, played in the garden and on the PlayStation until a very harassed chef Shimon arrived to scoop up the energetic Noah. He refused all offers of a sundowner or a coffee as he was en route to the airport and even by my standards, was cutting the time very short before his flight was due to take off.

'What are you going to New York for?' I asked him, unable to contain my curiosity.

'To cook Thanksgiving dinner.'

So chef Shimon was travelling all the way to New York to cook a presumably kosher Thanksgiving dinner for people who had enough dollars in the bank not to bother going out, cooking dinner themselves or ordering take-away, which are my limited options in this world. Shimon was also quite the expert on wine, so maybe he was doubling up as sommelier too.

We once had a bottle of very special wine at his house, and I savoured the experience. A little too slowly as it turned out. We had a glass each, and just as I was wondering when we would be offered a top-up, the rest of the wine was poured down the kitchen sink by Noah's older sister who was helping to clear up. A tragedy. It seems Israelis enjoy a glass of good wine with food but aren't huge drinkers.

Shimon was in such a rush, I forgot to ask him where I could buy a turkey and how to ask for it in Hebrew. I knew how to ask for two chickens, so all was not lost. This, after a conversation in Rami Levi supermarket with a very flirtatious septuagenarian and an offer of private Hebrew lessons at his home. I could go with him then and there if I wanted, he offered. *Stein offum* is two chickens in Hebrew. *Bugger offum* was my mental reply; 'No, thank you,' my actual one.

The following weekend, which was yet another long weekend for one of the Eid holidays, we decided to travel to the Negev Desert. We took a picnic and appreciated the awesome views from the rim of the Ramon Crater at the start of the Great Rift Valley which extends down to East Africa. This was where Chris was born, in Nairobi, Kenya, to be precise. The view and the concept of how the Rift Valley came to be are truly awesome. We had the pleasure of looking at the valley from the other end of this geographic phenomenon on many holidays to Kenya when Chris visited his expatriate family there.

Ben Gurion is regarded as the founder of modern-day Israel and was its first prime minister. He led the country during the Arab-Israeli War of 1948 and formed the Israeli Defence Force (IDF). He also oversaw the development of Israel in terms of infrastructure, welcomed Jews who had been displaced by the Holocaust and sought reparation and recovery of property for those who had lost material possessions and property during the Second World War.

I was interested to learn that he was included in *Time* magazine's 100 most important people of the 20th century (posthumously). He had a vision of Israel settling the territory in the Negev Desert and developing it. Quite the pioneering spirit. I wonder how Middle East history and politics would differ if the Zionists had concentrated on settling and developing the Negev, the original vision of Ben Gurion. Would any of the wars and conflict have been avoided?

We toured Ben Gurion's house as I have a passion for houses and love looking around the homes of other people. I was surprised that it was so small and spartan. But it was charming, functional and was clearly the home of a man who was a reader, writer and intellectual. It was simple, uncluttered and strangely calming. There weren't many places in Israel I found calming.

25

HAIFA AND OTHER SAFARIS

A long weekend and yet more holidays from school prompted us to get out the map of Israel and head for Haifa, a port city in the north. In the past it was possible to catch a ferry to mainland Europe from Haifa, and friends of ours drove a car from Amman to the UK via Haifa at the end of a tour of duty with the United Nations. You can't take a passenger/car ferry anymore, and I believe that security is the reason why the service has been halted. It's a shame because that would be an interesting way to travel back to Europe.

We knew Haifa was on the coast, but that was about all we knew. We planned to use the city as a base to explore the Carmel wine region of the country then Galilee and to reach the northern border with Lebanon where there are some interesting tunnels and a cable car ride. An ambitious timetable, I know, and even more ambitious when we discovered a gem of a World Heritage Site within striking distance of where we were staying. We were unaware of all the treats and treasures in store that weekend. We tend to study guidebooks after we've visited places of interest as we don't want our initial impressions clouded by too much knowledge.

We stayed in a guest house in the old German Colony area of Haifa owned by the Haddad family. I was drawn to booking this accommodation because we knew a family called Haddad in Jordan, and they produced very drinkable arak (a popular alcoholic drink which tastes of aniseed and is often taken with a good Arabic meal as an aid to digestion). Our host later confirmed that this family did have relatives in Jordan and connections with the great arak makers.

In the German Colony, there's a wide main avenue called Ben Gurion Avenue which is lined with traditional houses built in blonde stone. Many have been converted into guest houses, restaurants and cafés leading from the port level of the town up towards the hills and the famous centre of the Bahá'í religion. Pilgrims travel to this holy site from all over the world. I have to confess my ignorance. I had no idea that Israel was the home of a fourth religion, and I'd never heard of the Bahá'í faith before.

The Bahá'í shrine and the immaculate Persian Gardens which surround it are seen in perfect symmetry from the main thoroughfare through the German Colony. By day the shrine and gardens are colourful and architecturally stunning; by night they're beautifully lit and create a serene backdrop to the many restaurants and cafés which line the avenue. It was clear as soon as we arrived that we'd chosen the perfect location to stay. After a day of driving to the north of Israel through beautiful forested hills, we simply parked up, checked in and could stroll to any number of great eateries.

Bars and restaurant gardens were strung with fairy lights, and trees were decorated with bright, colourful, hand-blown glass baubles. The area was lively with diners and strollers alike and buzzing with atmosphere and gentle music.

Haifa is one of the few places in Israel where Jews and Arabs live together in relative harmony. It's built on the slopes of Mount Carmel, and as such, it can be tiring to get around when you're heading uphill. It's always a bit easier on the way back down. It's a place apart, and the one city in Israel where public transport runs on the Sabbath. It also has a dinky underground railway with four stops, which avoids the need for climbing hundreds of steps if you want to get from town up to the Carmel area of Haifa town where there are hidden garden restaurants, cafés and independent shops selling arts, crafts and handmade toys.

Although there's a huge port and the usual assortment of commercial shipping and cruise ships, there are also lovely Mediterranean beaches a short drive out of town. The place has a relaxed atmosphere, and it seemed on the surface that there's the possibility of a great quality of life for those who live there. We headed straight to the beach for a swim and loved the family feel and less frantic activity levels than the ping-ponging, jogging, volley-balling beach bods which hung out and hardly ever had an inactive moment on the beaches of Tel Aviv. This was taken at a much gentler stride, with people swimming and enjoying the sunset, sitting and schmoozing. Altogether a different pace of life. Yes, my preferred views at the beach are from a horizontal position on a beach towel.

After our swim we decided to head up towards the Persian Gardens, which were closed by the time we reached the main gates. Never mind. We would definitely be back to explore them as the vast estate which houses the shrine looked so beautiful that it was now on our must-see list.

On our way back down through the labyrinth of staircases, we came across a housing development of bleak apartments which looked cell-like with bare light fittings and appeared to be very old, tired and run down. We tried to ask directions of a young dad who was supervising his child on a stride-and-ride toy in the warm night air. He didn't speak English and sounded Russian, but with hand signals and physically escorting us to the path, he led us to the beginning of the right track back down towards the centre of town. I looked up at a resident on the second floor standing over a simple stove, stirring a pot by the bare window, alone in a loose undervest. I got the sense that perhaps some immigrants came here in search of a new life and never left. I later learnt that there's a large population of Russian Jews in Haifa, which would account for the variety of vodka on sale. There couldn't be many Brits as there was no gin on offer in the supermarket, but I was happy to note that there was a vast selection of deli goods including forbidden pork products. It's amazing how delicious food becomes when it's forbidden.

From the outside our guest house looked great. On the inside we were greeted by the proprietor, and it was clear that painting and redecoration of the small reception area were underway. Our room was snug and basic with no frills. We enjoyed sitting in the communal hall space upstairs and meeting our fellow guests. Without this overflow space, it would have been almost impossible for all three of us to stay in the room at the same time as there was barely room for the double bed and the extra child's bed pre-ordered for Morgan. It was very hot and stuffy when we arrived, and we had to jam the door open.

Two women of differing ages who could have been mother and daughter arrived, one blonde, one very dark-haired. They asked our advice on cooling and airing their room and then left for some shopping. We stayed where we were, sipping our wine and enjoying a quiet few minutes alone. We speculated on this odd couple of travelling companions who seemed to have little rapport; one was bubbly and chatty about her travels and religion, and the other more reserved. It turned out that they were Jehovah's Witnesses who had journeyed to Israel to meet other Jehovah's Witnesses and enjoy the fellowship of people with similar beliefs before going forth and spreading the word to the rest of the world. The younger blonde woman, who was very jolly and friendly, shared with us during one of our conversations that her ambition was to learn Hebrew so that she could read the whole of the Bible in the language it was originally written. A much loftier ambition than a need to learn Hebrew so that you can telephone the Hot Cable Company and add a channel to your TV selection.

The next morning we drove further north towards the border with Lebanon. We were heading for Rosh Hanikra which is the furthest north we could travel along the Israeli coast. The area has been developed for tourists, and there's a café with panoramic views of the waters and the sea border with Lebanon, marked by buoys and patrolled by Israeli coast defence boats. It was easy to see how arguments could arise as to where the boundary line should lie. I wouldn't mind betting that there will be many arguments and skirmishes to come now that the Israelis have discovered vast reserves of natural gas under the sea bed, enough to provide for all its needs for decades to come.

This spot has amazing views from the top of the cliffs. A short but scenic cable car ride lowers you down to the base of the cliffs where you can view the grottos and weird structures eroded from the rock over the centuries by the waves' crashing.

We were told a tale of a beautiful young bride being brought for marriage to an old codger she wasn't keen on. The usual inverse fairy tale of old. It was said she was so unenthusiastic about the forthcoming nuptials that she threw herself from the clifftop and was never seen again. Legend has it that you can still hear her calling through the grottos at Rosh Hanikra. This tale made quite an impression on the junior member of our party who brooded on the unhappy outcome for the fiancée for the rest of the day.

There are some old railway tunnels which were used during both World Wars to transport troops, their rations and other necessary supplies. The British Army also used the tunnels to invade Lebanon from this strategic point. During the Arab-Israeli War of 1948, the Israelis blew up the bridges linking the tunnels to prevent a major influx of Arab fighters from Lebanon. There are so many stories of war and memorials wherever you venture in this land of contrast. It's a historically noteworthy and picturesque spot.

When you exit the cable car at the top of the cliff, you can walk towards the border, but you cannot cross into Lebanon from there. There's a door which marks the crossing point, but no entry to Lebanon is permitted.

As I hung around the reception area of the Haddad Guest House the next morning, waiting to check out and return the room key, I spotted a framed certificate behind the reception desk. I expected to see a licence permitting a certain number of guests, or perhaps a framed TripAdvisor rating. I was flabbergasted to see that our patron was the grand master of the Masonic lodge in Haifa and was advertising that fact. I was labouring under the misapprehension that the Masonic lodge was a secret society. Perhaps I'd been reading too many Dan Brown books.

Apart from the comic images of rolled-up trouser legs and dodgy handshakes, I had no idea what the masons did, or what their mission was. I shared with Mr Haddad that my paternal grandfather was a grand master of the Masonic lodge in my home town of Kirkintilloch,

Scotland. I had a feeling that it was at that time a primitive social networking group, with a religious element, but I wasn't sure. I know my brother inherited my grandfather's Masonic jewel from my father, and that it was a highly intricate medal-like brooch made of pure gold. It must be worth a fortune now, the way gold prices have gone up. I made a mental note to ask to take a proper look at it the next time I was home.

26

CARMEL AND THE WINE COUNTRY

On the last day of our ambitious and enjoyable long weekend, we planned to drive through the Carmel Forest area and head towards the famous vineyards which were founded by none other than Baron Edmond de Rothschild, who is renowned for the pressing of many an excellent grape.

With his help the Carmel winery was founded, and it now commands a sizeable chunk of the wine market in Israel. The winery is the largest of Israel's wineries and the maker of some of its award-winning labels. The quality of winemaking has improved so much over the years that Israeli wines regularly feature in international competitions and do well. Wine has been made in the Holy Land since biblical times, but the consumption of wine has increased dramatically, and it's now used for both sacramental rituals and social imbibing.

Many of the wines are kosher, and they're exported to Jewish communities all over the world. The United States of America is the largest export market, not surprisingly, having the largest Jewish population in the world. To be certified as kosher, the wine must only be made by Shabbat-observant male Jews.

You can visit many of the wineries (including the very small boutique ones), and we were on a mission to start with Carmel. The shop was large and with such a tremendous variety of wine on display, it was a little confusing. Luckily it was also well staffed, and we were given an impromptu mini tour with tasting by a knowledgeable and friendly English-speaking assistant who knew his cabernet sauvignons from his merlots. He insisted on opening bottles for us to taste. Sadly Chris was driving, so I had to do the polite thing with no spitting out! We loaded the car with three cases of our favourites, a couple of bottles of bubbly (truly the best bubbly I've tasted in Israel, confirmed by our visitors who enjoyed it later in the year). The assistant threw in a pair of oversized wine glasses, beautifully boxed with no tacky logo, and all in all, we thoroughly enjoyed the experience.

Our excellent wine assistant, who had made Aliyah from the Midlands of the United Kingdom a few years earlier, was obviously missing speaking in his native English tongue. He invited us around for dinner at his house that evening as he and his British wife were hosting an English-speaking gathering. We were sorry to decline the invitation as we had a long road ahead of us back to Jerusalem with precious cargo. We hoped that when we went back, we'd be invited again.

After that we wandered through the centre of Carmel town, which is very quaint with lots of little independent shops selling artwork, colourful crafts, hand-painted mobiles (baby toys not phones) and handmade clothes. There was no shortage of cafés and places to eat. We found a lovely book shop down a lane and bought several titles about Israel, by authors I'd never heard of before moving there. Yet another world was opening up for us.

Not long after our drive through the forests and wine country of Carmel, there was a massive forest fire which tragically resulted in the loss of many lives. By the time the fire was brought under control, after four days of battling it, 44 people had died and thousands had been evacuated from their homes. It was the worst forest fire in Israel's history, and the smoke from the burning forests, which were totally razed, was visible from space.

The fire had spread quickly, and it seemed that the country wasn't equipped with firefighting planes which were necessary to halt the destructive inferno. I was heartened to see that other countries offered help which was accepted by the Israeli government, normally shy of any outside interference.

I'll never forget watching the Haifa chief of police being interviewed from her car near the blaze as she updated the public through a local television news channel on the dire situation. Only a few hours later, it was reported that she too had been killed in the fire. For me she was the personal face of that tragedy. It was heartbreaking.

We were hugely conscious of the risk as our house was situated on the edge of the Jerusalem Forest which faces the same fire risk as Carmel, if not more so. The summers are long, hot and dry, and the forest is used by Jerusalemites as an escape from apartment and city dwelling to a place of nature walks, picnic tables and play areas for children. Barbequing is a national pastime. This, taken with youth groups on camp-outs and people who just want to sit around a fire and relax at night, places the Jerusalem Forest at extremely high risk if people aren't careful and responsible. The thought of another Carmel-like fire on our doorstep was terrifying, but that was a nightmare we hadn't faced—yet.

27

TEL AVIV

When we wanted to enter a whole different world, we drove down Highway 1 from Jerusalem for about 45 minutes in the direction of Tel Aviv. The time difference was decades. The city skirts the gorgeous golden beaches of the Mediterranean Sea, with a wide promenade fringing the sandy shores which are enjoyed by residents, day trippers and tourists. It's possible to walk along this promenade to Jaffa quite easily, although you have to be careful of the mad, speedy cyclists who jostle for space on the footpath with characteristic pushiness, bordering on aggression. If you survive the cyclists, it makes for a picturesque stroll to the Old Port.

Jerusalem is beautiful, with its modern and Old City, historical architecture, colourful gardens and tree-lined streets. However, Tel Aviv is regarded as a happening place, more relaxed than Jerusalem (it would be harder to be more uptight than Jerusalem). The hunched and harried bodies of orthodox Jerusalemites hurrying along in ankle-length baggy denim skirts and training shoes are replaced by fit, healthy bodies jogging, roller-blading, cycling and posing along that promenade in various stages of undress. This beach attire would be unthinkable on the streets of Jerusalem where verbal abuse and haranguing are a risk if you venture into the wrong area of town in the wrong clothes.

I spent a happy half hour in the Jaffa market flicking through a stack of vinyl LPs (long-playing records for those of you who have fallen through the gap of time between the original popularity of vinyl and popularity regained). Apparently vinyls are making a comeback, and Scott, one of my nephews, collects them. Having chosen a few to send back to him with Liberty, I was asked by the Israeli stall holder, 'Where do you come from?'

'Jerusalem,' I replied.

He thought a bit, scratched his stubbly chin and sympathised. 'It's very difficult for women in Jerusalem.'

It wasn't so difficult for me, as a foreigner, who didn't speak much of the lingo. I think it was probably helpful that I couldn't understand insults. It was also a plus that I wouldn't dream of strolling around any city in micro shorts, whether there was a beach or not. But I could imagine that the restrictions of dress code might be infuriating for women who were born there and fought in the army or had chosen to live there permanently and make Jerusalem their home.

The thing is, he's right. You won't see an advertisement in Jerusalem showing a woman, and I didn't notice this until it was pointed out to me. There are no advertisements on the city's buses showing women wearing jeans, or of waterproof mascara or advertising movies. Even when a woman was running for the office of mayor of Jerusalem, she couldn't have her picture on billboards or buses. It was explained to me that the buses would be damaged. Such is the strength and power of the orthodox view in this city. Although they're a minority of the population, the orthodox pack a punch well above their weight.

Female doctors were excluded from a lecture on gynaecology and obstetrics at a medical conference as it was considered inappropriate for women to be in the same room as men when the subject matter was covered. An outrageous decision for secular Israeli women, or any woman or man to accept. A group in the city was working at addressing these issues and discrimination against women generally.

The influence of the minority of the population, who would

segregate buses, streets, stop advertising and ban female doctors from conferences on gynaecology drives many residents of Jerusalem to move to Tel Aviv, or further afield, permanently was terrible to witness.

On the other hand, some religious residents of Jerusalem view Tel Aviv as a hotbed of sin. 'Sodom and Gomorrah' is how one Jerusalemite described the city after an alleged gang rape on a Tel Aviv beach in the middle of the afternoon. It was then reported as a group sex session where the only woman involved had allegedly consented. It then became, for some, an issue of morals when it transpired the woman had mental health issues, and it wasn't the first time she had engaged in sexual activity in public. The fear was that in her vulnerable state, she had been taken advantage of by a group of young men. What shocked many Israelis was that people had watched and even photographed the spectacle for an hour, but only one woman had called the police who had turned up but found nothing amiss and had then pursued some pickpockets. Pickpocketing and petty theft were rife on the beach, although we hadn't fallen victim to them. Thankfully sex on the beach in broad daylight, consensual or non-consensual, appeared to be a very rare occurrence.

Against this backdrop, and although enjoying the atmosphere and fun of the beaches in Tel Aviv, we explored other options and found a new regular beach haunt further south of Tel Aviv and Jaffa, far from the maddening crowds. We discovered a pretty cove near the town of Ashkelon, very close to the Gaza border, perhaps explaining its quietness.

Later during our time in the country, the beach area had a bit of a spruce up and now also sports shiny new changing rooms, showers and a garden promenade. It's still far less crowded and commercialised than the beaches further north, and so far as I know, the beach bums keep their swimming cossies on. The only offensive sight you might catch is that of a tanned Israeli gentleman striding forth along the beach in his budgie smugglers, and you can always close your eyes.

The downside was that we had to carry beach chairs, sun umbrellas and other paraphernalia from the car park to the sea shore as there were no sunbed rental concessions. We also needed to bring sustenance—a flask of coffee, a cool box and lots of water. So it took a little planning and effort, but it was worth it.

Ashkelon has a strong Russian influence. The Russian Jews who have settled there eat food which isn't kosher in the eyes of other Jews. They're also a fun-loving lot. We often stopped at Tiv Tam supermarket on the way back from the beach where we'd found a bar with beer pumps and wine in the middle of the supermarket. If we went on a weekend, there was live music and some old-timers, heavily made-up (the women not the men), waltzing to the band. As we could purchase pork, bacon, ham, prawns, fresh scallops and other contraband, it was a favourite stop for a shop. I could finally tell the difference between Russian and Hebrew.

We often crossed the road by the beach in Ashkelon to a sports bar and pub for some grub, and it was clearly owned and run by Russians. The food was really good in a no-nonsense sort of a way, and it was open on a Friday and Saturday.

The only drawback to this quieter beach experience was that we had to be fairly sure that there were no incoming rockets from Gaza expected. We gave it a wide berth when there was tension and skirmishes on that border.

Another issue which was troubling in Tel Aviv was tension between residents of South Tel Aviv and several African refugees and asylum seekers. This had led to some friction on both sides, with some Israeli residents claiming they were afraid to go out at night.

Tel Aviv is also host to a vibrant gay community and to a world-renowned Gay Pride parade, a week-long festival of events for the lesbian and gay community which is officially promoted by the Israel Ministry of Tourism. The parade now attracts in excess of 200,000 people annually with participants from all over the world. This city has become a gay travel destination throughout the year, mainly because of its reputed tolerance and positive welcome to all who want to party here. It's hard to imagine that such an open-minded community can exist within a country which requires all heterosexual Jewish couples who aren't 100% Jewish to travel abroad for marriage. Rabbis still have a monopoly in the marriage market.

Most of the buildings in Tel Aviv are of the ugly concrete school of architecture, apart from the Bauhaus treats, but my eye was drawn to the lovely pavement cafés, trees and city parks and of course the beach. So the 1960s-style apartment blocks could be forgiven.

We decided to book into a hotel in Tel Aviv for the night and pretend we were on holiday. It wasn't hard to do as there were fish restaurants, inflatable boat shops, flip-flop stands and cheap, gaudy beach clothes stalls—all we needed for a beach break.

The sandy shores were kept beautifully clean, and there were large permanent wooden pergolas which provided shaded areas if you weren't a sun worshipper. There was also a Bay Watch-style lifeguard hut elevated above the throngs with a fully functioning loud hailer. As I frantically beckoned Morgan and his friend Taymor to come ashore for lunch, on a previous trip to the beach, I was told by the life guard, through the loud hailer and in English, not to worry about them. The same guard told a local mum to get up off her sunbed and take care of her children.

There's also a selection of bars and restaurants, so we could go for the day with minimal preparation, lie on a sunbed and people watch all day. We often scoffed unhealthy meals featuring French fries, calamari or chicken, all deep fried of course. Was this really the Mediterranean diet?

Our hotel in theory fell within the 'luxury' bracket. The price was luxury, but the hotel wasn't. It was run down and in need of a facelift. As we stepped out after a welcome gin and tonic sundowner, we almost immediately stood on a litter of business cards carpeting the walkway which led to the seaside restaurant promenade. Business cards dropped by prostitutes. Morgan's eyes were on stalks. He glimpsed pneumatic breasts and black strips of lace, and I uttered the now famous words, 'Put it down, Morgan,' as he giggled awkwardly.

We strolled along the seafront and were drawn into a performance by a man who sat at a small table doing the three cups and one squidgy ball trick. He started his show, shuffling the cups quite slowly so that we could all tell exactly which cup was harbouring the ball.

'Who wants to bet 100 shekels on knowing where the ball is?'

A stooge standing beside him put his money on the table and was of course rewarded immediately when he tapped the right cup.

'Come closer, come closer,' the man beckoned like the wicked wolf in a fairy tale.

'It's easy, Mum. Can I try, can I try next time?' asked Morgan, hugely excited by the prospect of winning money.

I uttered the usual reply, and we were on our way without participating in the farce. A gentleman of African origin followed us as Morgan was still harping to return and have a go, upset by the missed opportunity.

'Do not give money to that man. He is a bad man who cheats people,' advised our new African minder.

Chris then explained to Morgan the disappointment of shysters in the real world, and we carried on with our stroll, ticking off another life experience on Morgan's list of lessons to be learnt.

That was when we encountered one of the strangest sights I'd seen in Israel, and believe me I'd seen a few—a group of young disco goers, dancing in unison, but with certain individuality, to total silence. A headphone disco. They were all given earpieces in exchange for shekels and could listen and gyrate to ear-splitting music without disturbing the peace. What a great idea. It did look a bit silly though. I decided to give that disco a miss.

After a lovely break, and feeling as if we'd been on holiday, we packed our overnight bags and headed for home, a shortish drive away. No airports, no security checks and no lengthy questioning on why we'd visited Egypt, Jordan, Oman, UAE, Syria, Malaysia, Brunei and a few other predominantly Muslim countries. On attempting to leave Israel on a previous occasion through Ben Gurion International Airport, and after one such question and answer session, a young border official asked me, 'Why do you visit such places?'

'Because they're pleasant and lovely,' was my honest reply.

We decided we must go on 'home holidays' more often. It was only when we were on the highway that I realised the extent to which our pockets had been picked. At well over $200 a night for a very average room, we thought we might save up and have a fortnight in Spain next time.

28

WINTER SUN AND WAR

The weather was still unusually warm for November. We were able to visit the beach and bask in 28°C degrees of sunshine while the UK was under a blanket of snow and the coldest November nights since records began.

In this sunny paradise we now called home, the sirens blared from Jerusalem. At 10 a.m. they were tested as Jerusalem prepared for war. If this became the real deal, as opposed to a 'normal' drill, there would be a long siren call followed immediately by a short one. Or it might have been the other way around.

Bizarrely it also appeared that Israel might be one of the few countries in the region not to be damaged by the WikiLeaks disclosures of diplomatic cables from the US to various governments about Iran's nuclear capability. It seemed that Arab leaders had been saying privately what Israel had been shouting from the rooftops for quite some time—Iran's nuclear ambitions posed a threat to the entire region.

We also woke up to the news that two nuclear scientists in Iran had been targeted in co-ordinated car bomb attacks. One had died, and the other was critically injured. The foreign press suspected American and

Israeli involvement. A senior member of the Jordan royal family believed war in the region was imminent.

All in all a rather unsettling day. I couldn't help but wonder if it was just me who felt this unease. Were the Israelis so used to the uncertainty, drills, threats of possible war and assassination attempts that it had become the norm?

29

THE LADIES OF UBEIDIYA

I travelled out of Jerusalem, through a security check point which was so civilised that I didn't even notice it (I wasn't driving), towards the small village of Ubeidiya which lies to the east of Bethlehem. The landscape and scenery on this drive were spectacular, and Penny, Nas (a friend I'd made through school) and I arrived on the hilltop with vast views of rounded, stony outcrops. The panorama was immense.

The Al-Sabaya Centre in Ubeidiya had a plaque announcing that the premises were 'adolescent-friendly'. We climbed the stairs of the freshly painted concrete building and entered through a doorway which was hammered out of the concrete wall. The jagged entrance led to a neat doorway and a long bright workspace.

This area had been set up as a large naturally lit and airy sewing room. Long cutting tables stretched down the centre of the workspace, and at the far end, a group of ladies were using several smart industrial Singer sewing machines. The Japanese government had donated the machines which stood in a row in front of large windows which lined one side of the room, affording the best light. Palestinian women could, upon the payment of a small contribution, sew and work from the premises.

Penny and Nas had established and nurtured the project towards financial viability so that it provided a source of income for 25 families in the West Bank. It's often difficult to find work in the Occupied Territories, and impossible to travel into Jerusalem, so many families face financial hardship. The women employed the traditional skill of Palestinian embroidery, but with a modern slant. The designs were stitched on quality linen fabric, but not in the conventional predominantly red and black colour schemes. The ladies were stitching pastels and brightly coloured threads (only the best quality was used) onto white and cream linens. There were also red and green linens, beautifully embellished baby clothes and adult shirts and dresses. It was a busy day as they were making the final preparations for the Christmas bazaar at the American Colony Hotel in Jerusalem. This is one of the world's leading small luxury hotels, and the annual bazaar, hosted by the hotel, provided one of the main sources of income and marketing for this fledgling project.

Nas and Penny bought the fabric and threads in Jerusalem and supplied the women with design ideas. Before moving to Jerusalem, Nas was a designer with Ralph Lauren in New York. Today they'd brought swatches of pale linens for the summer collections and some children's dress patterns Penny sourced during a trip to the UK. Penny was an actress and appeared in one of the Bridget Jones movies, which I've now watched again just to see her.

The Palestinian ladies had ready the garments ordered for the upcoming sale, and the clothes were inspected for quality, cleanliness, sizing and eye appeal. They were beautiful garments, and the intricate embroidery which appeared on the front and the back of every piece was a pleasure to see. Each item was logged in a notebook which served as a register, and the women were to be paid for each one. Not one of the garments was rejected. After the sale in Jerusalem, it was hoped that enough income would be generated to pay the women and buy the next batch of fabric for the spring/summer collection. It was all very hand to mouth, and the project survived on a small annual UNIFEM grant which had been given for the last three years. It was no exaggeration to say that the craftsmanship and hard work of the women of Ubeidiya was a feast for the eyes and also put bread on the tables of West Bank families.

Ubeidiya is remote in terms of the tourist trail and any potential expat market, so the link to Jerusalem and the local community was essential for the marketing of the products. I left this project inspired by the warmth and cheerfulness of these Arab women who were doing their best in very challenging circumstances, and inspired by my friends Penny and Nas who had made it all possible.

30

HEBRON

Hebron is the largest city in the West Bank and one of the hotspots for trouble and unrest. It's home to around a quarter of a million Palestinians who live alongside no more than eight hundred Israeli settlers (population 2014). The Jewish settlers returned to Hebron in 1980 and are constantly guarded by the Israeli police and the army.

The Old City of Hebron displays typical Arab architecture with thick stone walls, traditional old stone houses and narrow cobbled streets which house the souk.

It also hosts a site which is of huge importance to both Jews and Muslims. After a walk through and past the small shops which are set back from the ancient footpath and, in typical Arab souk style, display many wares on the pavement outside, we encountered modern, airport-style security screening to enter the area of the Tombs of the Patriarchs and Matriarchs. Chris, Morgan and I were the guests of a local family on this particular visit and passed through the first security barrier with no difficulty. The second barrier, which screened visitors to the part of the Herodian building known as the Ibrahimi Mosque, proved a bit trickier. One of our unofficial tour guides wore traditional Arab headgear (that is, her hair was covered by a white headscarf closely wound around her head and neck and secured by pins), so her ethnicity was obvious to the IDF soldiers. They quizzed the rest of us about our religion and nationality. After a longer conversation between the soldiers and Dr Sharif, they permitted us entry.

'What did they say?' I asked Dr Sharif as the conversation was lengthy and all in Arabic. My Arabic isn't much better than my Hebrew. A few words and phrases picked up here and there.

'Oh, they wanted to know why you were covered in paint.'

We'd forgotten that this cultural visit was an unexpected bonus after a day of painting two local schools in Hebron, one boys' school, one girls' school, and planting trees for shade in the playground. Dr Sharif, a member of Chris's senior management team, had organised the charity painting day. We were invited to dinner with him in his family home later that day. Both schools were badly in need of a coat of paint, and the classroom furniture was dirty, dilapidated or broken. After a whole day in the sun, hard at work, we were all dusty, sweaty and paint-smeared, and our appearance would have led to questions at the entrance of any holy site in the world. The local TV cameras at the schools had also filmed several interviews for the local news channel, and we must have looked such a sight.

I was spared the embarrassment of my messy clothes at the mosque as I was asked to don a long brown robe with a pointy hood before entering. I then resembled a short monk. Noor, Dr Sharif's sister-in-law being covered already, simply put on some stretch elastic clothes in a fetching 1950s floral apron print, and we were almost in. I say 'almost' because we then had to leave our footwear in the shoe cubby holes at the entrance to the mosque.

I managed to suppress a smile as I thought of a Jordan-based deputy British ambassador who shall remain nameless. He was on a day trip to Damascus on business and had been taken to the Umayyad, or Great Mosque, as part of his official visit. After the tour was completed, he returned to the starting point to retrieve his shoes, left in a neat row outside with many other shoes. The only ones left in his size were a rather fashionable pair of white plastic patent 'leather' pointy ones. His dapper leather shoes by Church's, a famous London shoemaker, were long gone by the time he returned for them. His newly acquired footwear must have raised a few eyebrows in diplomatic circles for the rest of the day.

Unlike the Blue Mosque in Istanbul, there wasn't the all-pervading smell of sweaty socks and shoes. No thanks to us, I hasten to add.

The ceilings and decorations were magnificent, but my personal favourite was the wooden stairway which dated back to somebody the great (probably Suleiman again) and had verses from the Quran carved into the sides. I like to think of it as a stairway to heaven, regardless of who your god might be.

Neon clocks in the next room displayed the times of prayer. When we lived in Brunei, and before Google was a household word, we were puzzled by the green arrows we saw pinned to the ceiling in random corners of hotel rooms in Brunei and Malaysia. They were pointing the faithful in the direction of Mecca for prayer time. Just to highlight the need for cultural awareness, in the UK if you're not a Muslim but pointing towards Mecca, you're on your way to a bingo hall or a bookmaker. Such activity would be frowned upon in Islam, and by the majority of the population of Edinburgh.

The worst terrorist atrocity in Israeli history took place in the Ibrahimi Mosque. On the 25th February 1994, during the holy month of Ramadan and on the day of the Jewish celebration of Purim, 29 Palestinians were shot and killed and 125 were wounded as they offered up morning prayers at the mosque. They were shot in the back by an American-born local Jewish doctor who was reported to have emptied four magazines of ammunition into the praying masses from behind, only stopping when his gun jammed.

The legacy of that attack is apparent on the streets of this city, especially around the Tombs of the Patriarchs. Measures were put in place to separate the Jewish and Palestinian communities for security reasons. After a two-month curfew following the massacre, shops remained shut and barred, depriving shopkeepers who had traded for generations of their livelihoods. To this day, tensions run high.

When we left the mosque, we were herded onto a cordoned-off narrow pavement on one side of the road which was the walkway for Arabs. When we reached an IDF checkpoint a hundred metres from the mosque, we were forbidden entry because it was the Jewish

Sabbath. We turned back and walked in the other direction along the walkway while small family groups of Jewish settlers sauntered back home, spread across the road and the other pavement. We were met by another imaginary, but very real, dividing line. We couldn't walk further than ten yards past the Tombs of the Patriarchs without being stopped. This beautiful green park was for Jews only, and we could only stand and look at them sitting on the grass, while children played.

We chatted to a shopkeeper, who told us that although his home was metres away from his shop, he was barred from crossing the line in this street, and he had to walk a long and circuitous route home. His livelihood had been threatened, as had his shop. It had in the past been ransacked and his stock destroyed by Jewish settlers who wanted him out.

Almost on cue, as we chatted to this friendly and surprisingly gentle man, a tall heavy-set orthodox Jew in a long black frock coat, with black peyot swinging on both sides of his face, strode past us with his family and across the line. He stared at us in an intimidating way. I'm not one to be easily riled, but his look bore us all ill will. I was told that he was a wealthy American Jew who donated millions of dollars each year to ensure the wellbeing of the Jewish settlers in Hebron. I can't imagine choosing to move my family to a community of 800, needing the might of the IDF to protect me and mine on a daily basis, but I guess it takes all sorts.

I hated the atmosphere of fear and intimidation on that imaginary line. I experienced first-hand what it feels like to be in the ranks of the occupied and learnt what it was like to lose the right to live on a street, lived in and walked on by generations of your family before you.

The main industry in Hebron is stone-cutting. We saw young men, faces white with dust, working in the stone-cutting area of town.

'Look at their faces,' I said to Chris. 'Their lungs must be in a terrible state.'

'The dust can't help the lungs of the local population either,' he replied, 'but without this industry, operated in a very primitive way, many Hebronite families would go hungry or starve.'

'Can we stop and watch this man?' Morgan asked as we walked past one of the many glass-blowing businesses.

'Of course,' I told him, fascinated by the process myself. 'Just look at all those different colours. It's incredible that all those beautiful pieces are handmade.'

There were several factories, and it was like stepping back to the industrial revolution with large open fires and ovens and a man sitting on a short stool, blowing glass like crazy with cheeks for bellows.

We drove to Hebron again during the Christmas holidays in search of the wonderful multi-coloured hand-blown glass balls which are made and sold there. Liberty had in mind personalising the balls she planned to buy in the Holy Land for all her friends back in Scotland by painting messages on them. I wanted to buy enormous glass balls to hang in our trees on the moshav and ultimately to arrange artistically in the garden of our house we'd yet to build in Italy, bought in hope and excitement before our family jigsaw was broken. But we planned to plan again. Who knew; dreams can come true.

To get the effect I'd conjured up for our imaginary home, we needed to buy really big glass globes. I'd seen them strung up in the café gardens of Haifa when we visited, and they looked very appealing.

We visited the first workshop where they had a formidable fire going and a glass blower turning out glass balls and vases a lot quicker than you might imagine. Another man painted beautiful pottery in the adjacent pottery workshop, outlining timeless designs as his colleague coloured the patterns with pastel shades which would turn into vibrant blues, greens and turquoises after baking in the kiln.

On entering the shop, we found a collection of small- and medium-sized baubles along with wine goblets, pitchers, tumblers, hanging plant holders and loads of bells and other decorations in every size and colour.

'Do you have big balls?' I asked the shopkeeper in all innocence.

'Feast your eyes,' was the reply. 'I have the biggest balls in Hebron.'

'Excuse me, sir, that's my wife you're talking to, and she only wants to purchase some Christmas decorations,' Chris chipped in.

This conversation was made up by my lovely family in the car on the completion of our shopping mission. There's no way that I would ask a gentleman such an embarrassing question and more to the point, there's absolutely no way a gentleman of Hebron would speak to a lady in this brash and unsavoury manner.

I had a really good shopping session and snoop around the Hebron glass shop. It was so hard to choose, so I bought two balls in every colour. In this life of being a global nomad, you never regret the things you buy, only the things you don't buy.

Words of the day: min fadlak — please (Arabic)

31

HANUKKAH

The date of Hanukkah moves each year, but it usually falls in the holiday season, and that year it almost coincided with our Christmas celebrations. Liberty labelled this holiday Chrismukkah in her Facebook photo album. There was a real festive atmosphere around town and in the malls.

The eight days are marked by the lighting of the Hanukkah candle at nightfall, and it must burn for a minimum period of half an hour. You can buy small and cheap Hanukkah candles in the shops, but why would you purchase short-burning candles for the ritual when you could enjoy the wonderful, warming, longer-lasting benefits of candlelight from everyday ones? Families usually have a candle holder or candelabra which can hold nine candles, one for each of the eight days plus an extra candle which is lit every night. On each night of the holiday, a candle is lit along with the extra candle as well. Families gather, and someone will be given the honour of lighting the Hanukkah candle that day. The whole point is for the candles to be seen from the outside of the house, so they are placed in windows or on prominent places near windows. In the Old City, some of the very old houses have small glass boxes mounted on their stone walls. I saw an Orthodox Jewish gentleman open the door of such a glass box and light the Hanukkah candles inside. It was such a traditional and timeless scene that I would have loved to have taken a photograph but didn't want to intrude. Like so many memories in this town, the record I have of it is in my head.

The Festival of Lights celebrates the fact that when there was only enough oil left to burn a lamp for one day in the temple (as part of a purification ritual after the temple had been defiled), miraculously the oil lasted eight days. Hence the eight-day holiday and celebration and the eight candles, with one extra.

There's also the equivalent of selection boxes on sale in markets and in the shops at this time of year. There are dreidel (spinning top) shaped colourful cardboard containers holding a selection of sweets, chocolate money and a plastic or wooden dreidel.

The children play a game with the spinning top and win or lose the chocolate money, depending on how the top falls. It's the custom for children to receive a small gift on each night of Hanukkah, but nothing like the gifts our children ask for at Christmas time. You won't see iPads and electric guitars exchanged each evening but sweets, games and books instead.

The shopping malls are much busier than usual on a weekday evening, probably because the children at local schools have a holiday. The kids at international schools don't, nor do most of the grown-ups. It's work as usual for most Israelis, although an effort is made to get home early for the ritual lighting of the candles.

Morgan and I popped into the Jerusalem Mall for something essential and saw that it wasn't only busy but bustling with children's entertainers, games, musicians and colouring-in contests. All this fun and frivolity is normally sponsored by the corporate world.

We got caught in a people jam and then realised that it had been caused by a man who had collapsed into unconsciousness at the top of the escalators. We took a diversion in an effort not to contribute to the chaos. As we climbed down the stairs to the lower level, Morgan observed, 'That's so sad, Mum. He's really not well, and on the sixth day of Hanukkah too.' I had no idea it was the sixth day of Hanukkah, but it was a shame. Things didn't look any better 45 minutes later as we were trying to leave the mall, and the poor man was still lying there, surrounded by people and paramedics but motionless. I fear that story may not have had a happy ending.

Another big treat at that time of year is Hanukkah donuts which are delicious and handed out free at the Mamilla open-air mall. Neither Morgan nor Easton, who was staying with us for the Christmas holidays, missed a trick. Despite being perilously close to dinner time, both boys managed to scoff down one each. Traditionally the donuts are fried (fried food is popular at this time because of the oil in the temple connection) and filled with strawberry jam. However, the huge selection we were offered also had chocolate and many more fillings. We took some home from one of the many bakeries which displayed temporary trestle tables full of donuts lined up like the soldiers of the Chinese Terracotta Army. We chose huge chocolate-covered ones with long fat syringes of extra chocolate sauce for squeezing in the centre of the bun. A chocoholic's dream come true. When in Jerusalem, do as the Jerusalemites do!

32

NAZARETH

We visited Nazareth in winter when the Christmas lights were strung all around the Church of the Annunciation. The church is said to be built on the site of Mary's house, where she heard the news that she was pregnant with the baby Jesus. We were in the company of Christian pilgrims on a tour of the Holy Land, and the church was uncomfortably busy. There was no opportunity for a quiet moment of thought or prayer on this visit. It was hectic.

Nazareth is situated in Northern Israel where Jesus grew up. It's a real mix of old and new buildings, of churches and commerce. We visited one of the markets which looked a bit like the Arab section of the market in the Old City of Jerusalem, but on a much smaller scale.

There's a good range of restaurants, and we managed to find a very reasonable one with the usual breads, salads and dips and a decent mixed grill and chicken shish tawook—nothing fancy, just delicious, fresh food cooked well.

The population is predominantly Muslim (70%), with some Christians (30%) as well. It's regarded as an Israeli Arab town as its inhabitants are citizens of Israel.

It's also home to a hotbed of anti-Israeli sentiment and prone to outbursts of violence. I was struck by a large sign displayed prominently on the side wall of one of the buildings which read:

> *And whoever seeks a religion other than Islam, it will*
> *never be accepted of him, and in the Hereafter he*
> *will be one of the losers.*

(HOLY QURAN)

It's easy to see how provocation arises on both sides and how that can lead to outbursts of violence. We enjoyed our day out there, but I was happy to leave.

33

JAFFA

Before moving to Israel, my thoughts on Jaffa were mainly food-related. Who doesn't love a Jaffa Cake[1] or two? Jaffa oranges were also a bright and colourful display in the greengrocer's shop of my childhood, Malcolm Campbell's. This was in the days before you could buy kiwi fruit and papaya in Tesco most days of the year. It was also in an age before pineapple was found outside of a tin in the United Kingdom, and the sweetness of exotic fruit like mango was found only in the realms of my young imagination. Growing up in the 1960s in Scotland led to a choice of apples, oranges and bananas, rhubarb from the garden and tinned peaches. To question whether there might be another choice (grapes were only bought when someone was sick in hospital and the trick was to buy, bring and eat during the visit) was dangerous. It could lead to stories of parents who didn't see a banana until they were nearly ten years old because of the Second World War, or the equally harrowing tale of the lucky child who was good all year and rewarded with an orange in their Christmas stocking. The naughty child got a hole in their stocking and maybe some coal. It was a hard life back then.

When I grew up and migrated south to work as a solicitor in the offices of a large London law firm, I worked beside another solicitor whose surname was Jaffa. I never associated him with food or fruit although he may have had ginger hair.

So it was with not much more knowledge than that, and no guide book, that we spent 'just another Saturday' in this gem of a coastal town.

Perched above the twinkling waters of the Mediterranean Sea, the port town of Jaffa is lively, culturally diverse and a wonderful eclectic mix of old and new. Some of it is very old, and the museum is built on what remains of an ancient crusader fortress. A tremendous amount of money was being spent on this charming town, and we could see the influence of its Arab culture everywhere we looked. The renovations of old stone buildings and cobbled streets were being undertaken with vigour and sensitivity to the original designs and atmosphere of this unique place. Jaffa is only a short walk along the beach front from the slick tower blocks of Tel Aviv, but feels as if it could be in another country.

It thrilled me to live within driving distance of places like Jaffa, although when you look on the map, many would say (well, mainly my mum) that it's too close to Gaza for comfort, or for lunch.

We usually started with a hearty lunch at the famous restaurant The Old Man and the Sea, presumably named for the novel by Ernest Hemmingway and not the proprietor. This restaurant was always busy, and at the weekend we expected to queue for a parking space and a table. A few hundred metres along the coast road there was another eatery, designed in the same vein, but which was never busy, possibly because most people didn't get past The Old Man.

The approach to lunch at The Old Man was very Arab. We would sit down at a table without frills, inside or out. A waiter set down a pitcher of freshly squeezed lemonade with a tower of small stacked glass tumblers. My palette was then tempted with a variety of Arab mezze-style starters, from roasted aubergine dip (*mutabal*), mini haggis balls (*kibbeh* (my definition, not theirs)), salads such as parsley and couscous (tabbouleh), toasted bread salad (*fatoush*), goats' cheese, grilled halloumi cheese, green and black marinated olives, pickles (including bright pink cauliflower), hummus and a constant supply of fresh, warm flatbread (Arabic bread) for dipping. We called it the 28-

starter restaurant and, believe me, after 28 starters, I was willing to throw in the towel. I'm possibly exaggerating a little, probably more like 15 or 20. The original 28-starter restaurant is in Puglia in the south of Italy, and we counted them, so the name has become a bit of a jingle in our family folklore.

After picking our way through a lovely selection of food, both hot and cold, the waiter invited us to choose chicken, fish or lamb for our main course. This was no airline-style choice of pre-cooked, mediocre food. This was protein, grilled on charcoal and served when hot and delicious, full of flavour and fresh, fresh, fresh. I always chose fish as it was caught, not farmed, and sitting next to the sea in the hustle and bustle of this restaurant, I could taste the difference. The waiter, who treated us to excellent service with a smile, brought fruit and traditional Arab pastry with strong, short, freshly brewed coffee and a bill when we requested it. With one price for the full meal and the only decision you needed to make being the choice of protein, it wasn't surprising the place was so popular.

We headed north along the coast and back into Jaffa Town proper. Layer upon layer of old stone buildings provide a spectacular backdrop to the promenade area around the Old Port (which is a natural harbour and dates back to the Bronze Age). This area has many restaurants directly overlooking the port and one perched on the clifftop. It must have the most beautiful views due to its situation, but we never tried it, which is again The Old Man's fault. The historical area around the Old Port has been beautifully restored, and the light-golden original stone of the old fortifications gleamed in the sun. Narrow alleyways led us up and towards the real town where the people of Jaffa shop, eat and play. The old houses in the alleyways have been renovated to reveal magnificent stellar stone ceilings, the likes of which I hadn't seen since I was last in the south of Italy. Most now house expensive art galleries, handmade locally designed jewellery shops, craft, quirky furniture and home accent shops. There are no chain stores, chemists, opticians or anything pragmatic. All is given over to the celebration of creativity and aesthetics. The art galleries and our walk through alleyways worn shiny with the passage of feet and time were interesting to the eyes and a peril to the purse.

This gentrified area was redeveloped for everyone to enjoy but is really only used by visitors to the town and is in stark contrast to the flea market and souk of the centre where the commercial action happens. The markets in Israel tend to be very well used by locals for daily shopping. The outdoor flea market in the open square has a range of goods from ancient small electrical appliances to second-hand, very large panty girdles. There are also tenanted, second-hand shops where you can find some interesting pieces of furniture and antiques.

I've found some treasure in my trails, but without fail, everything I've tried to buy has just been sold. The happy purchaser has just gone to fetch a friend to carry or drive it home. Like everything in Israel, second-hand, attractive, one-off pieces of furniture aren't cheap. I found a beautiful, aged chest of drawers in warm honey-coloured waxed wood which would have fitted under our staircase for the camouflaging of my collection of clutter. Back home in the UK in a flea market setting, I would probably have paid a couple of hundred pounds at the most. There in Israel, it was priced at over $1,000 and had been snapped up.

We wandered through a covered souk with rows and rows of shops mainly selling cheap imported souvenirs and clothes. One whizz around was enjoyable, but I wouldn't rush back unless I needed another large cotton beach blanket—my only real find of the day.

Walking along the main street of Jaffa, I inhaled the sweet smell of the Arabic pastries, and could be tempted by the falafel and shawarma shops.

'Look at those shoes!' I nudged Chris, pointing to some white, imitation patent-leather footwear, presumably for bridal wear. 'They're the most atrocious shoes I've seen since I was a child.'

'This shop looks better,' he replied as he moved on next door to a quirky Aladdin's cave of a boutique.

'Just look at those artfully lit stone display niches.'

Morgan yawned as I gazed at the handmade whimsical shoes and boots alongside designer clothes, bags and accessories.

On the surface it seemed that like Haifa, there was room for everyone to do their thing in Jaffa. Sadly this wasn't the case.

Historically many Arabs who had lived in Jaffa for generations had been forced to leave with their families. In what was previously regarded as an Arab neighbourhood within Israel, there remained only 16,000 Arabs, the majority of the population being the 30,000 Jews who inhabited the town.

December is the month when the Jaffa orange harvest begins in earnest. Then we would find juicy oranges, fresh from the farm, grouped in huge flimsy net bags. I only needed to lift my netted treasure from the boot of the car to discover how easily three kilogrammes of sweet, juicy squeezing oranges could break free. The harvest was so abundant, and the fruit so relatively cheap (less than $1 a kilo) that we invested in a citrus press. A heavy, cast-iron, vice-like hand press, the device was primitive in design and appearance but oh so efficient at squeezing every drop of juice out of a Jaffa orange. I used it to squeeze the bejesus out of pomegranates and lemons, so it was worth parting with almost $100 in the Arab Quarter of the Old City of Jerusalem. It was a good investment, because even though we lived in one of the most renowned countries in the world for growing oranges, a bottle of freshly squeezed Israeli orange juice would set us back just under $10 at the very least.

In December and June, we had a glut of huge shiny yellow lemons which our gardener plucked from our two magnificent lemon trees. One had a branch so laden with lemons that it couldn't support its own weight. We counted over 40 of them on just one branch.

They weren't as amazing as the lemons of the Amalfi Coast in Italy, which vary from a modest grapefruit globe to the proportions of a decent-sized honeydew melon, but ours were impressive nonetheless. So twice a year, I took up the process of making homemade limoncello in preparation for our retirement to Italy. That dream was receding as the world economy, stock markets and property market fell and our pensions diminished. It looked as if we'd need to wait until we were in such established old age that we'd hardly be fit to pick our noses never mind lemons.

Apart from our fruit trees, we had fresh mint, basil and thyme growing in the garden and a local lemongrassy bush, the leaves of which I added to hot tea for an aromatic, citrusy flavour. I could've become a domestic goddess had I stayed any longer. Well maybe a kitchen goddess. I would always be writing in the dust.

It was only after living in Jerusalem for three years and meeting Suad Amiry and reading her *Sharon and my Mother-in-Law* that I realised the artists' colony I'd so enjoyed visiting was originally an Arab village. All the villagers had been displaced. I also took to heart her physical pain in her attempt to find the home in Jaffa which had been her parents' home and was now, like most of the rest of the town, occupied by Israelis.

Beit Zayit Limoncello

This is a recipe I've tried and tested to much praise and the enjoyment of friends and family. It's well worth splurging out on a bottle of vodka for this homemade digestif.

Ingredients
5 or 6 unwaxed lemons, well-scrubbed
1 l vodka
500 g sugar
700 ml boiling water

Method—stage one
Carefully pare the zest of the lemons and ensure that you don't collect any pith or this will make the drink bitter.
Slice the zest into thin strips and place in a large glass bottle or bowl with the vodka.
Cover and leave to sit for a week or two (in a cool place if you live in a warm climate), stirring every day if you remember. Don't worry if you forget the odd day.

Method—stage two

Pour the boiling water over the sugar in a heatproof bowl and stir until the sugar is dissolved. Combine the vodka-peel mixture with the sugar-water mixture, stir, cover and leave for another week.

Strain off the peel, bottle, chill, serve and enjoy!

I made double batches so that I could serve it at our dinner parties and have plenty for second and third glasses.

---

1. Biscuit-sized cakes with three layers—a sponge base, a layer of orange-flavoured jam and a coating of chocolate on top.

34

OH, LITTLE TOWN OF BETHLEHEM

It was bizarre, but unless we travelled to Bethlehem in the West Bank, passing through the intimidating security wall and long tunnels en route, there was very little evidence that it was Christmas in the Holy Land.

The Old City of Jerusalem was spookily bereft of tourists, and the absence of hustle and bustle meant that we could look at the goods on display in front of the shops without being pushed and jostled. It was also possible to enjoy visiting the Church of the Holy Sepulchre as there were no queues to commune in the area where Christ's body is said to have been laid out after crucifixion, nor was there a line to kneel and put a hand in the indent in the rock where the cross was allegedly erected. If we were in the Arab Quarter of the city, pushing, jostling and cart deliveries continued whether it was Christmas Eve or not. Apart from a temporary shop selling only Christmas tat 'made in China' at the Jaffa Gate on Latin Patriarchate Street (we couldn't fail to miss it with its life-sized blown-up Santa Claus tethered to the front door), there was no evidence that Christmas Day was approaching.

So to get into the Christmas mood, we decided to travel to the town of Bethlehem in the Palestinian Occupied Territories, the birthplace of Jesus.

Bethlehem is a popular stop on any Holy Land tour, so I was surprised when conducting an unofficial tour of my own (my mother-in-law to the Mount of Olives) to overhear two very well-preserved, middle-aged Liverpudlian ladies taking in the fabulous view of the Golden Dome of the Rock from our elevated vista point.

'That's where Jesus was born,' said one Liver Bird[1] knowledgeably to the other, pointing out the Old City of Jerusalem.

I'm no top Bible scholar (though I did win a Sunday school prize at St Mary's Parish Church, Kirkintilloch, for Bible knowledge) or official tour guide, but even I know Jesus wasn't born in Jerusalem.

'Jesus was born in Bethlehem.' I'd hesitated for just a second but had to correct the duff information the one friend had given to the other. 'Stick out your hand for a smack,' I added, as they both smiled sheepishly and laughed.

'We're going to Bethlehem this afternoon,' the unofficial tour guide confessed. 'How ignorant are we?'

How do you go on a Holy Land tour and not know that Jesus was born in Bethlehem? The mind boggles.

To get to Bethlehem from Jerusalem, we had to pass through a checkpoint and have our passports available for inspection. We weren't intimidated by the checkpoints, which had sadly become a normal part of our everyday lives. It was only when we were ferrying visitors around, or introducing new families to the joys of the West Bank (it made us feel like we were back in our beloved Jordan), that we thought twice about the crossings. Visitors and newcomers were naturally nervous and reticent to pass through the checkpoints until they saw how easy it was to do, as long as you had the luxury of a foreign passport.

Israeli settlers cross back and forth all the time as settlements have been established on the Palestinian side of the security wall. Such development has been regarded as illegal by the United Nations and internationally. Many Israelis dispute this and claim a right to live on the land of Judea and Samaria as they call it; a right, they say, which dates back to biblical times.

After passing through the checkpoint with ease, we drove down a street guarded by two emphatic no-entry signs, and took a right-hand turn, skirting the security wall. If we took this turn from the beaten track, we came to what is perhaps the most bizarre art gallery in the world. Many creative sorts have painted portions of the wall, making powerful statements. Someone once said that a picture paints a thousand words, and some of the work created on this concrete edifice is very poignant and expressive.

Even the famous, if elusive, graffiti artist Banksy has visited the West Bank and 'tagged' the wall with nine works of art. He wittily quipped that the West Bank barrier was 'the ultimate activity holiday destination for graffiti writers'. On a more serious note, his work on the wall, together with the reporting of it and his record of his experiences, continues to draw international interest and attention to the issue, not to mention the attention of the IDF. The following exchange reported on **www.banksy.co.uk** sums up the tension which we all felt there from time to time.

Soldier to Banksy: 'What the fuck are you doing?'

Banksy: 'You'll have to wait until it's finished.'

Soldier to colleagues: 'Safety's off.'

There are Palestinians who disagree with the decoration and acknowledgement of the existence of this monument to separation.

In another conversation, Banksy told how an old Palestinian man said his painting made the wall look beautiful. Banksy thanked him for that and was immediately put right when the old man said, 'We don't want it to be beautiful. We hate this wall. Go home.'

The images and sentiments expressed, often so articulately and with artistic passion, have a place in keeping the wall and the difficult issues surrounding it in the public eye. At the same time, I have great sympathy with the views of the old Palestinian gentleman.

One bonus is that I can guarantee no one will cut out the Banksy offerings on this wall to sell in an art auction overseas and live to tell the tale.

Banksy has now opened the Walled Off Hotel in Bethlehem, and regular auctions of his highly collectable work ensure that it survives and the proceeds are used for social causes.

When we visited Bethlehem on Christmas Eve, it was no exaggeration to say that there was no room at any inn, nor was it likely that any stable block would have been available, with or without a manger.

On approaching the town, it became clear that many tour buses had deposited hordes of pilgrims to celebrate the birthday of Jesus on this very holy night. Manger Square, cleverly named, which is in the centre of the town and is just in front of the Church of the Nativity, was packed full of representatives of every outside broadcast unit of every TV channel in the world, or so it seemed. A stage had been erected in the square where choirs and bands which had travelled, many internationally, were to sing and play from early evening until the small hours of the morning. TV reporters mingled among the crowds, interviewing visitors and shoving long furry microphones on elongated booms into the faces of passers-by. The place was vibrant and busy with all the hustle and bustle which accompanies a crowd with tourist dollars. Arab children peddled everything from chewing gum to small cheap plastic toys. This was a homage to commercialism and tourism.

It was only when we stepped inside the Church of the Nativity, leaving the carnival behind, that we could enjoy the peace and tranquillity of this holy place, and a space in which you might be able to muster up a smidgeon of spirituality.

On my previous visit in November, the interior of the church had been covered in scaffolding, the first major restoration work in over 100 years. It was such a pity that for many visitors, it was a once-in-a-lifetime opportunity to see this special place of worship and pilgrimage. To arrive on what resembled a building site must have been very disappointing. We were warned that it was normal to queue for hours to descend to the grotto of the nativity which contains a silver star marking the spot where it's said that Jesus was born. But to wait for hours in the noise, dust and detritus of construction must have tested the most stalwart pilgrims and dimmed the light of this most holy place.

We waited, it being impossible to think of visiting and not pausing for a while in the grotto. A priest in long flowing robes gave us a blessing and pressed a small colourful card with a picture of the baby Jesus into my hand as a memento of the special moment. It must have been a case of mistaken identity as I've never had any special attention before or since. We were witness to the intense emotion and devotion contained in that small grotto as pilgrims approached the place where the star is inlaid. 'Oh, Come All Ye Faithful' will never sound the same again after sharing a moment with the global pilgrims as they progressed to the most profound moment on their Holy Land tours on this special Christmas Eve. I keep the small and very special card in my jewellery box.

We climbed up to the Church of St Catherine and were treated to a packed Christmas Eve service in full swing. The music and singing were so beautiful that it was impossible not to well up with emotion. I was transfixed by the radiance and intensity of an older nun, praising the Lord from her Bible and her heart. The word adoration is the only way to describe the expression on her glowing face on this special eve, in this special place.

After a very meaningful and emotional experience, it was back to the real world for our family.

We strolled in the golden afternoon light up the steep flag-stoned hill towards the market place. En route, we made our financial contribution to Bethlehem and negotiated to buy several warm pashmina-style scarves for Liberty to take back to chilly Scotland. The negotiations were accompanied by the usual cheery chat and banter of the shopkeeper. We resumed our amble up the old stone steps into the main market where we wandered around stalls of fresh fruit and vegetables, mock Crocs (the really ugly plastic shoes which were so popular in Israel with adults and kids alike), spices, fresh ginger, plastic household goods and dusty antiques. It was an experience to be enjoyed. We were lucky enough to see a Palestinian lady wearing a beautifully embroidered traditional dress, something which was becoming a rarer sight.

On the way to the market, we also passed cages of rabbits. I'd lost count of the number of 'Can I have a rabbit?' conversations I'd had with Morgan on our visits to Bethlehem. I had a suspicion that the rabbits might be bought for food there, not as pets. I couldn't share this thought until he was a bit older, especially as he was so close to Sugar, the class rabbit who came home for sleepovers at the weekend.

We left the market and walked away from the crowds and craziness, through stone passageways and arches up to amazing views across the belfries. Church spires and the minarets of Bethlehem were illuminated in a beautiful rosy light as the sun set on Christmas Eve.

We would usually have stopped and admired the arts and crafts for sale. I was particularly fond of the hand-painted Armenian pottery made in the Holy Land. I'd previously bought the olive wood nativity scenes as presents for family as keepsakes from this special place to be hung on Christmas trees. That day it was just too busy to contemplate, and we even bypassed our usual Arabic coffee stop just off Manger Square.

After a lovely cup of coffee in the lobby of the Holy Family Hotel, which was fully booked for Christmas three years ahead, we travelled back to our moshav to snuggle in safe and warm for the night.

On other trips to Bethlehem market, we'd bought delicious ginger vinegar, a huge curry pot, scarves and pashminas aplenty, old-fashioned wooden clothes pegs and a single silver dessert spoon which my mother-in-law Ann found at the bottom of a box of junk and bought to transform into a bracelet. Sounds a bit like the items passing on the conveyor belt on the UK TV show *The Generation Game*. It also seems like a fair start to one of our favourite table memory games, I Went to the Market, which we played with the children when they were small, hungry and waiting for food to be served in a foreign country. On a serious note, I think shopping is important as it keeps the local economy ticking over. Well that was my excuse for the day.

Word of the day: ahlan—hello (Arabic)

---

1. A reference to the mythical liver bird which is the symbol of the City of Liverpool, England, and a UK TV comedy programme.

35

THE ARAB SPRING

Breaking news in January was that the Hot Cable Company added an English language option to its customer helpline. Sadly it was mere window dressing. If I carefully selected the required digit for English, I was transferred to a person who couldn't speak a word of it, barked at me in Hebrew, put me on hold yet again with annoying mus-ache and then disconnected me.

Morgan was named pupil of the month and was indeed reading *Harry Potter*. Who knew he was interested or had it in him? Like most JAIS kids, he developed an unhealthy obsession with Lego, which culminated in him filming John F. Kennedy's life story in Lego, with animation. One of the best minute-and-a-half animation clips I've ever seen, and it only took him and his cameraman (me) three days of our lives that we'll never get back.

The real breaking news in January 2011 was that a fruit vendor in Tunisia, who set himself alight the previous month, led to a winter of discontent and the uprising known as the Arab Spring. Egyptians protested and demanded democracy, and the ruling Hosni Mubarak was eventually ousted from three decades of power. This was unsettling in Israel as deals had been agreed with the old regime, but no one really had any idea as to whether the new democratic Egypt would continue to tolerate the relationship of practicality with Israel. Mutterings of the Muslim Brotherhood seizing power could be heard, and yes, after the Egyptian elections, the Muslim Brotherhood indeed governed and led the new Egypt, albeit briefly.

Bahrain attempted to quell protests and demands for democracy, and the Libyan people followed suit. The Libyan protests quickly developed into a potential humanitarian disaster as the Gaddafi regime attempted to beat down and extinguish the rebel protests. The international community, mainly the UK and France, stepped in, and after a battle, Gaddafi was ousted from power. Quietly protesters started to demonstrate in Syria and Jordan. In Syria a battle raged between the Bashar al-Assad's regime and the rebel forces. Over time the identity of the rebel forces became blurred, with reports of foreign infiltration and fighters. There was also a chemical attack against innocent civilians asleep in their beds which led to a harrowing loss of life. I was worried about living where we were, but not so much that I felt we had to leave. Chris and I always kept an eye on the news, and we were aware of our emergency evacuation plan. This was a very uncomfortable time to be surrounded by less-than-friendly neighbouring countries, in a country which was experiencing its own internal conflict and power struggles. This state of affairs continued to develop, with tragic humanitarian consequences for years to come, as a new Middle East political map and jihads were pursued by Islamic State in the Middle East and the rest of the world.

36

HOLOCAUST MUSEUM—YAD VASHEM

As Chris worked in the Palestinian Occupied Territory, his weekend was usually Friday and Saturday, so for the first time in years of parenthood, during our time there Chris and I had Fridays off together which we usually spent doing the school run, tracking down a delicious Israeli breakfast with the weekend newspapers and exploring Jerusalem and beyond.

For months the weather had been glorious, and we made the most of it and walked in the Old City, on the ramparts and beyond. Jerusalem is a beautiful city to look at and live in. We were both learning a lot about world religions, history, art, architecture and language. We were eager to explore the museums and art galleries which are scattered throughout Jerusalem but could never bear to be inside when it was sunny and warm outside. A phobia of missing out on sunshine is a hangover from my Scottish childhood. As children on the wet West Coast of Scotland, which is warmed by the Gulf Stream (although you wouldn't notice), we made the most of every glimpse of summer sunshine, and sometimes we even took our cardigans off.

So on a wet and dismal Friday in February, when the sky was grey and the trees dripping, Chris and I travelled up the hill to the Holocaust Museum. I really didn't want to visit as I was afraid of how sad it would make me feel. In my personal life, I work extremely hard at staying cheerful for the sake of my family, my friends and my sanity. Since we lost one of our lovely daughters so suddenly, I could so easily teeter into a very deep dark hole and stay there. I make it my mission to pull back from the edge of that hole whenever I see it looming.

But some places must be visited. I felt that despite my fears and nerves about visiting the museum, it simply had to be done, with heart and soul.

As a child, whenever I saw any documentaries or films on television about the Holocaust, I used to seethe with rage. I felt let down that the world as it was before I was even born had allowed this to happen. I was certain that if I'd been around then, I would have stopped it. I simply couldn't understand why other humans hadn't done so. The innocence and naïvety of children can be touching.

The Holocaust Museum sits in a huge memorial garden site perched near the top of the Jerusalem Forest. As it was pouring with rain, we made our way briskly from the light and airy reception building to the museum.

The architecture is modern, and the grey concrete walls on two sides of the vast museum lean together and join in a triangular structure. As my eyes were drawn to look upwards, I could see natural light flooding through the glass apex. We journeyed with hundreds of other visitors through the main thoroughfare to the chambers of despair, death and destruction. There are nine underground galleries off the main atrium which tell the story of the Holocaust. While walking through the timeline of the events leading to the 'Final Solution', it was frightening to see just how quickly Nazi Germany and Adolph Hitler occupied Europe.

There were pictures, photographs, displays, films and personal belongings, menorah, books and rescued remnants of Torah scrolls. Particularly poignant, a display of heaps of shoes, shoes of every shape and size under glass. There were stories and drawings by teenagers alongside beautiful drawings by established artists. Musical instruments, books and the clutter of creative and fulfilling lives pulled us into this harrowing experience.

By far the most compelling and moving exhibits were the personal accounts and testimony of the survivors, relayed on small television screens. One boy, who was eight, had his break for freedom bought from a guard who looked the other way in exchange for money. His mother passed the guard a large bank note and pushed her child under a fence and told him to run. At eight years old, he wouldn't have been old enough to visit this museum where visitors must be aged ten at least. How did that small boy escape the Nazis and learn to survive alone? I hoped that he was taken in by a caring family. That poor mother.

Tributes were also paid to those non-Jews who helped save lives during the process which led to the decimation of Jewish communities throughout Europe.

We read tales of families being rounded up to be transported to ghettos where they would work on starvation rations. Particularly harrowing was a tale of one young girl who had been hidden in a wardrobe with her sister when her parents were taken away. Her mother had persuaded the Germans to allow her to get her coat before leaving. She opened the wardrobe and said, 'Goodbye, children.' At that point I sobbed. The children had been given instructions in advance by their parents to go to another family, and they never saw their mother or father again.

When things must have seemed that they couldn't get any worse, they did. The ghetto communities were required to give up their children as they couldn't work. Six million Jews were killed in the Holocaust, and one and a half million were children.

Eventually all roads or tracks led to the gas chamber, the gas trucks or the pits, where the bodies dropped as they were shot. There were some terrible tales of young boys surviving under a weight of dead bodies, only to crawl out and hide under cover of darkness. The tragedy, the trauma and the tremendous loss will continue to be felt acutely for generations.

A moving tribute was paid to a young talented writer and artist who died during the Holocaust. His drawing of the moon was taken into space by Ilan Ramon, Israel's first astronaut, on the American Columbia space shuttle. Tragically that flight was a disastrous one, and the space shuttle disintegrated on re-entering the earth's atmosphere with the loss of all on board.

When we watch something scary on television, like dinosaurs or *Doctor Who*, we often say to Morgan, 'Don't worry; it's only a story.' It's impossible to reduce the horror of the Holocaust for our children, but when the time is right, it's something they must learn about so that we're all aware that atrocities can and do happen and maybe, with knowledge and an understanding, we and our children will ensure that similar ethnic cleansings are relegated to history and won't be part of our future.

We didn't see the Hall of Names, which sets out the names and personal details of victims. Nor did we visit the symbolic tombstones filled out by survivors in memory of their loved ones. We missed out on the Museum of Holocaust Art, the Children's Memorial, the Valley of the Communities and the Avenue of the Righteous Among the Nations which was planted in honour of non-Jews who risked their lives to rescue Jews during the Holocaust. Like the Eternal Flame in the Hall of Remembrance, this place will always be there, and I won't be afraid to return and reflect.

As we emerged from our drive home through the forest, I noticed that the blossom season had begun. The trees started with the palest of almond blossom, and then there was apple, pear and the deep pink of cherry. This flower and the tree it beautified would bear fruit again.

37

ISRAEL MUSEUM

As the weather stayed wet and grim, we all enjoyed a family outing to the newly refurbished Israel Museum. It was one of the few places which opened on a Saturday, so we had an excellent opportunity to enjoy it as a family.

It was Shabbat so the orthodox community didn't drive and usually just walked in their neighbourhoods, to and from synagogue. It was the time of year when black fedora hats were protected from the rain by large shower caps and natty carrier bags from my favourite book shop, cleverly rolled and moulded to fit.

The Israeli Museum was housed in a series of modern concrete and glass buildings spread out on a spacious campus-like enclosure. It had a vast collection of ancient artefacts.

What captured my interest and imagination was the Jewish Life Cycle exhibit, which took us from birth, with all its ceremonies and traditions (not to mention the surgical removal of infant male foreskin), to the marriage paraphernalia and onward to death and mourning. The precious household objects of worship, celebration and ceremony were beautifully represented with menorah candle holders and platters aplenty.

There were also four real synagogues moved from three different continents which had been dismantled and shipped from their original locations and faithfully reconstructed within the museum. The synagogues were originally from Italy, Germany, Southern India and South America. The South American synagogue was light and bright with sand on the floor, true to the original.

It was during our tour of this wonderful exhibit that I learnt of the issue of assimilation. When Jews lived in communities in which they were persecuted and had to hide their synagogues inside innocuous buildings, they tended to remain a homogeneous group. However when they were accepted by the societies in which they lived and could openly worship, building free-standing synagogues, as in the case of the sandy beach one, they assimilated so much into the wider community that they melded in, and gradually the strong ties to synagogue were lost.

We also explored the vast section on archaeology. Great swathes of Israel are given over to digs, and it's possible to join in and help for a day or more if you have the time. (Visit the tourist information office at the Jaffa Gate for information and to sign up.)

The Dead Sea Scrolls exhibit was a major one, housed in its own building on campus. We even got to see the model of Jerusalem previously displayed at the Holyland Hotel, which used to be the only way Jewish children could see the city when it was under Jordanian rule. Like many exhibits this had been acquired and brought to the museum in memory of a lost loved one.

A thoroughly enjoyable and fascinating family day out was only improved by shopping for some vintage Visit Palestine posters designed to tempt many innocents abroad. I'd seen them in a friend's home and was very happy to find copies in the museum gift shop. We had them framed, and they hung in our home throughout our time there.

Words of the day: ahlan wa sahlan — welcome (Arabic)

38

HEALTHCARE ISRAELI STYLE

Since arriving in Israel, we'd spent more time seeing doctors, or trying to see them, than we would have liked.

Israel is famous for its research and development in the fields of heart surgery and many other specialist areas. The chances are, if you've had an angioplasty, the umbrella-like device inserted to widen your clogged artery was designed and patented in Israel. The Hadassah Hospital in Ein Karem is known throughout the world for its pioneering and lifesaving surgery.

My first meeting with a GP had been to get a school medical form completed, confirming that all immunisations were up to date and in line with the recommended US immunisation schedule for children. Miraculously all were in date and all issues covered, and there I'd been, feeling guilty that Morgan would have an extra few weeks' holiday while my oversight in having him regularly jabbed with a sharp needle was remedied. The all-important school medical form was signed with the recommendation that one shot, which expired at the end of the coming year, was updated when the time came. Mumps was at epidemic proportions in Israel, so it was important to note. Measurements of our happy student were taken, weight recorded, and we left the clinic confident that we were in good hands.

A couple of weeks later, we returned to the same doctor to complete our mandatory USAID medicals. Chris had wisely had his medical exams completed while in Amman before his move to Ramallah.

We appeared at the clinic, having had a great deal of trouble with the satellite navigation system we'd stuck on the dashboard of the car; equipment which performed as it should only some of the time. When we crossed to the West Bank, it took us on the longest route to avoid travelling in the West Bank at all and told us we were in an unsafe area. Maybe it needed a 'politics-optional' button.

It isn't legal for Israelis to travel into many areas of the West Bank, and it's not unusual to see large red road signs warning of imminent and dire danger if you enter into certain areas, so this might explain the programming. I never did work out how the device dealt with the 'beware landmines' warnings along the Israeli side of the Jordan Valley. There was no beep like you would get when approaching a speed camera in another country.

The location of the clinic had been saved from the previous visit, but the satnav took us around in ever-increasing circles until I simply switched it off. After cruising around the leafy suburban avenues for a while, I spotted a landmark which enabled me to find the clinic very easily. So much for technology.

We arrived late, but the good doctor very kindly saw us and completed our USAID medical forms post haste.

He gave no indication that he'd seen Morgan recently and proceeded to ask him the same questions and take the same measurements until Morgan had a fit of the giggles and told him straight that he'd been there before. It was a busy clinic, so he'd probably seen hundreds of patients since our last visit. In addition to the requirements of the school medical, Morgan had his testicles inspected which caused a great deal of hilarity on his part. Thank goodness he's such a jolly child as one with a different temperament may have been traumatised by the experience. The USAID medical examination is designed to be thorough and to ensure that you're fit to serve in the country you're sent to, which may have limited medical facilities.

I had deep concerns about the rectal examination which was required as part of my examination. Chris, always one to look on the bright side, said, 'You ought to be happy you're getting a "free" health check courtesy of USAID.'

'I'm just grateful you've not left me a Facebook-wall post saying, "Wishing Linda good luck with her rectal examination."' This wasn't an irrational fear. Friends of ours regularly post interesting details of their marital bliss on Facebook. One of our personal favourites is: 'M is wishing R good luck with his colonoscopy.' And the previous post: 'M feels sorry for R who is only allowed to drink apple juice in preparation for his colonoscopy tomorrow' also raised a sympathetic smile.

Imagine my relief when our Israeli doctor said firmly that he wouldn't be doing the test.

After the completion of two lengthy forms, we left with a list of other tests for us to complete—blood tests, TB tests, eye tests, stool tests, urine tests, a chest X-ray, cardiogram; the list went on.

I'd been suffering severe constant headaches, and the good doc was very attentive in his examination and in considering the options for diagnosis. He referred me for a CT scan, and his receptionist kindly phoned around and made the appointment. I was told to fast for four hours before the procedure and given an appointment only a week away.

After paying 50% more than we'd been quoted for the scan (common for foreigners apparently) and waiting nearly an hour beyond our arranged slot time, I was asked for my blood test.

'I was only told to fast, not to bring a blood test,' I told them.

The hospital doctor was adamant that creatinine levels had to be established before injecting me with the contrast dye. I was to return the next day after more fasting. I also needed to pay again but was assured the first payment would be deducted from my credit card bill.

So while the top-end Israeli health care is reputed to be world class, for day-to-day treatment, the system is busy, a bit like the NHS in the UK, except in Israel you'll actually see a doctor while you're still sick.

To get over my frustration at the time wasted on the abortive CT scan, we decided to have supper out. Morgan had spotted a blue

McDonald's on the approach road to the hospital and was very keen to go as it had been months since his last fix. I was too worn out to argue, so we all trekked, in a wind which had suddenly become too icy for March, to the famous, blue-signed, super-kosher McDonald's. The fries were served in blue boxes; the drinks cups were blue, as were the trays. The food was just the same. When McFlurry time arrived, as it always did, we were required to leave the restaurant and enter through the outside door to the ice cream section. As I'd dined on a falafel wrap and not a Big Mac, I was the only member of the party who could legitimately buy and consume an ice cream under the kosher rules. No interrogations were made, and Morgan completed his feast.

As we were sitting waiting for him to have the last lick, Chris received a call. Settlers had attacked a car carrying one of his employees on Highway 60. The car had been damaged, the windscreen smashed and unfortunately the employee had been hurt but, we were relieved to hear, not seriously. The security manager at the office made a report to civil defence. It was important to ascertain whether this was a random attack or another premeditated one on the USAID contractor building a US-funded road to Ramallah. This road was of no interest to settlers who weren't permitted to enter Ramallah. It was a worrying new development at the end of a stressful day.

39

SOS CHILDREN'S VILLAGE, BETHLEHEM

Following the cycle ride from London to Paris which took place in September in memory of Amber, we'd reached our target of buying a brand-new vehicle for the SOS Village in Amman. Amber did most of her growing up in Jordan, and we'd only moved to Dubai the year before she died. She'd missed Jordan so much she said that she could even smell the sheep, so that's why we chose to support the village in Amman. We bought the small silver Toyota car to benefit the orphaned and disadvantaged children who lived there as it would ferry them to and from town for appointments and help in the running of the village for years to come.

This is the point at which I would like to pause and reflect on the bum-numbing five days of cycling, and to thank the gods we pray to for delivering our young riders safely, if a bit saddle sore, to Paris as planned. So to Callum, Dominic, Easton, Emily, Julie, Katy and Liberty (in alphabetical order), a huge thank you. You were all focused, fit, determined and an inspiration to me. I found the journey exhausting, and I was just driving the backup vehicle. I should also thank Easton for packing 'an insane' amount of luggage. The quote courtesy of Julie, one of Amber's best friends, who picked up his bag by mistake. My upper arms had never been more Madonna-like. I mean the singer, of course, and not the serene one with the enigmatic smile.

We owe thanks to all our friends and family the world over who supported us and donated generously to this truly worthwhile cause, and to my lovely mum who was a happy passenger in the backup vehicle and supported us all and the cause very generously.

The scenery of Northern France was haunting and beautiful, the villages a florist's dream, bedecked with flower beds and baskets spilling cascades of blooms over their edges. The vistas were panoramic as the countryside there is so flat. It was excellent cycling country with bike-friendly tracks, unlike our first leg of the race in the South of England when I feared for the lives of our cyclists as the route was so busy with commercial vehicles all trundling at speed to the port of Dover. One day I hope to return and to cycle the route at my own pace, a gentler one more suited to my level of fitness.

It's impossible not to feel the pang of the great loss of youth and opportunity for the generations which sacrificed so many young lives during both World Wars. Cemetery upon cemetery containing a staggering number of simple graves, all immaculately kept, one the same as the next, lined our route out of Normandy and towards Paris.

It was also personally poignant that on day two of this amazing endeavour, the funeral of my lovely friend Elaine took place. She'd lost her battle against the cancer which struck so suddenly and took her so quickly from her husband, sons, young grandchildren and all the friends she'd gathered during her travels around the world. I promised myself a glass of wine and some quiet time in the evening, after the driving, as I was unable to attend the champagne lunch planned for Elaine's friends and family to gather and remember a great lady. I will always treasure her friendship.

Having accomplished our first fundraising mission of buying the car, we decided that we might be able to help SOS Villages in the Palestinian Occupied Territory and set out to find the village in Bethlehem. There were two villages, one in Bethlehem and one in Gaza, but the Foreign and Commonwealth Office (FCO) of the British government advised against travel to Gaza. The ceasefires announced by Hamas and Israel following conflicts in 2010 were fragile, and tensions remained high. The FCO also advised that there was a possible risk to Westerners of kidnap by terrorist splinter groups opposed to Hamas.

This made me think of a T-shirt I spotted in the German Colony in Jerusalem on a sunny weekday morning, after a coffee with my favourite almond croissant. It was stretched across the chest of a burly young gent and sported the slogan 'Fat people are harder to kidnap'. Gallows humour is popular in this town, as are pastries.

So we gave the Gaza SOS Children's Village a miss, which was a great pity as they probably needed help and support the most.

We arrived at the SOS Children's Village in Bethlehem with no appointment, but as with our experience in Jordan, we were welcomed and given a tour. It's a bright, warm and happy place and was established over 40 years ago. The mission statement of the village is to provide a loving home for every child. This particular village had twelve houses, all named by the children after Disney characters. An SOS mother lived in each house with between eight and ten children, aged between one and fourteen. Her calling was to care for and nurture each child. Siblings were kept together, and we were told of the arrival of three siblings at once, including a very young baby, which touched everybody's hearts in the village.

We visited on a Saturday afternoon after the village children had attended school. Delicious cooking smells came from the house, and our mouths watered. The children proudly showed off their bedrooms and character cushions (a different one on each bed). The boys had Ben 10 and Spiderman, the girls Hannah Montana and Bratz. There were three siblings in this particular house, and the youngest resident was tiny, although four years old. Our translator was ten, the same age as Morgan, and he practised his English by translating for his housemates. We then showed our talent in Arabic by counting to ten, twice, and the children laughed loudly and joined in the chant. Our Arabic was never great, being limited to basic greetings and pleasantries, the odd useful word and the ability to sing word perfect 'Happy birthday to you'. It's odd what you remember. There are days I find it hard to remember my Apple password, but I can sing 'Happy Birthday' in Arabic. We left knowing we had well and truly made some new, very happy friends and that we would be back again.

In Jordan one of the houses in the SOS Village was funded by Angelina Jolie and Brad Pitt who visited with their children from time to time. I smiled when I heard that they'd taken their tribe of Jolie-Pitts to the Lickilicious ice cream shop in Rainbow Street, Amman, for a cooling treat. When they walked in, the shop assistant promptly fainted on the floor.

When we'd visited the village in Amman the year before, around the time when Liberty was planning the cycle ride, we were given a tour of a house and met a wonderful house mother and her charges. As we talked there was a knock at the door. Two teenaged girls who had moved out of the house and were now in further education had come back to see their house mother on the weekend. What a lovely bond that one seemed to be, and hugs and news were exchanged with excitement and a great display of affection.

After the age of fourteen, as the children reach puberty, they're moved to a Youth House, where they learn about life and gain independence. The boys and girls are separated at this stage of life, the girls having a house mother and the boys a house father. It must be hard to be an orphan in any circumstances, but to be an orphan in the Occupied Palestinian Territories has additional challenges, emotionally and physically.

One of the many wonderful achievements of the SOS Villages worldwide is that they work at integrating the children in the local community. So it wasn't unusual for an SOS child to marry locally, work locally and to have children of their own. There was a real sense of belonging.

In Bethlehem there was an SOS school which the village children attended, but it was also open to local children, so the village children and local children learnt and socialised together from a very young age. It was a recipe for creating long-term security within the wider community and forming lifelong friendships.

The following weekend we returned to Bethlehem for a tour of the school and to meet some of the people who made the village and the school the successes they clearly were.

We wanted to understand better how we could help and what they needed. Chris's employing company, hearing of our visit the previous weekend, had pledged $1,000 to help in an appropriate way, so we were keen to find out just how the money could be best spent, along with money we would raise personally as before.

At this meeting we learnt that although the children live a 30-minute drive from the Mediterranean and the beautiful beaches, they'd never been given permission to cross the border to Israel and visit the beach. Their only knowledge of the sea was from what they read in books. Applications had been made to take the children on a school trip to Jerusalem, another 30-minute bus ride away. The applications had also been refused. I could respect the need Israel felt it had to protect its citizens, especially in the wake of the horrendous suicide bombings on buses, in cafés and in markets in Jerusalem which were regular occurrences at the time of the last Palestinian uprising. However, it saddened me that the SOS children, together with many other children in the West Bank, had no prospect of walking around this beautiful old city and of gazing at the golden Dome of the Rock and Jerusalem skyline. It's a tough world.

It was possible to sponsor a child locally. One of my friends, who was married to a Palestinian gentleman, sponsored three girls for a time. The girls were brought from the village to visit in their family home and given birthday presents and an extra dollop of care by this thoughtful family, who also treated the other children in the same house as the girls. Inevitably bonds formed but were sadly to be severed. The father of the girls was serving a 25-year prison sentence. He was a freedom fighter (Arab version) or terrorist (Israeli version). After many years he was released under an Israeli/Palestinian prisoner exchange. His wife had remarried and given up the girls as her new husband hadn't wanted them. Upon his release the father remarried and brought his daughters to live in the new family home. Sadly the sponsors were advised to step away from the children. Years on, my friend still worried about what became of the girls and whether they were ever accepted by their stepmother and treated well.

As we left the village, we learnt from our security advisers that five members of one family of settlers had been murdered in their home in the settlement of Itamar, near the Palestinian town of Nablus. The Fogel family had lost a mother, a father and three of their five children. The youngest victim was three months old, and we learnt later that they were all stabbed to death—an indescribable loss.

Shortly after that, we heard that colleagues had their car attacked by angry, stone-throwing settlers, but while the passengers were shaken, this time they weren't injured. We headed for home in despair that there could ever be an end to this cycle of occupation and bloody violence. We were warned to keep a low profile, so we headed back on the main road instead of winding our way back to Jerusalem through West Bank villages filled with smiling, waving children who shouted out their welcomes and hellos. I probably should have been more nervous than I felt at the time. I wondered when we would get back to see the village. The last blanket ban on travel in the West Bank, imposed for safety reasons by Chris's employing company, had only recently been lifted.

Word of the day: afwan—you're welcome (Arabic)

40

SETTLERS AND PRICE TAGS

Unlike the forested hills of Jerusalem and the leafy, tree-lined streets of its attractive suburbs, much of the West Bank landscape is characterised by a huge backdrop of rolling hills. Hills which are pale, rocky and appear to be barren, but it's astounding how many sheep and goats are fed on the meagre, dusty, dry pickings of the landscape.

From a hilltop vantage point, the views are usually spectacular and vast, stretching as far as the eye can see. In the more cultivat*f*ed areas and in the West Bank villages, olive trees have been planted, and you're treated to magnificent scenes which must look much the same as when Jesus was a boy, walking deep in thought and dusty leather sandals.

We could drive along, enjoying the wide-open spaces and the dramatic desert scenery, when suddenly, totally out of place, we would see a town or village of Mediterranean-style houses. They were usually quite large (by British standards), European in style with red-tiled sloping roofs and verdant gardens. The towns were well kept and often displayed a bouquet of bougainvillea in every colour imaginable, together with a bouquet of barbed wire.

The red-tiled roofs were an immediate giveaway from a distance, indicating we were approaching a West Bank settlement, populated by Jewish settlers. Most roofs of Arab dwellings were flat and the buildings constructed from pale golden stone or painted concrete. As we got closer, there was another clue as to what this strangely out of place development of dwellings actually was.

In Israel most water tanks are placed on the roofs of houses and apartment blocks. Israelis buy white water tanks, and from a distance, you can see hundreds of them in the built-up areas of Jerusalem. Palestinians or Israeli Arabs buy black tanks. So we could see at a glance the ethnicity of the neighbourhood we were passing through. It was interesting when we were in a 'mixed' neighbourhood. In Abu Tor, Jerusalem, we could see black water tanks down one side of the road and white ones down the other.

As we reached the apparently idyllic-looking town of red roofs, we faced the grim reality that it was surrounded by barbed wire fences and security gates, had armed guards and was often given IDF protection.

The focus of the Fourth Geneva Convention is the protection of human rights of civilians who live under occupation. Article 49 (6) of the Fourth Geneva Convention states 'The Occupying Power shall not deport or transfer parts of its own civilian population into the territory it occupies.' Israel is a signatory to this convention.

The United Nations is of the view that the construction of settlements violates the Fourth Geneva Convention. The continued expansion of settlements is seen as a major stumbling block to achieving peace, or even talks on peace. It's estimated that during nine months of peace talks brokered by former Secretary of State John Kerry, an unprecedented number of new settler houses (13,851) were built.

The Israelis also believe that the settlements form a first line of defence against any incursion into the more populated areas of Israel. There have been two intifadas by the Palestinians. The first was in December 1987 and lasted until the early 1990s. Some commentators believe that it came to an end with the signing of the Oslo Accords in 1993, while others are of the view that the popular uprising came to an end in 1991.

The Second Intifada in 2001 was characterised by suicide bombers in the markets and cafés, bus bombers and lethal bulldozer drivers who drove into crowded places with devastating effect. This led to the security barrier, separation barrier or apartheid wall, depending on your point of view, built by Israel, purportedly to protect the lives of its citizens. While hugely unpopular with the Palestinians and most of the rest of the world, it seems to have reduced the number of terrorist acts in Israel substantially. Most now come from within Israel.

The settlers are a tough bunch. It's not unusual to see a young settler dad pushing a cute baby in a buggy through the streets of Jerusalem, with a serious automatic weapon slung nonchalantly across his chest. Nor is it unusual to see a similar sight in the Jerusalem Mall at Malha. I found this a little odd as the Jerusalem Mall has airport-style security, and my handbag was searched every time I visited. I was also required to walk through an X-ray machine as if I were off to board a happy flight somewhere. So how do these young parents get in while flaunting such heavy-duty weaponry? And what was the security guard searching for in my handbag if not firearms?

There's friction among settlers and West Bank villagers. For years there have been complaints about the settlers cutting down ancient olive trees. The settlers argue that olive trees provide great camouflage for snipers or potential attackers. On the other hand, the Palestinian olive grower relies on the crop for his livelihood and personal needs, and his family have farmed olives on the land for generations.

I've known many Palestinians over the years, and there are constants in this society—a love of God, a love of family and a love and connection with the land. So this divorce from the land is not only a disaster economically for farmers, but often a heartbreaking emotional wrench from land on which families have been rooted for generations.

Children have been shot dead playing in olive groves because the soldiers say they have no way of knowing if the person behind the tree is planning to shoot them. A shepherd or local farmer, or a ten-year-old boy collecting stones for a primitive game in the dust can be mistaken for a threat.

Settlements are undoubtedly a barrier to the negotiation of a two-state solution, and the policy of the government is that they will continue to build.

Word of the day: nakba—a disaster (Arabic)

41

PURIM

Purim is the happiest of the Jewish holidays, and that year it just happened to fall on my birthday. Double celebrations!

This is the time of year when adults and children alike dress up in Halloween-style costumes and multi-coloured wigs (bright pink, purple, yellow and rainbow effect rather than just the usual bad hair-dye jobs).

The festival is even celebrated in the ultra-orthodox area of Mea She'arim, the area which is populated by the modesty enforcement brigade, and where some very unlikely, normally sober, Jewish males get more than a little tipsy.

It was with some excitement that the annual Purim Carnival to be hosted by the PTA at JAIS was prepared for. The school issued the usual edict—'No scary costumes and no weapons, even pretend ones.'

The first dilemma was this. Morgan had taken an enormous growth spurt and was almost being cut in two when wearing his all-in-one, not-so-scary skeleton costume. It was permitted for the Halloween costume parade, but he wasn't allowed to wear the mask in case he scared other children. So we had to find a suitable replacement costume.

Now here was the problem—where to find a non-scary, dress-up costume which was cool enough for a ten-year-old boy to wear. We trawled the arcades of shops in the Jerusalem Mall where there were more costumes than you could poke a stick at. The choice was either Walt Disney satin and sparkle at one extreme, or Dracula, a vampire or a nail ball-wielding costume at the other. The tackiest, most basic costumes were ridiculously expensive even for a very average, stretchy polyester number. I've never lived in a country where so little costs so much.

We couldn't reach agreement. Everything my World Wrestling Entertainment fan would even consider wearing would be banned from school. Anything remotely within the school guidelines was uninteresting to Morgan and dismissed as geeky.

We did the only thing we could agree on after trailing for at least five kilometres around the mall and looking at the same cheap (in the quality rather than expense meaning of the word) shops we'd looked at before. We went to our favourite café for pizza, cake and drinks. Yes, that was another 100 or so shekels. At least our landlord wouldn't be going bankrupt any time soon.

Eventually we found a wonderful Mariachi hat which Morgan LOVED. We cleverly added a pair of black plastic slit-lensed glasses, and we had the basis of an outfit. Hallelujah. All we needed was a red waistcoat, sash, wide-sleeved white shirt and some black bell-bottom trousers. Sewing the rest of the ensemble was a morning well spent. Morgan looked fandabidozi, as UK TV personality wee Jimmy Krankie from my home country would have said.

On the big day, we turned up for the costume parade and festivities. We watched and photographed lots of the little darlings and their teachers and generally entered into the spirit of this new-found Jewish-Israeli jollity.

We were then treated to what was described as a Purim skit, performed with great enthusiasm by the teachers. The skit was a minor pantomime and, from what we could gather, the story went a bit like this:

An evil king rolled metaphorical dice hundreds of years ago and decided that he would kill (they may have used the word murder) all the Jews. What the flip! The kids at Morgan's school weren't allowed to scare each other with masks, but it was perfectly okay to tell the whole school about a planned mass murder, decided on a whim. Was it just me, or was that slightly strange given the background to this school party?

Another parent shared with us the insight that all Jewish holidays run to the same plot: They tried to kill us. They didn't succeed. We will stuff our faces with food in celebration.

On this day of celebration, it was exactly a week to the day since I'd been reduced to tears watching on live television the Japanese tsunami wipe out thousands of people. Our school had told the students not to talk about it because some of the Japanese students didn't know about it and would be upset. Reality check. It was hugely upsetting, but surely it would be more so if picked up on CNN at a friend's house on a play date, while an unsuspecting parent was catching up with the Dow Jones. Surely it was better to tell the children in an age-appropriate way and allow them to raise the worries or questions they may have had at home, or at school with friends and a trusted teacher. Yet again we faced cultural differences. Tragedy and disaster don't go away. They need to be dealt with. As for the scary mask concerns of the school, we were living in one of the most volatile areas in the Middle East, and the children participated in emergency lockdown drills and bomb-scare drills on a regular basis. Enough said.

Thankfully Morgan dealt with such events very well. On one occasion, which wasn't a drill, he and his classmates made their way to the bomb shelter. The siren had sounded. I'd been in the shower at home at the time. I spent the next twenty minutes or so in our safe space, wrapped in a towel feeling damp, chilly and a tad lonely until the all-clear was sounded.

On collecting Morgan from school, I asked, 'Are you okay? Were you frightened?'

'It was awful, Mum.' He offered up. 'Zaid,' (one of his classmates) 'was crying his eyes out. My legs wouldn't fit inside the door, and just when I thought it couldn't get worse, our music teacher started singing "If You're Happy and You Know it, Clap your Hands".'

Lemon Drizzle Cake

Penny baked a lemon drizzle cake for my birthday, and as it's a delicious cake on any day of the year and a great way to savour some zingy Beit Zayit lemons, I'll share a favourite recipe.

Ingredients
Cake
225 g unsalted butter, at room temperature
225 g caster sugar
4 eggs
Finely grated zest of one lemon (avoid the white pith as it's bitter)
225g self-raising flour

Drizzle
Juice of 2 lemons
90 g caster sugar

Method
Heat oven to 180°C/fan 160°C/gas mark 4.
Beat together softened butter and caster sugar until pale and creamy.
Add the eggs one at a time, slowly mixing through.
Sift in the flour then add the finely grated zest and mix until combined.
Line a loaf tin (23 cm by 13 cm approximately) with greaseproof paper and spoon the mixture into the tin and level with a spoon.
Bake for 45-50 mins until a thin skewer inserted into the centre comes out clean. (I use wooden kebab skewers for this job.)
While the cake is cooling in the tin, mix the lemon juice and caster sugar to make the drizzle.
Prick the warm cake all over with a skewer or fork, then pour the drizzle over it. The juice will sink in, and the sugar will form a crispy topping. Leave the cake in the tin until it has completely cooled. Remove and slice.
The cake can be kept in an airtight container for 3-4 days or frozen for up to a month. Our preference is to scoff it immediately.

42

SHATTERED PEACE

We woke up to grey skies and dripping trees in our moshav. It was quite mild and reminiscent of a Scottish summer day from my childhood. After school we were invited to Penny's house for her daughter Mae's third birthday party. It was such a shame it was raining, especially when all weather forecasters had already told us categorically that we'd seen the last of the rain until the autumn. I was glad I still hadn't got around to cleaning the windows.

Dominic, Mae's daddy, was back from the Libyan uprising where he was reporting on it for *Sky News*, covering the regime change in Egypt, not participating. He would be able to celebrate her third birthday at home. So never mind the rain; it never hurt anybody.

I got organised for a busy day, prepared to be out until early evening, and wrapped the birthday girl's present. Just before leaving the house, I switched on the news. Nas's husband, Kevin, who was bureau chief of CNN in Jerusalem, was telling the world that there had been an explosion in central Jerusalem. There were scores of emergency vehicles at the scene. Someone had attached a suitcase containing an explosive device next to a busy bus stop near the central bus station. We'd driven past the exact spot 24 hours earlier when I was doing the lunchtime school run back to our moshav and had taken a change of route to collect a visitor from the city.

It was an odd feeling to be watching what would normally be fascinating news but had become so immediate, personal and horrific. Instead of having a fifteen-minute tea break before going to school to collect Morgan, I left straight away, knowing that the roads would be chaotic.

I chose to avoid the main Tel Aviv Highway, my normal route, to bypass the congestion and to save clogging up roads which may be needed by emergency vehicles. But the journey was still slow. People were disregarding traffic lights, and the pushiest got through the junctions. You have to be really pushy to push a pushy Israeli out of the way. I reached school more or less on time and lent my mobile phone to a friend who had visitors from the United States scheduled to be returning to Jerusalem via the main Tel Aviv Highway from a trip to Galilee. She was anxious to re-route them before they became hopelessly lost in detours.

Morgan's photography teacher, a capable and game girl, emerged from school looking ashen.

'Have you heard the news?' she stammered.

'Yes, we have,' I murmured. 'I'll get you home,' I reassured her.

I normally gave this teacher a lift home after photography club but this meant risking heavy traffic on the usual route. She looked shocked and very upset. There were no buses on the roads, and lots of people were walking along the pavements and hitching lifts, presumably to escape the city to the safety of home. There were also rumours that another device had been planted.

When we got in the car, she turned to me and explained, 'My family made Aliyah from the United States just months before the Second Palestinian Intifada in 2000. I lived through the violence of bus bombings, mall bombings and café bombings, so reports of the explosion today have brought back traumatic memories of that time.'

'I'm so sorry,' I said.

'I'm scared that, with the build-up of events over the last weeks, this is just the beginning of the third uprising.'

'I so hope not.' I sighed. It was a frightening thought.

The roads were chock-full, but at least the traffic was moving slowly. I was extremely anxious when we entered a long underground tunnel on Begin Boulevard as we approached her home near Ramot, as the traffic came to a complete standstill. Loudspeaker announcements were broadcast in Hebrew, but neither of us could hear them properly as the sound system was badly distorted. I regretted not sticking to my planned safer route through the Jerusalem Forest. We were trapped, and if another device had gone off at that point, there would have been carnage on a truly massive scale.

When we emerged from the tunnel, we saw flashing lights up ahead and wondered if there had been an accident. There were several vehicles with blue flashing lights parked at an angle across the central reservation of the three-lane highway leading to route 1 towards Tel Aviv. There was no accident, just security and lots of it. At bus stops, at junctions, even at our moshav slip road from the highway, rigorous checks of vehicles were being made in both directions. As we sat in another tunnel, four armed soldiers walked past the stationary traffic. Clearly Israel was preparing to defend itself. I had goosebumps and couldn't remember feeling so unsure of the future since we'd witnessed jubilation on the streets of Jordan post the 9/11 attacks. Then the advice was to go home, close our shutters and sit tight. The mood on the streets had changed to one of shock the next day in Jordan when the enormity of what had happened at the World Trade Centre had truly sunk in. Who knew what tomorrow would bring in Jerusalem?

I did get to the birthday party, much later than planned, but sadly Mae's daddy Dominic didn't. He was just behind a bus near the bus stop when the explosion took place, and as a foreign correspondent on the spot, he spent the rest of the day reporting the dramatic events. So he wasn't in Libya or Egypt or Bahrain but at home base and still missed this special gathering. To think that our only concern that morning was about the rain dampening the party.

The children played and had fun, blissfully unaware of what had happened earlier.

If you visit the Old City on a Friday, you see Arab children running, playing and kicking footballs without a care in the world. If you then wander into the Jewish Quarter, you'll see a similar sight, children skipping along, playing, laughing and sometimes bravely saying a shy, smiley *shalom* to a stranger. Like our children, they don't deserve this legacy of conflict and tit-for-tat attacks and retribution. The never-ending cycle of violence on both sides was letting all our children down, letting the world down. The grown-ups needed to take their position in the cockpit of peace missions and work towards sorting this out once and for all. Not only for themselves, for the next generation. How could people live like this?

One woman was killed in the attack, a British national. She was a mature student engaged in Bible study. Many were injured, three critically. The security and routine of life for Jerusalemites was shattered in a moment. It was hoped that this was a one-off attack and not a strategy, or God help us all.

43

PASSOVER

I didn't know whether it was because the sun was shining and the cherry blossom was out in obscene abundance, or if it was because it was nearly Passover, but there was a distinctly cheery mood on the streets of Jerusalem, and I made two new friends out of strangers. On both occasions the conversation was initiated by the normally taciturn locals.

Cillit Bang cleaning spray was on special offer in the supermarket —two bottles for the price of one—and I always say there's no bang like a Cillit Bang!

The Jewish holiday of Passover requires deep cleaning throughout the whole house. All crumbs and any traces of yeast must be totally removed. I read somewhere that every book in an orthodox home has to be taken out and given a good old shake through, lest there be a crumb lurking between the leaves of the pages. It sounds like quite a job, but it's akin to a general spring clean elsewhere in the world.

So cleaning products were on offer and sold in abundance. I was told that some wily Jewish householders would find a non-believer to hold onto the yeasty items until Passover is over. The items are then reclaimed and returned to base. This strategy carried an element of risk. If one of my neighbours were to ask me to take care of a delicious baked yeast, cinnamon and nut loaf until after Passover, I couldn't guarantee that it would be returned if left in my store cupboard temporarily. It really was scrumptious.

The other marker for motorists was that on Passover, we were permitted to switch off our headlights when driving on the highway in daylight hours. Until Passover, even if the sun was splitting the trees and you were on the way for a day at the beach, you had to switch on your headlights at all times. Failure to comply with this rule of the road could give rise to a hefty fine.

One of the joys for Jews who have returned to Jerusalem is the ease of shopping for Passover food which must be kosher and without leavening agent. One of my new Passover friends confided in me that before she made Aliyah from the USA years earlier, unless she got out and shopped at the crack of sparrows, the only food available to her and left on the shop shelves was coconut macaroons. Oh, the joys of Jerusalem at Passover time, more matzo bread than you could stack, and festive food stalls set out in the malls with delicacies to satisfy the most cosmopolitan tastes.

Despite this temptation, we were off to the USA for Passover. The Jewish holiday coincided with Easter, and we took full advantage of the school break to visit Grandpa Fred and Granny Barbs in Dahlonega, USA. That, coupled with my natural tendency to avoid excessive house cleaning, sealed the deal. I usually only engage in a frantic deep clean of our nest on a voluntary basis if I'm in the early stages of labour.

At Passover, kosher cows must eat corncobs and not their normal feed, or the milk produced will be unsaleable. Corn feed is more expensive. My natural yogurt purchase for breakfast in the USA was certified as kosher for Passover. A bit of a surprise and no more or less delicious than usual.

However, when we popped into the Back Porch Oyster Bar for lunch, I was surprised to see on the menu a beef burger with cheese and bacon and a kosher pickle. Kosher pickle? Was someone having a laugh?

There's a special meal called the Passover Seder which is an important part of Jewish family life. When our landlord asked us for family reasons to leave the home we'd rented on the moshav, well before the expiry of our lease, his rather glamorous mother shared with me her ambition to be sitting in my dining room by the Passover Seder in several months' time. Bloody cheek.

For Passover Seders held outside Jerusalem, the words 'next year in Jerusalem' are often said at the end of the meal.

Who knew where we would be the following year and whether we would be homeless.

44

INDEPENDENCE AND REMEMBRANCE

In May three important dates of remembrance and celebration fell and were marked in very different ways.

The Holocaust Remembrance Day fell on the first of the month. On this day the sirens were sounded at ten in the morning for two minutes, and Israeli Jews stopped what they were doing and stood in remembrance of the Jews who died in the Holocaust. It was almost impossible to believe that this was the entire population of Israel when we first moved there. Motorists pulled their cars to the side of the road and got out, standing still as a mark of respect to the victims. Chris was in a meeting in Tel Aviv and reported that the meeting stopped as everyone was silent and still for the wail of the sirens which are sounded across the country. From sunset the night before until sunset on the next day, normal broadcasts are replaced by documentaries on the Holocaust and interviews with survivors. Almost all satellite channels are off air, except for one or two news channels.

There are still a number of Holocaust survivors, although as time passes the number gets fewer. They receive visits from the prime minister or other senior government officials at this time. Ceremonies of remembrance are held at the Holocaust Museum, including a wreath-laying ceremony. Survivors, often very well decorated with military medals, take part. Other survivors and second- and third-generation descendants of survivors gather to watch, remember and lay individual tributes to their relatives who were lost. It's a sombre time for reflection.

Memorial Day fell on the 8th May in our first year in Jerusalem. Again, the siren was sounded for two minutes, but this time at eleven o'clock in the morning, and again everything came to a complete standstill as the country stopped to pay tribute to the fallen. The day was officially known as Israeli Fallen Soldiers and Victims of Terrorism Remembrance Day. Cars stopped, and the bustling Jerusalem Market was frozen for two minutes. It was as if someone had pressed the pause button on life itself, and then, as soon as the siren fell silent, people carried on shopping, driving and working as normal. This was the mindset of a tough nation: we defend ourselves; we suffer tremendous losses and hardship to live our lives in relative normality; we are thankful to our army and mourn our losses, but life has to go on. Again, the TV channels went off air, except for news and the odd documentary channels.

After sunset, Memorial Day morphed into Independence Day. It's now more than 70 years since Israel gained independence, and the day is celebrated officially at Mount Herzl, where the founding fathers and past presidents of Israel are buried.

There was a ceremony at which the prime minister addressed the nation, and an amazing fireworks display which we enjoyed from our house as Mount Herzl is one of the highest spots in Jerusalem. The fireworks were fabulous and worthy of a grand metropolitan celebration anywhere in the world. Then the loud music and partying started. The party on our moshav continued into the wee small hours of the morning, as did spectacular firework displays in surrounding areas and at private parties. It was hard to get any shut-eye at all on this special night.

As the new day dawned, there was yet more celebrating to be done. Families set off to picnic in Jerusalem's parks and the forest, while others headed on Highway 1 for a day on the beaches of Tel Aviv.

Friends had invited us to join them at the Independence Day celebration of the Israel Newsmakers Forum (INFO). Although we weren't journalists (I completed a Diploma in Journalism and had a press pass before we left Jerusalem), television news presenters or politicians, we were warmly welcomed by the association as newbies who wanted to meet people in Israel and settle well.

The event was hosted in Ein Yael, an old Roman villa and terraced gardens which have been converted into a 'living museum' and are available for private hire. Morgan's teacher invited us to her wedding there which we were sad to miss as we were travelling.

The association laid on a tour of the Roman villa (which has its own spring), and bow and arrow games for the kids. I was reminded of my archery lessons with Mr Juba who represented the UK at Olympic level and put me through my paces in my early 20s at the Allander Centre in Milngavie, Scotland. I must have been a disappointment to him, as despite constant haranguing and pushing on his part for my entire six-week beginners' course, I never made it to the Olympics, or even his intermediate class.

There was also a drumming circle, set up out of doors under the shade of some ancient-looking trees where 25 junior guests and some keen parents were taught how to tap out a beat following the ringleader. Morgan and his friend Taymor ended up leading the circle in a non-traditional but hugely enjoyable round of that great Queen classic 'We Will Rock You'. The workshops (pitta breadmaking, ceramics and basket making) together with the petting zoo meant that we ran out of time to do everything which had been organised for us.

This was mainly because we were treated to a delicious barbecue lunch in the gardens of the villa. There were white tablecloths and newly cut flowers with the fabulous array of fresh Israeli salads, breads, dips, desserts and fruit and all sorts of kosher barbeque meat and sausages, lamb burgers and hot dogs. In short there was something for everyone.

As the wine and beer were topped up throughout the afternoon, we met lots of people, and conversation flowed easily. I was thrilled to talk to a *Sky News* cameraman who had just returned from an assignment in London covering the royal wedding of Prince William to Catherine Middleton. I cross-examined him mercilessly on every insider detail. The wedding must have made an interesting change for many of the

cameramen as this entire Arab Spring they'd been returning from
Tunisia, Egypt, Libya and other places of revolution, change and
danger. Places where lives were at risk daily to get the news out of the
war zone and into our comfortable living rooms.

I knew first hand just how good these families were at putting a
brave face on to the outside world when the father is in Libya and the
mother is trying to carry on as normal in Jerusalem with young
children and school runs to manage. I remember casually calling
Penny one morning to offer to do the morning school run as I was
going into town on an errand anyway. Our arrangement was that she
did the morning run, and I collected the children from school in the
afternoon. There was no reply on her mobile phone, so I called the
landline. She was shaken and scared to have received my early
morning call, fearing the worst news as very few calls were received
on landlines, on our street anyway.

But on this sunny day, the mums, dads, children and friends all
enjoyed good food and great company. Dominic even encouraged
Morgan to repeat his repertoire of slightly rude jokes to our entire table
of newly formed acquaintances.

There was only one blight on this enjoyable day. As we travelled
into town later that evening, we drove past Sacher Park, a beautiful
huge green open space just at the bottom of the hill on which the
Knesset stands. The crowds were thronging the pavements which were
double parked with cars, transit vans, taxis and buses. Exhausted
parents ferried home coolboxes, buggies and hordes of tired and
grubby children. The amount of litter and picnic junk left behind all
over this beautiful spot was a disgrace. I couldn't imagine how long it
would take the municipality to clear up the forest if this was the state
the park was left in.

Not long after the partying, fireworks and general fiestas of Israel's
Independence Day, the Palestinians mark Nakba Day, or disaster day.
It's a day which is marked on my emotional calendar as it's my late
and dearly loved dad's birthday.

Independence Day is celebrated in Israel with reference to the Hebrew calendar, and so there's a gap between both sides of the wall, not only on their perspective on Israeli independence but on the day it should be marked or mourned.

Palestinians inside and outside Israel and the Occupied Territories mourn the loss of their land from which they were removed and the villages which were razed or lost when the State of Israel was formed in 1948. At that time many Palestinians were displaced and fled to the West Bank, Gaza, Jordan, Syria and Lebanon. Over 70 years and generations later, many of the refugees still live in camps with no hope of jobs, travel or prospects of any kind. Many refugees are born, live and die in the camps. They have no right to travel into Israel and to see the homeland or village in which their families tended olive groves, herded sheep and goats and worked the land. Or their family villas, which are often repurposed, the Museum on the Seam being a good example of how a family home can be taken over. The previous Arab owner of this beautiful building baulked at having to pay an admission charge to what had been his former family home.

Their prospects and the prospects for the next generation of refugees will depend on the will of the world to push for a lasting peace and a workable agreement between both sides, and the will on both sides to make and keep the peace. The parties couldn't talk about peace as the Palestinians couldn't accept the precondition that Israel should be recognised as a Jewish State (Arabs and Christians and others also live in Israel). It seemed unlikely that peace talks would be held, never mind get anywhere during our time there.

On our first Nakba Day in 2011, thousands of Palestinians and other supporters from the West Bank, Lebanon and Syria were reported to have marched on the northern militarised Israeli border, towards the fence. It was believed that the fuel of this unprecedented confrontation with the army was fanned by the uprisings of the Arab Spring in neighbouring countries. The inevitable clashes between the IDF and the protesters resulted in many deaths and injuries, mainly from live ammunition used by the IDF in an effort to hold back the protesters from the border.

After Nakba Day was what we think of as Israeli bonfire night. Its official name is Lag B'Omer, and bonfires are lit all over the city. We worried as we watched the flames lick the ridge of the hill above the Jerusalem Forest. It was easy to imagine how this night of celebration could end in tragedy and another forest fire, but thankfully the fires were contained on this occasion. Like bonfire nights in the UK, there were always injuries and visits to accident and emergency on this night of outdoor fires, singing and dancing. It was a time when families gathered and barbequed food. It was also a time when the air quality was so poor that it was best to close all windows in advance and stay in the house if you were asthmatic. The school warned us that if by the next day the air quality wasn't good enough, children would be kept indoors at playtime.

Two weeks after Nakba Day, Jerusalem Day is celebrated big time in Israel. This marks the liberation of Jerusalem from Jordanian control after the Six-Day War in 1967 and the reunification of the city.

Shortly after Israel declared independence in 1948, its Arab neighbour launched an offensive, and East Jerusalem and the Old City fell under Jordanian control. An Israeli taxi driver who drove us between real estate viewings in our early days there reminisced with us about the time, before 1967, when he and his friends would kick their football into the Arab-controlled Old City, from an area close to where the new Mamilla Shopping Mall now stands, near the Jaffa Gate. It was surprising to hear that more often than not the football was kicked back again.

After day one of the Six-Day War, Israel gained control of the Old City once more. It was a war Israel started in response to the building up of troops along its borders with its Arab neighbours Egypt, Syria and Jordan. After the conflict, Israel had taken and occupied the West Bank, Gaza, the Golan Heights and the Sinai Peninsula. Israel also took East Jerusalem, including the Old City of Jerusalem. For the first time in many years, Jews were able to enter the Old City and pray at the Western Wall of the Second Temple, the holiest site in Judaism.

Jerusalem Day was an Israeli holiday and an early release day for our school. Due to gatherings and marches during which the Jewish population celebrated the reunification, there were road closures and moving around some parts of the city proved difficult. Thousands of settlers were also expected to come into town and march through the city. Clashes and violence were always a possibility, and we were told to steer clear of potential trouble spots. So we made our way home, through much lighter traffic than normal, and enjoyed a sunny afternoon in the peace and tranquillity of our garden.

Just as there was a risk that our children would be in school for a whole week without a holiday or an early release day (I've never been part of a school community which enjoys so many holidays), the Jewish holiday of Shavuot was celebrated.

The religious significance was that it marked the giving of the Torah on Mount Sinai, so the Ten Commandments were read in synagogues, just as they were read in the desert thousands of years ago. The Book of Ruth was read too as she was a true convert to the Jewish faith. Shavuot is also the date of death of King Noah who was directly descended from Ruth. The celebration takes place seven weeks after the Passover Seder.

It was a happy harvest festival time, and flower stalls sprung up on the pavements throughout the city, much as they did on the Sabbath. It was said that although Sinai is situated in the desert, when the Torah was given, the mountain bloomed and sprouted flowers. For Shavuot, people decorated their houses and synagogues with flowers, fruit and greenery. Young children wore lovely garlands of fresh flowers in their hair like little bridesmaids, and there were gatherings and parties outside. We had a party on our village green. We seemed to have one every holiday.

It's also traditionally a time when dairy produce is eaten. I found a recipe for 'The Perfect Shavuot Cheesecake' which I was reliably informed stars at the end of every Shavuot meal. Who knew that this delicious baked dessert dates back to Roman times? I thought New York was the birthplace of the baked cheesecake. Clearly I'm no food historian. So we celebrated desert and desserts at this special time of the year.

You could either choose a straightforward religious gathering and reading of the Ten Commandments at your local synagogue or go for a religious/dairy combo celebration.

'Join us for a reading of the Ten Commandments and communal ice cream party' was one invitation I was tempted by.

Chris is rather famous for his unbaked lemon cheesecake, so with his permission, I'll share the recipe. It was given to us by a good friend in Amman and is best made the day before so that it gets a chance to set. We used our Beit Zayit lemons from the garden but any lemons will do.

Lemon Cheesecake (Unbaked)

Ingredients
125 g Marie biscuits
60 g butter
250 g cream cheese
397 ml tin condensed milk
1 tsp vanilla essence
125 ml lemon juice
Crumbled Flake or grated dark chocolate to decorate (optional)

Method
Crush biscuits.
Cut butter into cubes and melt gently in a pan.
Add crushed biscuits and stir.
Press the mixture into the base of a cake tin and chill in fridge for an hour.
Beat the cream cheese until soft then add condensed milk followed by the vanilla essence and lemon juice.
Top the biscuit base with this mixture and leave overnight in the fridge before serving.
Crumbled Flake chocolate or grated dark chocolate make an attractive and delicious topping.

45

ABU GHOSH

When we were desperately missing the smell of gently spiced grilling meat, falafel, hummus, tabbouleh salad, kibbeh and a decent mixed grill, smells which usually signalled that an Arabic restaurant was handy, we headed down the road to Abu Ghosh, a Christian Arab village which lies just off the main highway from Jerusalem to Tel Aviv. The drive from our house, through forested hills (not our usual ones), was quick and picturesque.

This event usually also coincided with a drop in the pressure of our gas bottle for our home cooking needs. We knew it was getting dangerously low in pressure when it became harder and harder to light the gas rings.

Gas wasn't piped by suppliers direct to the house. Gas cookers were fed by gas bottles of various sizes, stored conveniently and safely outside the main house in the garden. The bottles lasted a while, so it wasn't as inconvenient as it sounds. It was normal to have two bottles so that when one ran out, it was simple to swap the connection to the spare bottle and carry on cooking.

When we lived in Jordan, I had the maddening experience of stirring my porridge over a warm cooker in a cosy kitchen while it snowed outside. It does snow in the Middle East, although many people who haven't lived there find that hard to believe. Suddenly the gas flame died completely, which was odd because we'd just bought a new bottle from the noisy, hooting gas-bottle vendors who trawl the streets of Amman beep-beeping to let you know they're there and ready to trade.

I grabbed the key to the gas-bottle cupboard just outside the kitchen door and was horrified to see that someone had stolen both of our gas bottles. Two long thin plastic hoses swung empty from the open cupboard door which hadn't been locked properly after the last gas delivery. When I spotted the huge, very recent footprints in the snow, I decided not to pursue my detective work but to go back inside and cook my porridge in the microwave oven. We didn't hear the gas lorry hooting for the rest of the day. Presumed innocent until proven guilty. I inspected and noted the size of the delivery man's feet when the next delivery happened.

In Israel they also have gas-bottle deliverers, but you need to place an order, in Hebrew, so we drove to the nearest gas vendor and went through a simple empty-bottle-to-full-bottle mime.

Driving into Abu Ghosh village was like driving into a village in Jordan. The pale, flat-roofed buildings, faced in chiselled stone, which appeared to have sprung up without too much interference by town planners, with room for expansion and wild shrubs, were fairly typical of what we might have seen in Jordan. Abu Ghosh welcomed us all like an old friend. It was reasonably affluent as hordes of Israelis and tourists flocked there on a weekend for a decent Arabic tuck-in. After many visits we had our favourite place to eat, a Lebanese restaurant as we entered the village. There were many more restaurants as we climbed the hillside and more opening all the time, which was just as well as our favourite was always packed full. The restaurants were basic, but the food could be superb.

Most had terraces or gardens which were lovely if we were eating lunch out from April onwards. Most of the pavements were just dirt and rock, although one or two of the more established places had paving just outside, which was a fairly typical Arab approach. It was an altogether different experience to eat, relax and enjoy a weekend outing in the same room as Jews and Arabs (albeit Christian Arabs) who were eating and relaxing in the company of friends. There was no tension. People ordered in Hebrew or Arabic (we ordered in English and just ate what they brought us, usually a pleasant surprise). This was a hangout of the secular Jew. I never saw an Orthodox Jew in Abu Ghosh, probably because the food wasn't kosher.

Music festivals were held in the church, crypt and outdoors which we hoped to visit and enjoy.

Meanwhile we were amazed to see that Abu Ghosh, our wee slice of the Arab world in Israel, was included in the Guinness Book of World Records. If you happen to have a 2010 copy handy, you'll see that its claim to fame is producing the biggest bowl of hummus in the world. Disappointingly Lebanon very quickly snatched this record back the following year, but who knows what the future holds for Abu Ghosh. I wouldn't mind helping to polish off a record-breaking bowl of *mutabal* either, or poor man's caviar as it's sometimes known.

Hummus

Here's my recipe for hummus which is so easy and delicious. It's great for parties or to serve with sundowners. I made huge portions of it for Penny and Dominic's leaving party before they headed off for a posting in Washington. The lovely Nas and Kevin hosted the party in their beautiful old stone villa in Ein Karem. That was the end of another chapter in Jerusalem but the beginning of a new one.

Ingredients
350 g can chickpeas, drained (saving the brine) and rinsed
A shake of dried chilli flakes or smoked paprika to taste
½ tsp dried cumin
1 clove garlic
1 ½ tbsp tahini
4 tbsp good olive oil
2 tbsp fresh lemon juice to taste
Salt and fresh ground black pepper to taste

Method

If using chili flakes, pound in a pestle and mortar.

Crush garlic or whiz it in a food processor.

Add chickpeas, chilli or paprika, cumin and tahini and whiz in food processor.

Add salt and pepper, olive oil and lemon juice and whizz again. You can adjust the consistency of the hummus by adding some of the drained-off chickpea liquid.

It's as easy as that. Eat with warm pitta bread and chopped vegetables.

46

EILAT

It was with realistic expectations that we all piled in the car with swimsuits and summer clothes and headed for the beaches of Eilat on Israel's Red Sea coast. This was a different experience from the Med or Dead Sea experiences we'd enjoyed since we arrived.

Our relocation agent, a great lover of the arts and classical music concerts, had proudly advised us, 'You have to see Eilat.' It was a clear imperative.

We'd been too busy exploring other parts of this amazing and varied land and never quite made it there before, partly due to a limited amount of available travel time, and partly because we'd enjoyed so many family trips to Aqaba, Jordan's Red Sea resort, a short distance from Eilat.

We were also told by an American friend who had visited that it was very expensive and 'just like the Jersey Shore[1]'. From the tone of Jan's voice, I gathered this wasn't a compliment.

I had no idea what the Jersey Shore was like, imagining it to be on a par with one of our British seaside holiday resorts. Maybe not as boring as Eastbourne but less tacky than Blackpool. Morgan was forever chiding us that he hadn't been to Blackpool, when all his friends in Kirkintilloch, who he saw and spent time with every summer, had. He left us in no doubt he felt deprived. I'd been many times and suggested to him that he should visit when he's a grown-up. I had no strong pull back to that seaside town.

We drove to Eilat on the Dead Sea Road, dropping down from the ear-popping heights of Jerusalem to the valley where the smell of hot sand and baked earth acts like a mild astringent on the nostrils. The dusty, salty smell, coupled with road signs, alerted us to the fact that we were driving below sea level and headed for the lowest place on planet earth. As we drove along, we passed Mineral Beach, the place where we celebrated Liberty's 21st birthday; Ein Gedi, where we hiked and enjoyed the hyrax, antelope and waterfalls; and the formation which represented Lot's wife, turned to a pillar of salt. There was another Lot's wife on the other side of the Dead Sea, but I thought this one was better. At the right angle, it really did look convincing.

Our only problem was that heavy traffic had delayed us in Jerusalem, and our journey time extended into darkness and also encroached on a carefully researched restaurant booking for a birthday dinner.

We arrived in Eilat at 8 p.m. in the dark, and our first impression was that it was nothing like Blackpool. There was a string of large Las Vegas-style resort hotels and walkways, making it difficult to navigate to our destination by car. We could see the hotel, but we couldn't get to it as inland waterways and pedestrian bridges blocked our way.

We eventually reached it, and although it fronted a lovely marina, only the back entrance from the car park appeared to be used. The whole of the front of this large hotel was glass, and although it was evening, and there was no danger of the sun beating in, the semi-transparent floor-to-ceiling curtains were drawn. This seemed such a waste of a prime waterside location.

We checked in, having booked a triple room rather than a double with a child's bed. Morgan was now taller than Chris, so we wanted him to have a proper bed.

Frustratingly we were shown to a room with a double bed and a child's bed, not the one we booked and paid extra shekels for. Our complaint fell on deaf ears (customer service, or even just getting what you paid for wasn't a priority in the hotel industry in Israel, as we discovered time and again).

We freshened up with amazing speed and jogged to our recommended restaurant. Although we were very late, we were welcomed to our table and served a mediocre but hugely expensive meal with a rare smile.

The next day we enjoyed strolling in the sunshine, people-watching at cafés and promenading along the boardwalk with the other tourists. Morgan went on some scary rides which involved either being dropped from a great height or being spun around in a chair at a great height. I wasn't tempted to enjoy the promised aerial views. I did notice that all rides operated even on Shabbat. There was a sign on the pay kiosk informing people that the business was leased to a non-Jewish person on Shabbat. I'm paraphrasing, but that was the message.

The hotel resorts were massive, with casinos and cabaret shows and vast outdoor swimming pools fronting the Red Sea and beautiful sandy beaches.

We took a boat ride and were excited to see the shores and beaches of Aqaba in Jordan and a Jordanian flag flying in the breeze, and then we saw the Egyptian border and flag. This was quite the frontier.

We explored a couple of other places for dinner and found the food to be more delicious and the atmosphere much better than on our treat night. It's often the way.

We never did get our hoteliers to accept that we should only pay for an extra child's bed, rather than a triple occupancy room. We've come to learn that life is too short for some battles which you can never win.

---

1. The coastal area in New Jersey, USA, not the American reality TV series.

47

BID FOR STATEHOOD

It was an interesting and tense week in Jerusalem after the Palestinians announced they would make a bid for statehood at the September 2011 meeting of the United Nations in New York.

We were given several security warnings from our usual sources and a strong one from the US Embassy, not a usual source. Although we'd registered with the British Embassy in Israel, I had yet to receive any warning or security guidance from either the embassy in Tel Aviv or the consulate in Jerusalem, only warnings picked up on the grapevine.

We were advised against driving within 100 yards of any IDF vehicles (America still uses imperial measurement, although most of the world went metric over 40 years ago). The reason for this warning was that IDF vehicles were potential targets for missiles of a rock or a missile of an even more sinister variety. I was alarmed one Friday, when driving to school along Highway 9, to spot an IDF vehicle right behind me in my rear-view mirror. He wouldn't overtake, but I shook him off by taking Begin Boulevard South, and the IDF vehicle headed on up the hill in the direction of the West Bank.

It wasn't known whether any major trouble would erupt. There was a concern that the settlers might try and provoke trouble by marching into Palestinian-only territory.

The IDF was also geared up for any trouble or flare-ups at the security crossings. They have one particularly foul weapon which we called the skunk truck. I don't know what its official army-inventory title is. Demonstrators are drenched in liquid which smells of decomposing flesh and excrement. The smell gets worse if you try and shower it off later, and why wouldn't you?

That's what happens when foreign correspondents of international news channels go out looking for trouble and get caught in the crossfire. As if tear gas wasn't bad enough.

So in view of tensions and the possibility of trouble, on Friday 23rd of September 2011 we were banned from going into the Old City of Jerusalem where the Muslims would pray at the Al-Aqsa Mosque and the Jews at the Western Wall. That Friday was the day upon which President Abbas, leader of the Palestinian people, was due to present a bid for recognition of Palestine as a member state of the United Nations.

For the past week, great pressure had been put on the Palestinian leadership to resist lodging such an application for recognition.

Israel made it clear that it would oppose the application; the USA had made it clear that it would exercise its power of veto over any such application which came to a vote, and France suggested that the Palestinians content themselves with the watered-down status of 'observer nation' within the UN. The Palestinian leadership was holding its ground and sticking to its guns. After all, in this troubled part of the world, guns and ground were what it was all about.

Eleventh-hour meetings were held in Israel. People who were normally below the radar in this part of the world popped up to help. People like Tony Blair, former prime minister of Great Britain and the Middle East envoy at the time, gave the first public hint as to why he was paid to undertake that role. I believe that the EU representatives were also in town to broker a deal and keep the bid from statehood off the agenda. There was talk of the USA stopping all financial aid to Palestine if it insisted on presenting the application, and if it insisted on putting the USA in the embarrassing position of having to veto any vote. We learnt later that congress had frozen all aid to Palestine, a move which President Obama opposed and hoped to reverse.

I'd seen the results of the USAID work at first hand: the wells drilled, roads made and schools and communities directly helped in infrastructure, agriculture and social programmes. The threatened withholding of USAID funds to Palestine was no minor matter.

For their part the Palestinians had run out of patience. The peace talks had stalled, with no real progress for years. The parties couldn't even agree on the preconditions to talks taking place. From the Palestinian perspective, there was anger and frustration that the settlement- building programme in the West Bank had resumed at a pace, following a negotiated moratorium on further building which expired in September 2010.

From the Israeli point of view, they had as a precondition the requirement that Palestine must recognise Israel as a Jewish State, which the Palestinian leadership was unable and unwilling to concede.

'We recognise Israel as a State,' they would tell you.

'What of the Muslim, Christian and Druze Israeli nationals? Where would such a declaration of Jewish Statehood leave them?' It was a question often asked.

'We don't ask for Palestine to be recognised as a Muslim or an Arab state, but to be recognised only as Palestine,' we were told more than once.

As the parties had been unable to agree on the preconditions to talks, no substantive talks had taken place.

So the die was cast. President Abbas did in fact deliver the application for full recognition as a Palestinian State to the secretary general of the UN at the time, Ban Ki-moon. That brave political and fiscal act was followed by an impressive and memorable speech to the United Nations in which all of the frustrations and hardships of the occupation of the Palestinian Territories and the division of families and communities by the security wall, which it was alleged was illegally annexing additional land, was conveyed in an eloquent and measured way, in what must have been one of the most important speeches of President Abbas's career.

Prime Minister Netanyahu also spoke, emphasising terrorism and security, both a part of everyday life in Israel. After highlighting the events of 9/11, he went on to emphasise that his number one priority was the defence of Israel and the protection of its people. He cited the deterioration of security for Israeli citizens after Israel withdrew from Gaza and after settlements were dismantled there.

On a personal level, I was also worried that if USAID money stopped, we and many others would have to leave and find other postings. When it came to the bigger picture of Israeli/Palestinian relations, I was deeply disappointed that the US wasn't more supportive of President Abbas and used USAID money as a bargaining chip, in order to persuade him to withdraw his bid for statehood.

The bid was unsuccessful and the continuing status quo after the failed bid was disappointing and depressing. No progress has been made towards a peaceful resolution in the years since the UN vote was passed.

Words of the day:(Laa) afham—I (don't) understand (Arabic)

48

THE FORESTS

We enjoyed living next to the Jerusalem Forest. It amazed me that it wasn't a natural forest but had been planted 60 years previously by some far-sighted landscape sculptor. It's driven through, picnicked in and jogged and cycled through every day by hundreds of Jerusalemites. It was responsible for possibly the most beautiful school run I would ever do.

Everything isn't always idyllic when you live so close to a forest, as I was to discover. Mid-afternoon one day, Morgan and I were aware of even more aerial activity than normal. It wasn't unusual for us to have Israeli Air Force jet planes flying low over our rooftops, or helicopters buzzing our windows into vibration mode, as they flew in formation, usually in threes to goodness knows where. However, that day the activity level reached frantic as the countryside in front of our moshav, right by the Motza junction of the main Jerusalem to Tel Aviv Highway, went up in flames. Initially there was quite a bit of light grey smoke, and the fire was about half a kilometre from the main road. The winds got up, and the orange flames rose. The fire spread with frightening speed, and all vehicles on this fast-moving highway came to a complete standstill. It must have been terrifying to be trapped there with the flames of the fire threatening to cross the road. The electricity went off, presumably as a precaution, and we were cut off from the news. As the smoke increased, the highway was closed completely as the visibility levels were so bad. We watched as the fire threatened to leap across the tarmac surface to the main forest. At that point I began to think about a possible escape route.

The main highway wasn't an option, jammed with many emergency vehicles trying to get through. I could see from our upper terrace that the traffic approaching the road was backed up to the village and going nowhere. This left only one route out of the area— through our beautiful forest in the hope that the fire didn't cross the road. In the end we decided not to take that risk, to sit tight, watch and wait.

We hung over our balcony upstairs, observing as the flames leapt and small aircraft dumped loads of water time and again to no avail. The wind dropped, and the battery of small aircraft started to win the battle. When a different sort of payload was dropped, bright red dust of some sort, the fighters got the fire under control, and we could breathe easy once more. The electricity even came back on quite quickly, unlike the previous year when part of the forest closer to town went up in flames and the electricity was off until nearly bedtime. This was no fun in the hot Israeli summers where a fan or air conditioning was helpful to a decent night of sleep and avoided the feeling that you were lying in a sauna.

On this occasion we had a lucky escape. One of our neighbours told me, 'The fire was started accidentally by a householder who was burning rubbish. A piece of paper blew away and caught quickly.'

'Was he charged by the police?' I enquired, assuming there would be repercussions for such major mayhem.

'No! He's Israeli. If he'd been Palestinian, they would have put him in jail,' laughed one of our many Israeli neighbours, who shall remain nameless.

49

THE DOG

The path to happiness on the moshav never ran smoothly. We'd been asked to uproot ourselves and move there to participate in a programme which was expected to roll on for years. Unexpectedly Chris's employing company came second in the bid process to fulfil Stage II of the USAID infrastructure needs programme, despite herculean efforts by all concerned. The company was to transition the programme to the winning bidder at the end of September, with our exit scheduled for the end of the year.

'I can't believe we're in this situation again,' I said to Chris one evening. 'We were supposed to be settled here for years.'

'Yes, I know, but we're lucky compared to some. At least we have options. What about Qatar? We have a lot of work in the pipeline there, so that's a possibility. It's being hailed as the new Dubai.'

'Well, I'm not sure that's a selling point. Our finances wouldn't survive another Dubai-style crash. We're still recovering from the last one.'

'The house in Dubai is rented out now, and the property market will recover if we give it time,' he countered.

'I know, but I'm just saying that moving to what might turn out to be another boom and bust economy doesn't appeal. Not to mention that it's as hot as a pizza oven most of the year. I'd miss our long walks and the garden. I'd miss our life on the moshav. I'd miss Jerusalem.'

'I think you should still check out the international schools. See if there are spaces, just in case.'

As it happened, all suitable schools were full and only had waiting-list places. We've always made a point of moving as a family. So any posting which wasn't family friendly, or had no schools available locally so that we could stay together, wasn't an option.

Chris could leave the employing company of the past quarter century and join the winning team of the bid process. He'd been headhunted for this role and others. We were very fortunate that there was no shortage of opportunities, just a lack of will to get on the road so soon after the last two moves. For many reasons, mainly political but also related to the global slow down, our posting before this one in Amman, our second posting to Jordan, was cut short to ten months. Calls from headhunters which had fallen on deaf ears in the past were now seriously considered as real options. The family could settle; Morgan could stay at the school he was enjoying, although we were a wee bit worried about the number of times a day he uttered the word 'awesome' and the phrase 'challenge accepted' in an American accent.

In the end common sense prevailed, and we decided that three international moves in three years were just too much. Chris jumped ship, and we all prepared ourselves for another three years in Israel and the Palestinian Occupied Territories with the bid-winning company.

This was a huge decision for our family. There were issues of long service and loyalty, not to mention the impact on pension and other employment benefits. However, we took the decision, and the day arrived when we were secure enough in our tenure to fulfil Morgan's heart's desire. We decided we would welcome another addition to our family and get a dog.

We all wanted a medium-sized dog, nothing too big and strong as I had no wish to have my shoulder dislocated on a daily basis, and the boys insisted on nothing small and yappy. Dreams of dressing my handbag-accessory pooch in bejewelled collars and raincoats weren't realised.

I remember visiting the pet department of Harrods on a home-leave trip when our girls were small. They picked out wardrobes for our imaginary dogs—Dolce and Gabbana—yes, they'd even named them by the time we left the shop. They'd also established with the shop assistant that the puppies they'd picked would grow no heavier than ten kilogrammes, the weight limit for taking your doggy in the cabin with you on a flight. Needless to say, no dogs were purchased that day.

The grown-ups (or donuts as our offspring affectionately call us) decided that there were enough dogs in Israel needing a home without importing one. We were prepared to take the big step and responsibility of being dog owners. Worries of quarantine regulations (or doggy jail, as we call it) were alleviated by the plan that we would route back to Europe via a pet-friendly European Union country, renting a place for the summer if required, and then we would take it from there.

So on a bright Friday afternoon in September, Chris and I collected Morgan from school and drove to an animal rescue centre. It was quite a drive, but excitement levels were high on this landmark journey.

We'd been on a preparatory visit the week before to see if there were any possibilities and to discuss the process. Morgan had a puppy in mind, which we'd taken on a trial walk on the leash and which had been very well-behaved and loveable. Sadly someone else had also found him so well-behaved and loveable that they'd taken him home.

We spotted Mat, an adorable russet-red spaniel who looked very handsome indeed. I was drawn to him, as I had been on the previous visit.

The rescue centre adoption lady warned us against taking a puppy as they're so much work but did a great marketing job on Mat. He'd come from a family home, was house-trained and wasn't like a puppy. We were prepared for the work and disruption of a puppy but took Mat for a trial walk anyway.

'Hold up, Mat,' chuckled Morgan as he was tugged forward at a pace across the barren stony lot just outside the kennel walls.

'He's just a bit enthusiastic, Morgan,' I told him. 'I think he's thrilled to be out with you.'

'I'm really excited to be taking him for a walk. See, he's a good dog.

Heel, boy,' tried Morgan hopefully. 'I don't think he speaks English,' he observed as Mat ignored his command and pulled him forward some more.

'Never mind, we can teach him,' suggested Chris. 'I think we should bring him home with us if you'd like to, Morgan.'

'Oh, yes, please,' was the predictable response.

We all adjourned to the rescue centre office to sign the official adoption contract and pay the $150 adoption fee.

'Do you have a dog bed already?' asked the boss.

'No,' I replied.

'Shall I add one to the bill?'

Her questions kept coming.

'Do you have dog food? I'll add a twenty-kilogramme bag of premium doggy chow to the bill. Do you have a collar…a lead… bowls…worm tablets?'

After the grand addition, Chris and I felt we could have just about been buying a Crufts Best of Breed. But what is money, if not to spend?

It was all worthwhile when on the way out of the office to be reunited with Mat, Morgan declared, 'This is the best day of my life… so far.'

Mr Mat, with his film-star good looks, sat beautifully on the back seat of the car next to Morgan who proudly held his leash. We drove him to his new home with large grassy doggy runs and a very comfy bean bag, just for him. We'd been assured that it was fine to rename him, and we all felt Mat was a little incongruous. So he was christened Pedro on the way home.

He settled beautifully and was totally reliable to pee and poo on his regular walks.

Then our Israeli gardener arrived, as he did twice a month. Pedro went nuts and tried to bite his feet, thankfully protected by his thick gardeners' boots.

'Linda! Where did you get that crazy dog?' he demanded.

'He's a rescue dog and obviously doesn't like tall dark men or their heavy boots much.'

We struck a deal that he would text ahead of his visits, and I would keep Mr Pedro inside the house until he left. I also gave him a bottle of homemade limoncello as a peace offering.

I took Morgan and Pedro to school every morning, and after dropping Morgan, exercised Pedro on his leash in the Jerusalem Forest. We walked for miles, and I lost three kilos rapidly. The Pedro Diet!

The first time we saw another person on our walk, our doggy friend launched an attack. If I hadn't shortened his leash, he would have had the person between his teeth.

So I kept Pedro on a very short lead with him tucked between my legs to control his movement if we were near people. One of the JAIS school teachers who was a real animal lover bent down to pet him at the school gate, and he snapped at her finger. By now he was displaying a behaviour pattern that wasn't particularly sociable, and I was getting worried.

Chris and I took him to the vet for his check-up and were shocked to learn that his teeth needed dental work as they were covered in plaque. I was surprised given he did so much biting.

We warned the vet's assistant that he bit, and she was very gung-ho. He went for her ankles and missed by a whisker.

A young man in the waiting room wanted to pet Pedro, but we warned him off. He couldn't believe that such a lovely woofer would bite, ignored our warning and got a sore finger for his efforts. When we spoke to the vet about his biting habit, he simply said, 'As long as he isn't biting you, that's okay.'

I didn't think it was okay and phoned the adoption lady at the rescue centre. She recommended a highly competent and successful Israeli dog trainer. The trainer insisted we were all at home for her first visit.

'Do you want the dog on or off the leash when you arrive?' I enquired.

'Off the leash, of course,' was her confident reply.

She arrived on a bright Friday afternoon, and Pedro went totally mad.

'Give me some food,' the trainer demanded from behind our gate in a polite but firm way.

She threw Pedro morsels of cold meat which reduced the frenzy, but he was still very aggressive.

'Are you sure you don't want him on the leash? He'll bite you,' I advised.

'I've never been bitten,' was the strong and unwavering reply.

She came through the garden gate, and yes, he went for her thigh and bit right through her trouser leg.

'Are you okay?' I asked.

'I'm fine, I'm fine,' she assured us, batting him off her leg and pretending nothing had happened. 'Perhaps you should put him on the leash for now,' she conceded.

The dog trainer was a regular visitor to the house and didn't come cheap. After weeks of her feeding Pedro cooked meat and winning his trust, he was just about tolerating her presence.

On a normal day, Pedro was like a sinister rewrite of that old children's story book *The Very Hungry Caterpillar*. First he ate the gardener; then he ate the teacher; then he tried the landlord; then he almost got a small Dutch visitor from Jordan, and the last straw was when despite having him on a tight rein at the garden gate, he went for one of Morgan's friends.

I'd lost sleep thinking about what would happen if he ever escaped our garden and encountered the little twins across the road who were now toddling around.

When I voiced my concern about his behaviour to the dog trainer, she just advised me that some things in life aren't perfect.

I phoned the rescue centre again to talk about the catalogue of biting. I was speechless when the adoption lady replied that he hadn't bitten in a while. Speechless and furious. I was in a situation where we couldn't safely keep a dog who only loved Deckers (and was starting to show signs of jealousy when I showed Morgan affection), but I was the mother of a child who really loved the dog, character flaws and all.

The rescue centre offered us a swap, but after a huge effort on all our parts to make this adoption work, we simply weren't ready for that and reluctantly had to return him. Instead of the apology we'd expected, the only words spoken to us were, 'What am I supposed to do with him now?' And then the adoption lady disappeared into the office, and we didn't see or hear from her again.

I think we were all hugely unlucky, including Pedro, who should have been homed in a different environment, and I'm not saying we won't adopt a pet again in another country.

I can't help reflecting on an old proverb and thinking just how apt it is.

Proverb of the day: once bitten, twice shy

50

THE NEXT MOVE

Just when we thought that our life was sorted for the next few years, our Israeli landlord started making serious noises about having our house on the moshav back for his parents.

We'd already gone through an interesting time when we discovered it on a real estate website. It was on sale for 6,000,000 shekels. I was astounded. It had lovely views and a great garden, but it was in no way luxurious or large. Just a normal four-bedroom detached house with quite small bedrooms at that.

Then we were asked to allow someone to view the house. I explained to the agent that we weren't even one year through a potential two-year lease.

'Ah, but the purchaser knows the right of the tenants will be respected,' he replied.

So a family came to view, and I asked them when they hoped to move in. They wanted to move quickly and were oblivious to our tenure.

The property didn't sell, and the landlord, in a rather droll way, asked if we would like to buy it. No, thank you.

Next he asked us to leave early and took to visiting on a Friday with his parents so they could plan their new home (they'd already sold their old one). At that point we told him that if another house came up for rent on the moshav, then we would move out early.

Within a couple of weeks, the landlord had established that a house a few doors along could be rented to us, so we moved all our worldly goods in the pouring rain just up the road. It was so wet that one of our removers wrapped himself in packing cling film in an attempt to stay dry. It wasn't successful, and we shared dry T-shirts, hot drinks and mopped shiny wet floors constantly in case of accidents.

The real estate agents who had handled our original rental and were based on the moshav very generously waived all commission on the second transaction and helped us in any way they could, given the circumstances. I really couldn't imagine us being allowed to terminate the lease early if it had been our circumstances which had changed.

Our new landlord was a kind and thoughtful man. We liked him from day one, and after his marriage, we got to know his lovely wife, and later on their new baby. Both made it clear that we would always have a place to stay on the moshav. Second time lucky.

51

EIN KAREM

If we ventured out on a Saturday, it was usually to walk through the countryside to the nearby village of Ein Karem, the birthplace of John the Baptist. I'd visited Machaerus in Jordan which is reputedly the place where John the Baptist was beheaded. It's contended that he may have been beheaded and his body entombed in Sebastia, near Nablus in the West Bank. I'd hiked from Sebastia to Nablus, which is a lovely walk, and then been treated to a traditional home-cooked meal with a local Arab family in Nablus. There's a consensus that John's mother, Elizabeth, discovered she was pregnant with him in Ein Karem and that Mary visited her there when she was expecting Jesus.

The church of Saint John the Baptist in Ein Karem isn't as grand or ornate as many of the churches in Jerusalem, but it offers a sanctuary and place of spirituality to those who need one. Surprisingly, quiet places of spirituality could be elusive in this part of the world.

Mary's Well is located in the centre of the village, and many tourists stop to drink the water there and bottle it to take home as it's thought to have magical properties.

We loved walking the dusty paths along the ridges of hills between Beit Zayit and Ein Karem, inhaling herbs trampled underfoot and the smell of pines needles warmed by the sun. Towards the end of the walk, which had an expansive view of hills, terraces and trees, and usually a percussion of goat bells, we climbed up old stone steps into the town. It was quite a climb.

Chris and I had our first gin and tonic of our posting sitting outside at sunset in Ein Karem shortly after our move. This was a memorable event as you don't sit outside drinking alcohol in street cafés in Jordan, or in fact in any of the places we'd lived in the previous twenty years. Now that we were settled, we usually set out for wood-oven pizza, a Roquefort salad and a glass of something cold and white around lunch time. Carloads of people trying to escape Jerusalem on a Saturday did the same, so it could get extremely crowded.

There was a take-away ice cream shop next door to our preferred restaurant which sold the most wonderful array of gelato I'd seen in the whole of Israel. This, and the other cafés and restaurants in the village, meant that we were unlikely to leave hungry.

We could walk off excesses of everything by strolling around little shops and galleries which were tucked down pretty flower-decked lanes. Artists, jewellers and craftspeople had settled in this haven of peace and creativity. We even discovered a chocolatier, and this business ran chocolate-making courses. I'm always happy to add to my skill set and eat chocolate.

A walk through the hills and forest to Ein Karem was a relaxing weekend treat for us.

I had dinner one evening with a colleague from Chris's office in Ramallah. She was an American Arab and a recent addition to the senior management team from the USA. She told us that she visited Ein Karem every weekend too, but for very different reasons. Her family home had been there, and her family had been forced to leave it during the hostilities in the late 1940s, around the time when the State of Israel was formed. So the beauty of the stone houses and lush gardens of this historic village is overshadowed by its past. Paradise lost for some and found for others.

If we walked in the other direction from our house, down into the valley and through the vineyards towards Jerusalem, we would reach the abandoned Arab village of Lifta. The population had been mainly Muslim with a few Christians. All of the houses stand empty. During the hostilities around the time of Israeli independence, several residents of Lifta were killed in a local coffee shop and others injured by Israelis who were trying to secure the western exit from the city of Jerusalem. The population fled to safety in fear of further bloodshed. It was an eerie sight and the last Arab village to stand unoccupied. The others have been re-inhabited (like Ein Karem) or knocked down.

I was horrified when one Saturday in the December after we arrived, two women were brutally attacked while hiking in the hills near Jerusalem. One, an American, Kristine Luken, was murdered, and the other, an English woman, Kay Wilson, was left for dead. Two Palestinians had stabbed them both. Although the attacks took place near Beit Shemesh, they were close enough to home to make me think twice about personal safety when hiking.

Later in our stay in Jerusalem, more terror and tragedy took place in our beautiful forest when a Palestinian boy, Mohammed Abu Khdeir, was beaten and burnt while still alive by three Israeli boys in retribution for the kidnapping and shooting dead of Israeli teenagers Naftali Fraenkel, Gilad Shaer and Eyal Yifrach, all in the summer of 2014. The Israeli teenagers had been hiking in the Occupied West Bank. They were kidnapped, shot and found near Hebron. A catalogue of horrific tragedy and a cycle of violence which plays on repeat.

Words of the day: ma'as salaama—goodbye (Arabic)

52

AN UNEXPECTED TURN OF EVENTS

On a beautiful April day in 2014 (which happened to be Holocaust Memorial Day), I sat in our garden in moshav Beit Zayit admiring a riot of red roses which had bloomed en masse while I'd been away. The sun shone, and the sky was a clear and brilliant blue. I had on my lap a robust cardboard envelope posted by Chris's aunt Madeline to my mother in Scotland for my attention. I'd collected it on our trip home for the Easter holidays but hadn't had an opportunity to open it and consider its contents. I felt a frisson of excitement, as my second mother-in-law (yes, I'm lucky enough to have two as my wonderful father-in-law married twice) had hinted at a family secret as a result of some research Chris's aunt had done into his family tree, after the death of his grandmother Lottie.

The envelope contained a manuscript, the memoir of the early childhood years of Madeline's cousin and revealed some of the family's past. We were aware of an Egyptian connection as Fred, my father-in-law, was born in Cairo. We were aware of an Arab connection as Chris's great-auntie Lizzie is said to have converted to Islam after marrying an Egyptian judge. What we were unprepared for was a Jewish connection, only discovered after the deaths of the sisters Lottie and Lizzie.

When I met my husband, I thought him very exotic as he'd been born and brought up in Kenya, before coming to Scotland for boarding school, university and a wife. I remember the usual humour around our Sunday dinner table.

'Aye, he's a keen yin right enough,' was one remark uttered by my late uncle Alex. My family have lived in and around Kirkintilloch for generations. My grandfather was an elder in the church my parents were married in, I was christened in and married in, and then our children in turn were christened in. I remember someone saying that my grandmother would have thought I was marrying a foreigner if my intended was from Bishopbriggs, the town five miles along the road.

I used to say that Chris's nationality was like a complicated immigration law exam question. If only I'd known.

It appears that Lottie and Lizzie lived their whole lives without sharing their Jewish heritage with their children or the rest of the world. It seems it was deliberately concealed as Lottie always described herself as French Italian and spoke in French as if it was her mother tongue, counting canasta card scores out loud in French.

Delving a bit deeper into the family history explains in part the deception. Chris's great-grandparents had both lost relatives in the Holocaust, and their memories of that time, coupled with the threatened status of Jews living in the Middle East in the 1950s, perhaps explained their very occasional visits to a synagogue and the petering out of the weekly lighting of a candle. But it was Lizzie and Lottie's strong determination to protect their offspring from prejudice or persecution which prevailed and led to the total erasure of Jewishness for the next generation. Madeline had no idea of this aspect of her mother's history until after her mother's death.

While it was interesting to us to find a facet of our family history which was relevant to where we were living in the world, we were lucky to live in a world in which there was a lot less racial prejudice and anti-Semitism than there was in Lottie and Lizzie's day. At least I hoped we did.

Having said that, I didn't know if Chris might be at more risk driving to Ramallah every day, working to improve roads, schools and water supply for the Palestinians, if it was known that his grandmother was Jewish. As Jewishness is passed down the maternal line, both his father and aunt had a genuine claim to Jewishness, while Chris and his sister did not. I hoped to investigate whether any distant relatives were living in Israel who might be interested in meeting their non-Jew relatives with branches of our particular family tree converted to Islam.

As we lived in a country where Jews were deeply suspicious and, I believe, a little afraid of Arabs, and Arabs tend towards a deep dislike of Israeli Jews and a fear of the IDF, I found it amusing that Chris's great-aunt started life as a Jewess and converted to Islam.

So it seemed we had a family tree abundant with Jews, Christians and one or two Muslims. What an inheritance our children have of these rich religions and cultures. We are all different, but it seems not so different with the passage of time. It may be naïve to pray for an understanding and tolerance of these great faiths. Let's hope that one day we can all live and let live, in peace, in freedom and in family, regardless of faith.

POSTSCRIPT

We continued to live on the moshav for five happy years.

We enjoyed the beauty and nature of the landscape and spent weekends walking, cycling and exploring our host country. We made the most of our special home and picked and cured our own olives, cooked, and relaxed in our garden. We certainly made the most of the country's produce and markets at home and away. When I spy a small packet of figs cling film-wrapped in families of four and for sale in supermarkets, I think back to the days when we strolled through the vineyards and picked warm, ripe, wild figs straight from the trees.

The religious festivals took on a familiar rhythm, and we became prepared for the total shutdown of services and road closures as well as the breaks from normal routine. A newly purchased book for a quiet weekend of reading was a treasured delight.

My lovely neighbour Talia popped in regularly to see us for a chat, often with one or two of her children. On one occasion she arrived at the door and insisted I join her for a run. I explained I walked for exercise, so we compromised on a jog, during which she asked me if Chris was a spy. I laughed out loud and made a special request that she never mention this suspicion of hers in his company. I would never hear the end of it if he were a suspected James Bond, nor would we get him out of his dinner suit. I was amused; usually I'm the one with the over-active imagination.

Chris and I became familiar with our emergency evacuation plan should we find ourselves having to leave Israel in a hurry for security reasons. We selected border crossings (Egypt to the south, Jordan to the east) and set meeting points in case the need should arise. We kept cash to hand as it was unlikely that any credit cards would be particularly flexible or friendly in a serious emergency.

During the rest of our stay, we experienced ups and downs. Some of the downs were tragic and extremely upsetting; others just inconvenient.

The Jerusalem light rail system was officially opened along with a brand-new bright and light multi-storey car park of the Park and Ride variety at Mount Herzl. This resulted in the purchase of a wheeled shopping trolley to promote trips into the market for food and Jaffa Street for fabric. My fabric collection continued to expand.

After the tragic deaths of the Israeli teenagers and the kidnapping and murder of a teenager from the streets of Beit Hanina in East Jerusalem in retribution, the light rail stations in East Jerusalem were seriously damaged during riots. When I left Jerusalem, it was still difficult to see which station was which in some parts of East Jerusalem as all signs had been damaged or removed in the unrest.

The light rail stops themselves were targeted, and queues of passengers waiting for trains in West Jerusalem were deliberately hit by moving vehicles in a new strategy to kill and maim.

When the light rail was being planned, concerns were voiced that the mere fact that the trains would travel across the city, from Mount Herzl to Arab East Jerusalem, was thought to be a major security headache.

Having loved the joy and the comfort of the friendships with Penny and Nas, where we spoke almost every day, it was time for me to explore other social possibilities like the Jerusalem Expat Network.

This social networking group led to many long-lasting friendships and the opportunity to continue to help and participate in some of the activities and fundraising the network promotes. After a while, I was happy to join the committee as the newcomer co-ordinator as it was a great excuse to meet up with new arrivals, chat and introduce to them to the many delights of living in Jerusalem.

I'd just spent a happy, chatty morning, strolling around spice stalls of the Jerusalem Market and stopping for coffee and freshly baked pastries when I received a call from Chris. One of his extended team working on a road project in the West Bank had been shot dead.

The young flagman was going about his normal duties and was required to ensure that vehicles entered and exited the site safely. He was reported to have been taken to work as normal that morning. A group of IDF soldiers alleged he was armed. This was denied. Apparently he was made to strip off his clothes and to walk up and down the road in front of the work site. He was then shot and died at the scene, aged 22. No one was charged as a result of his death.

In the summer of 2014, we were on holiday in Big Canoe, Georgia, USA, our base when we visit Grandpa Fred and Granny Barbs. We were alarmed by the reports of a war with Gaza. Having lived through sirens, safe places and school bomb shelters, Chris and I reached the view that we should look at other options for Morgan. We agreed that we would visit schools in Scotland, and Morgan was determined to go to boarding school and claim a degree of independence—a national trait for some in Scotland. Morgan spent the night at several schools as a taster and wasn't put off the idea of full-time school. After considering his options, he chose beautiful Glenalmond College in Perthshire, Scotland. This is the school which Robbie Coltrane (Hagrid in *Harry Potter*) attended, and I think J.K. Rowling and Harry are responsible for our children begging for boarding school in Scotland. Envisage the Glenfinnan Viaduct scene as the steam train chugs towards magic, friendship and adventure, and you get the picture. J.K.

Rowling is also responsible for making reading an enjoyable pastime for many a reluctant reader.

Morgan settled into the routines and rituals of a traditional boarding school quickly and easily. He enjoyed activities which hadn't been part of his international school life. He took up squash and ultimately became the captain of the team and a prefect, received colours and saw his name painted on the record of school sports' captains for eternity. He took flying lessons with the RAF cadets and flew out of the base in Leuchars in Fife when weather permitted.

Chris was convinced that it was the right choice for Morgan, being a former boarding schoolboy himself. I agreed but was bereft when Morgan left to live in school full-time. I felt the absence of his affection, humour and loveliness deeply, but I knew it was for the best. Chris and I settled into being a household of two again and made the most of our new-found freedom after a quarter of a century of parenthood. Our travels and treats were punctuated with Morgan's half-term holidays and weekend leave from school and we celebrated our reunions.

Before we'd reached the decision over Morgan's schooling, we returned home to Jerusalem and were shocked by the casualties of the Gaza War. Victims of the assault on Gaza, in response to rockets sent across into Israel, had made long journeys to St Joseph's Hospital in East Jerusalem where they received lifesaving treatment for extreme injuries.

I was drawn to talk to Amal who had lost her baby daughter in her arms when a rocket struck her home. Amal was in intensive care for her spine, which was fractured in the attack, as was her daughter Rania who had suffered burns. Amal made remarkable progress over several weeks, and we talked of life and loss, her beliefs and mine. We also made sure that Rania, who was three years old at the time and confined to bed with serious injuries, had her fingernails painted and had stickers and toys to distract her from her new reality.

Baby Ali, another victim, was such a sorry sight. He'd lost an eye and had an oversized bandage wrapped around his infant head. He was accompanied by his grandmother who chatted with the other women in the ward while keeping a watch over him. A cuddle with baby Ali was a precious treat for me as his innocent maimed body pressed into mine for comfort.

The older children didn't do as well. Although they were visited, and material and medical needs were met, they were carrying emotional wounds which may never heal. A lovely teenage girl struggled with multiple metal pins in her injured legs and with the grim prospect that she may never marry and have a family of her own.

I met many adults and children on hospital visits, but the last person I will share with you is brave Mohammed, a teenage boy who lost his leg in an Israeli rocket attack. Our friend John Cutliffe asked what he would like as a gift, and he asked for a football. The phantom pains in his leg tortured him, and he had no interest in food. He became painfully thin while waiting for the specialist treatment he needed abroad. Mohammed was accompanied by his grandfather, and it was from him that we later heard the very sad news that Mohammed had died in Turkey where the treatment was being made available.

Amal and Rania did return to Gaza, and I was happy to take a short stroll with Amal in the sunshine outside the hospital on her last day in Jerusalem. I was afraid to keep in touch with her while living in Beit Zayit for fear of the trouble and personal danger she might be in if connections with a woman who lived in Israel were established. I was worried that she might be suspected of collaborating with Israelis, for which the punishment was usually death. There were no explanations or trials, so I didn't want to risk any misunderstanding for this family who had been through enough.

The war in Syria continued, and we were reliably informed that Syrian casualties and children were dropped just over the Israeli border for treatment, which was given without advertisement or accolade.

On a lighter note, Morgan won't eat McDonald's and hasn't for years. His new fix is Domino's pizza.

Liberty and Easton were married in our family church in Kirkintilloch in September 2018. She became a fourth generation St Mary's bride. We celebrated with friends and family from all over the world. One of our guests travelled from Gaza.

I repacked the Hebron glass balls which now hang in the garden of our villa in Spain which, unlike our Puglia home, isn't imaginary. But that, as they say, is another story.

Thank you for joining me on this journey. Your company was much appreciated.

MESSAGE FROM THE AUTHOR

Thank you so much for reading this book, and I hope you enjoyed it. If you would like to see some of the photographs of our life and travels in Jerusalem, Ramallah and beyond, please have a look at my Facebook page (www.facebook.com/linda.deckerauthor) or website gallery (www.linda-decker.com/gallery).

I would be extremely grateful if you could leave a review on Amazon. I'd also love to hear your comments so do please get in touch with me:

Email: deckerwrite@gmail.com
Facebook: www.facebook.com/linda.deckerauthor
Instagram: www.instagram.com/deckerwrite
Twitter: www.twitter.com/deckerwrite
Website: www.linda-decker.com

BONUS MATERIAL—JEWISH CUSTOMS

BIRTH AND BAR MITZVAHS

When we were in Israel, we saw that, just as in the Arab world, the centre of Jewish life revolved around the family, whether that was an orthodox family closely guarding the laws and traditions of the Jewish faith, a moshav family—laid-back, barefooted and sporting faded hippyish clothes and enjoying the rhythm of a life marked by holy days and holidays—or a secular family, busy in a rapidly expanding and technically successful economy. Israel was seen as the start-up nation and boasted entrepreneurship as a near-national trait. It seemed to an outsider that most young Israeli couples jealously guarded family time with their partners and children. It also appeared that effort was spent creating nurturing home environments in which both mother and father played a part in the challenges and fun of childrearing and parenting.

Another visit to the newly renovated and recently re-opened Israeli Museum provided a wonderful cache of the paraphernalia of birth, death and marriage, Jewish style.

One of the best-known tenets of Judaism is that baby boys are circumcised. This circumcision takes place when the baby is eight days old and is performed by a person who has been specially trained for the task. He usually has a huge amount of experience as he regularly carries out the operation, although I do find it alarming that even in this profession, there's a first day on the job. The circumcision or brit milah (which means the covenant of circumcision) involves the removal of the foreskin of the infant's penis. It's usually performed in the family home but can be carried out at a synagogue or any venue the parents choose. The specialist who carries out the operation is called a mohel.

The eighth day is the optimum day for the baby's immune system and medical health, and the ceremony is usually carried out then unless the infant is too ill or weak.

It's normally done early in the day as it's a mitzvah (the carrying out of a commandment of Jewish law), and as such under Judaism you should be eager to perform it. After the procedure, wine is blessed and a drop placed into the mouth of the child. Then traditionally the baby is named. Biblical names are still very popular such as Rachel, Sarah and Leah for a girl and Nathaniel or Nathan, Samuel and Gideon for a boy. As in most aspects of Jewish celebration, there is then food and drink. I've seen a brit milah breakfast special menu catering many delicious dishes for a great price. Thankfully no mini sausage rolls. I'm not sure I'd have much of an appetite after the main event.

There's also a naming ceremony for girls, but this is without surgery.

I've never been to a brit milah, which tends to be a fairly small gathering of close family and friends. Being the sort of person who faints when it's time for fairly routine dental work, I don't think I'd have been good brit milah guest material.

As we all know, children grow up so quickly, and it's no sooner a boy's brit milah (just known as a brit colloquially) than it's his bar mitzvah. This is the right of passage of a Jewish boy into adulthood, and it takes place on his thirteenth birthday. It's also the day on which, under Jewish law, he assumes the age of responsibility. There's often a celebration for family and friends, again involving food and drink, but this doesn't have to fall exactly on the birthday, although the passage into the age of responsibility is determined by the birthday itself, not the date of the party.

Some Jewish families throw lavish bar mitzvah parties, and

websites sell suitable speeches for the father of the BM boy, Mother of the BM boy, the BM boy, his siblings, and so it goes on for a very reasonable $20 each, or a better value family package of speeches can be bought for less than $80. Do not under any circumstances embarrass your family by giving a homemade, unprofessionally written personal speech.

A wealthy family will plan a bar mitzvah event in the way people plan weddings in other parts of the world. The best of food, wine and entertainment is bestowed on the guests to celebrate the child becoming a man. The teenager is also usually pleased to be given generous gifts or money, so it's a win-win celebration. The girls have a similar story with a bat mitzvah celebration at age twelve.

The other bonus is that after his bar mitzvah, the spotty thirteen-year-old is then legally entitled to officiate at a Jewish divorce, which is just about as hard to get (no pun intended, all will become clear in the next chapter), as a house on a moshav.

I was also amused to learn that it was possible to qualify for a second bar mitzvah. All you have to do is survive to the ripe old age of 83! The logic is that the biblical lifespan expected is three score years and ten, or 70 years of age. So if you live 13 years beyond your allotted lifespan of 70, you're entitled to a second bar mitzvah. Sounds good to me...any excuse for a party. And you know what they say—people who have more birthdays tend to live longer.

MATCHMAKING, MARRIAGE AND DIVORCE

Matchmaking is an activity which is still widely practised in Israel.

When I came back from home leave to the UK after a long summer stay in Scotland, I was met by a very smiley and excited friend and employee at the international school Morgan attended in Jerusalem.

'I got engaged over the summer!' she was just bursting to tell us. This was a girl who was brought up in the US until her early teens when the whole family made Aliyah.

'That was quick,' I replied as there had been no mention of a boyfriend when we left seven weeks earlier at the end of June.

'Well, I was told by someone who knew a nice boy who was looking, and we met for ice cream, and the wedding hall is booked for November,' she told us, breathless with excitement and a little shyly.

This very confident, accomplished and talented young woman had been introduced to her intended, and a rapid courtship had led to a marriage proposal and a wedding date, all within five months. If the couple hadn't taken to each other, presumably the matchmaker would still be trying to make a match and catch a catch.

This was an example of how the match was made in a middle-class home of Americans who had made Aliyah. Now some very upper-class matchmakers advertise their esteemed services in the international press.

One international matchmaker regularly advertises in the classified adverts in the international edition of an American newspaper, offering global marriages and for those who may be shy of putting their goods on display in public, there is an assurance of protection of identity. So what kind of match can you expect to make through a top-of-the-range matchmaking agency? Here's an example of the sort of advertisement I came across (it's fictional, but you will get the gist):

Industrialist's Daughter
Representing the family-owned corporation worldwide, executing
business demands, this radiant young lady, 30, slim, 170 cm, exceeds
any expectations you may have in view of marriage. An articulate,
educated, feminine & happy beauty who now seeks to start her own
family.

There is also the do-it-yourself approach to matchmaking for the independently minded. This sort of advertisement appeared in the national press in Israel under the classified heading 'Matchmaking' (again it's fictional but fairly typical):

Private (no matchmakers): Female lawyer, blue eyes, Ashkenazi, seeks
Ashkenazi academic between the ages of 50-59, for a serious
relationship.

When we were back in Scotland one summer, Chris and I enjoyed a trot through the lonely-hearts ads, although there were no mentions of marriage. My other half penned this possible entry:

Balding, middle-aged man with a slight paunch seeks female travelling
companion on similar medication in case of lost luggage when abroad.

Tempting?
Secular Israelis (who make up the vast majority of the population) meet in the normal way young people do. You know, in the army,

while flirting over automatic weapons sexily slung across shoulders at a jaunty angle. I'm only half joking. As young people sign up for national service and are fit, healthy and active, there's bound to be mutual attraction and relationships formed in the most difficult of circumstances, and many lasting relationships are made while performing national service in the IDF.

There are also cafés, bars, cinemas, theatres shopping malls and all the usual places where secular Israelis can meet and match themselves.

One thing you have to be very careful about is not to tell any fibs to your date, or you could find yourself under house arrest for two years and then handed an eighteen-month prison sentence. This was what happened to an Israeli Arab man who was found guilty of rape by deception. He'd encountered a female in the downtown area of Jerusalem, and as one does, within ten minutes of meeting, they were in a stairwell having sex. Sex which was acknowledged by the court to be consensual, if not entirely conventional. Subsequently the female found out that the defendant wasn't a Jewish bachelor, as she had supposed, but a married man who was an Arab with two kids. So it's possible to be guilty of rape by deception, a scary possibility.

'Your Honour, I would never have slept with him had I known that he was overdrawn. He paid for the meal with a gold credit card. Who knew, your Honour?'

'Your Honour, I would never have slept with her if I'd known she looked so ugly without her make-up. I tell you, I nearly died when I pulled back the covers in the morning. She looked like a victim in *CSI Miami*!'

If a married man says he is single and has an affair, that sounds like it could be rape by deception, and he could be banged up, if you know what I mean.

The world we live in can be a harsh and cruel place. It's necessary to exercise sound judgement at all times when heading to downtown Jerusalem for sex of an evening. The Israeli Arab who was imprisoned for date rape had his sentence cut to nine months, but the case was cloaked in controversy.

Many young secular Israeli couples choose to live together before marriage. This is completely different from most Arab societies.

There's no way a young Jordanian girl would get to live with her boyfriend before marriage there. If that ever happened in the eight years I lived in Jordan among locals and expatriates, I never heard of it. This is hardly surprising in a country where there are still honour killings of women for a lot less than moving in with a man. But that's a different story.

Orthodox Jewish courting couples aren't even permitted to be in a room alone together before marriage, and if they find themselves left in a room, the door must remain open at all times.

So the way in which the romance is conducted, and the living arrangements of young adults in Israel, very much depend on their religious beliefs and which end of the rainbow of Jewishness they perch on.

Although about twenty percent of the population of Israel is Israeli Arab, romantic relationships between Jews and Arabs are still taboo.

Assuming a good match is made and agreed by the families and the youngsters, the date has to be set. There are certain periods in the Jewish calendar when weddings are prohibited. The Sabbath is out, as are Jewish New Year, Yom Kippur, Passover, Shavuot and the first and last days of Sukkot. Weddings can also be held on the intervening days of Sukkot, Purim and during Hanukkah.

In the seven weeks from Passover to Shavuot, it's a time of mourning, but depending on the Jewish tradition observed by the families, there are numerous days which may be acceptable for weddings.

So it's essential to consult a rabbi before you set a date. Yet another case of booking early to avoid disappointment.

The marriage ceremony itself varies from the most lavish five-star hotel experience to the more modest rented hall with food, dancing and wine. There are constants in wedding celebrations. The majority of Jewish couples will get married under the chuppah or canopy which may be decorated with flowers and fabric. Every chuppah I've seen has been white. The canopy gives a private place for the couple but is symbolically open on all four sides, symbolising the home of Abraham and Sarah which was always open to guests. It's a great honour to be asked to hold one of the four chuppah poles.

The bride and groom may choose to marry at the beach or on a rooftop, in a hotel or in a rented wedding hall. There's also the symbolic breaking of glass to signify the demolition of the second temple. So even on the happiest of days, the past is very much remembered as the couple look towards their future together, united as one soul. It's become a trend for couples to collect the pieces of the broken glass and have them made into a piece of Judaica artwork for their new home.

There's a marriage contract, or *ketubah* (the literal meaning is written or writing) as it's known in Israel. This document is usually elaborately written and decorated and sets out the obligations of the groom towards the bride. It's passed to the bride at the ceremony. It's really a pre-nuptial agreement in its earliest form and covers the rights of the bride during and at the end of the marriage, whether by death or divorce. My favourite *ketubah* shop is aptly called Azoulay and is situated in Yoel Moshe Salomon Street, a lovely old narrow street of art shops, handmade jewellery stores, a unique toy store and artisans' studios. It's between Jaffa Street and Hillel Street for those of you who would like to order an interesting wedding gift.

Although the street is one of my favourites and full of character, it's a little smelly on a Friday morning. There really should be more public toilets in Jerusalem, and that might deter the nightclub revellers from relieving themselves at every street corner in this part of town. It's not unusual to be driving along, minding your own business and happily humming along to 'Hips Don't Lie', or in the case of the other grown-up, something of a classical ilk, when you're suddenly confronted by a man with his man bits out in full display, no modest hiding behind a bush, relieving himself unselfconsciously by the side of the road. Maybe I'm just too sensitive having lived so many years in the Arab world, where such behaviour would be frowned upon and likely end up with a jail sentence.

I'm reminded of Liberty's flatmate who was travelling with her mother and boyfriend on a long road trip. After a few hours, nature called, and the boyfriend insisted on a potty stop. He carefully selected some verdant foliage to hide behind before relaxing into full flow. His relief was brief as his future mother-in-law yelled, 'Dick, there aren't enough leaves on that bush!' (Names have been changed to protect the innocent.)

Under Jewish law the moment of marriage takes place when the groom places the ring on the bride's finger. Traditionally only the groom gives a ring as a sign of acquisition or possession of the bride. Nowadays couples may choose to exchange rings if the officiating rabbi agrees to this modification of tradition. It just depends how orthodox the ceremony is.

In ultra-orthodox wedding ceremonies, there's also a circling around the groom seven times by the bride, representing him at the centre of her life.

A husband's obligations under Jewish law are to provide food, clothes and sex, kosher sex of course. The general idea is that any sexual act that doesn't lead to the destruction of seed (ejaculation outside the vagina) is permissible. There are also the laws of Niddah (the Laws of Family Purity) which require a man not to touch his wife after the first signs of menstruation until the evening of seven clear days after menstruation stops. This is decreed to be a minimum separation of twelve days. Apart from the dates to be avoided in the Jewish calendar, the rhythm of the monthly menstrual cycle has to be taken into account when setting the wedding date. The date must be calculated carefully to ensure that the bride is not Niddah on the wedding night. Although sometimes that can be the least of the bride and groom's worries.

In her book *Unorthodox*, Deborah Feldman tells of a bride who needed emergency surgery after her groom ploughed on in the act of intercourse and missed his opening, so to speak. The bride required hospitalisation and a colostomy bag. Such is the inexperience and ignorance of some of the orthodox brides and grooms. Others are simply unable to consummate the marriage on the wedding night, as was the case in Deborah's example.

I've read that in the scriptures, it's only the act of intercourse itself which is forbidden, and that touching between man and wife is permissible. Rabbis have chosen to interpret the scriptures more strictly.

You may have heard of the orthodox sheet, the marital sheet with a hole in it so that the other bits of the bodies of husband and wife don't touch during the act of intercourse. I have no way of verifying whether this item of the bride's trousseau exists but have heard conflicting evidence. Some allege that the holy sheet story is merely a myth. However, in *The Rabbi's Daughter*, Reva Mann relates a conversation she had with Mrs Frankel, her matchmaker and guide on the laws of family purity, before she herself became an Orthodox Jewish bride.

Mrs Frankel tells Reva that the sexual union between man and wife through a sheet is practised only by some.

Jewish weddings are huge events, and there will be photographers. If it's a non-secular wedding, the crowd may be segregated so a male and female photographer will be needed, and there's often a video photographer to boot. There are also the usual speeches, food, drinks, gifts and so on.

On the occasion of the wedding of Prince William to Catherine Middleton on 29th April 2011, a British-born Israeli scribe sent them an unusual and gift. The handmade wedding contract written by him in Hebrew and English reportedly combined traditional language with 'egalitarian' and omitted references to religion, there being no known connection between the couple and the Jewish faith. It was hand-delivered to the British ambassador to Israel at the time, Matthew Gould. He in turn undertook to deliver it to the happy couple via the diplomatic bag. The contract, which takes the form of an illustrated scroll reads, 'May we remain committed to each other's physical and mental wellbeing, and to each other's emotional and spiritual growth.' This was an original and very thoughtful gift.

While the writer wasn't an ordained Jewish scribe, he had produced scrolls in the Jewish tradition for special occasions, beginning with his wedding.

It's not possible to have a valid non-religious wedding in the State of Israel. Jewish, Christian, Muslim and Druze religious weddings are recognised under Israeli law. The legal system doesn't recognise interfaith marriages, same-sex marriages and non-religious or civil marriages. It's possible to marry abroad and then register the wedding on return to Israel, but many Israelis object to travelling away from home to take their wedding vows.

Israel is renowned for its tolerance of same-sex relationships as witnessed by Tel Aviv's Gay Pride parade in June each year. Some are rather cynical about this inclusive policy and call it a 'pink wash', designed to distract attention from the occupation of the Palestinian Territories. Others couldn't possibly comment.

Talking about washing, I was preparing Morgan's school snack box one morning when he asked me if I was a biological or a non-biological mother.

'Well, if your clothes are really, really dirty, I'll use biological washing powder, but I usually use non-biological powder in case it irritates your skin.'

'No, that's not what I mean. My friend at school has a biological mother and a non-biological mother, and I just wondered which kind you are.'

At our lovely small school at the time, we had several same-sex parents, and one of the boys in Morgan's class did indeed have two wonderful mums. It had taken him almost an academic year to notice this. I explained that I was his biological mother and that his dad was his biological father.

'Can you prove that?' he wondered, 'perhaps with a birth video?'

'Absolutely not,' was the reply. There was no video camera or in fact any camera present when I was giving birth to Morgan. We don't even have a wedding video, but the memories of both days are happy, colourful and sharp. He wasn't convinced.

'Okay, do I have any non-biological relatives at all?' he asked flatly, as if we'd let him down.

After quite a bit of head scratching, I came up with Granny Barbs, who has always been Granny Barbs to our children but is a non-biological grandmother. Bingo! The conversation then moved on to the creation of a kosher sandwich for the lunch box.

So despite the difficulties in overcoming the legalities of a legal union in Israel, when the difficulties are overcome, my experience is that there's an open, accepting approach to a person's sexual partners, male or female, with the strict proviso of course that if one is Jewish, the other isn't Arab.

The bill of divorce in most societies is just too high to compute, in monetary and emotional terms. In Israel, the Jewish bill of divorce is called a 'get'. Jewish law stipulates there can only be a divorce if a husband gives his wife a get. If the husband refuses, she can't get married again, start or expand her family, and her life is basically on hold until the get is got.

Even in cases where a court orders the husband to give a get, the process of enforcing the court order can take years if the husband doesn't co-operate. There are moves to amend the law in this area to provide for sanctions against a husband who refuses to implement the ruling of the court. It remains to be seen whether the Knesset will pass this bill. This is a problem which affects the life of many Jewish women who are locked into legal marriages which are at an end.

Assuming the husband is willing to grant his wife a get, the divorce hearing will take place in a court presided over by three rabbis. The husband and wife or their court-appointed representatives must be physically present (there is no such thing as a postal divorce in Israel), along with two witnesses. Naturally the witnesses must be kosher, Torah-observant males who have reached the age of legal responsibility.

The get must be handwritten by a scribe and is prepared specifically for the divorce proceedings. There is no such thing as a pro-forma court document for filling in as part of this procedure.

In this area of life, as in others, life isn't easy for women in Israel.

On the other hand, it's a safe environment for women, and personal attacks are rare. I had friends who lived in town and walked home from restaurants or the homes of other friends after dark without a second thought. Young men and women hitchhiked day and night as a mode of transport for short and longer journeys. It's just what youngsters did to get around, and it was considered a safe and normal activity. We weren't permitted to pick up hitchhikers under our local rules of employment (presumably for security reasons). I always felt guilty when I drove past the young people hitching a lift to town from the security post at the entrance to our moshav.

DEATH, YAHRZEIT AND MEMORIALS

Death is part of life in Israel. The atrocities of the Holocaust have created the deepest of wounds, leaving a scar which is still painful to this day. As time goes on, there are fewer and fewer Holocaust survivors left in the world. It's a tribute to the people of Israel that there's a support service for those who need help and that there are those who are willing to reach out. Yom Kippur is said to be the hardest day of the year for Holocaust survivors. I can understand that. It's the holiest day in the Jewish calendar and the Day of Atonement, when all sins are repented and your name is written in the book of life for another year, if you're one of the lucky ones.

It's also a quiet day. There's no driving; there are no shops or restaurants open, and apart from visits to the synagogue for prayer, it's a day of reflection, fasting and prayer. The hardest days for those who have lost a loved one are those in the calendar which were and are still meaningful. Days such as birthdays for our family are difficult days and can be long and lonely. We often engage in frantic levels of activity to distract us from tragedies in our lives which cannot be changed and have to be accepted and lived with. This is true when a much-loved one dies of natural causes. I cannot imagine how it feels when generations of entire families have been wiped out deliberately. When the activities stop, even for a day, the memories and thoughts of the past flood back.

In the Goldstein Youth Village which houses the school Morgan attended, there's a particularly poignant memorial stone amid the beautiful grassy slopes where children run, play, laugh and tumble around every day.

A DONATION BY

TILIA SMEIL

IN MEMORY OF HER HUSBAND

MAXIMILLIAN SMEIL

AND HIS DAUGHTER

EVA SMEIL

WHO WAS EXTERMINATED AT AUSCHWITZ AT THE AGE OF 2

Since the Holocaust there have been wars and conflicts which have led to loss of life. There are regular skirmishes and all-out conflicts as a direct result of the military occupation of the Palestinian Territories, also leading to loss of life on both sides. There's such a recent history of war and conflict in Israel which combined with intifadas and suicide bombings, has led to a population who appear to be resigned to death as a part of life. This is the cost of living in Israel and Palestine at this time, with no peace in prospect.

So even when a life is tragically cut short, it's regarded as part of God's plan. In the Muslim faith, while there are tremendous and heartbreaking displays of grief laid bare at a funeral, the overriding belief is that death is the will of Allah.

Under Jewish law, all parts of the body must be buried and come in contact with the ground. So there are no cremations, and if there's a coffin, holes are drilled in it so that the body can come in touch with the soil.

There are religious Jews who perform the mitzvah of collecting body parts in the event of a suicide bombing. This is a mitzvah of the highest order as the dead cannot repay the person for his courageous and selfless deed.

While all body parts have to be buried in the ground, there's no prohibition against organ donation under Jewish law. The reasoning is that the donated organ will eventually be buried when the recipient of the donated organ dies.

In the Jewish faith, life is just as important as death, and so life must be preserved at all costs. Euthanasia, suicide and assisted suicide aren't permitted, and like the Hippocratic oath taken by medical doctors in the United Kingdom, there's a general obligation to strive to keep alive. I'm paraphrasing, but that's the gist of it. There comes a point when it's no longer necessary to strive if it's clear that the patient is dying. Then nothing must be done to shorten his or her life, but there's no need to intervene to keep the patient alive artificially.

After death, funerals take place fairly quickly, usually within a couple of days. In the Muslim faith, burial must take place within 24 hours of death.

The most famous Jewish burial site of all, the most sought-after cemetery for all Jews, is the Mount of Olives. Jews have been buried there from the days when Jesus visited the Mount until this day. To be buried there, you have to have a huge bank balance. In fact, you have to take a whole different approach to the Decker family philosophy of perfect long-term financial planning, the WLCTB Plan (the write-the-last-cheque-to-bounce plan).

Jews believe that when the Messiah rises and leads them into the temple again, those buried in the Mount of Olives will rise and follow him.

For this reason the Golden Gate to the Old City was sealed off by the Muslims to prevent the Messiah returning. This sealed entrance can only be seen from outside the Old City walls. There's a great view of the Golden Gate from the Gardens of Gethsemane, a downhill stroll from the Lion Gate towards the valley at the foot of the Mount of Olives.

There's another major spanner in the works to this optimistic plan of passing through the Golden Gate. In the meantime the Muslim population of the Old City of Jerusalem decided to bury its dead just in front of the Golden Gate, in the shadow of the Al-Aqsa Mosque. It's thought that it's a strong possibility that the newly risen Jewish followers of the Messiah wouldn't want to traipse back into the Old City through a Muslim graveyard. Fair point.

I'll share a cautionary tale. The Mount of Olives is in what's regarded as Arab East Jerusalem. So I was surprised to see a large Israeli flag fluttering in the breeze on the top of a substantial villa at one of the highest vantage points. A prime property if ever there was one.

'Why is there an Israeli flag flying in this part of town?' I asked Chris in all innocence.

'Well the Arab owner was made an offer he couldn't refuse and sold the house to an Israeli for millions of dollars.'

'That was a brave decision.' I voiced my misgivings out loud while scanning the surrounding houses, all clearly still in Arab owner occupation.

'Brave or stupid, he was murdered shortly after he did that deal,' I was told matter-of-factly.

It makes me think of an old Scots adage which is regularly quoted to justify excessive spending: there are no pockets in a shroud. It will also serve as a deterrent for anyone else who might be tempted to take the jackpot and sell out.

There's another large cemetery in West Jerusalem, near the Jerusalem Forest. It has lovely views, and I'm not sure why the views are important, but there's something just a bit comforting about the prospect of being laid to rest in a place with a good view. It would be better not to be laid to rest at all, but when the time comes, as it inevitably will, a decent view might help.

This place has become so full that a concrete multi-storey car park-like structure has been built alongside the original hillside site to house the concrete box which holds the remains of the departed. A bit like an NCP car park, except when you're parked in your space, you stay there.

After the burial the family enter a period of mourning for seven days known as shiva (the Hebrew word for seven). This is the time when visitors will call to the home of the deceased to pay respects and comfort the family. It's called sitting shiva.

After that there's a 30-day period (*shloshim*, which means 30 in

Hebrew) of further mourning during which mourners won't attend celebrations or parties and don't listen to music.

The last period of formal mourning is only observed on the loss of a parent. This period lasts for twelve months after the burial. During that time, mourners avoid parties, celebrations, concerts and other live performances of entertainment. For eleven months of that period, there's a daily recital of the mourner's prayer by the son of the deceased.

Maybe it's because there's been so much death, or because life can be so short and end abruptly without illness, that the Israeli Jews memorialise their dead like no other people I've come across.

Sports halls, wings of universities, hospital facilities, MRI machines, play parks and picnic areas are often dedicated to the memory of a named benefactor, or named in honour of the deceased person by surviving family members. At the world-famous Hadassah Medical centre in Ein Karem, walls and walls list the names of benefactors who enable the centre of medical excellence, research and innovation to function and excel.

When I was walking through the Jerusalem Forest, I came across a memorial stone:

Picnic Area

In memory of Ingrid Bergman Sweden

A great actress and an outstanding person

What is particularly touching is the yahrzeit celebration. Yahrzeit is a Yiddish word for anniversary, and it's usual, on the anniversary of the death of a loved one, to make a journey to the graveside to pray and to light candles. I know that in the Western world we have a form of yahrzeit when we visit a place which is meaningful in the memory of our loved one, or perhaps insert an in-memoriam message in the local or national press. However in Israel, the memorialising is taken one step further.

The memorial to President John F. Kennedy is an enormous

modern concrete structure which houses an eternal flame (it was out when we visited), but the site, on the top of a hillside, has panoramic views over green hillsides and is a place of peace, grace and beauty. Families visit to picnic in the surrounding gardens and to enjoy the breathtaking bird's-eye views.

Former President George W. Bush Jr has been remembered by the Jerusalemites of Israel, although he is still with us in body and spirit, even if he doesn't always pay attention in class. A small triangular garden has been planted at the end of Jaffa Street, just large enough to settle one bench.

Our time in Jerusalem is so memorable that the experiences we had, whether good and bad, will stay with us forever. Every time I see a bougainvillea in full bloom, I am back in our beautiful village, Beit Zayit.

MY READING LIST

The Rabbi's Daughter—Reva Mann

The Marrying of Chani Kaufman—Eve Harris

The Israelis—Donna Rosenthal

A Woman in Jerusalem—A.B. Yehoshua

A Tale of Love and Darkness—Amos Oz

Unorthodox—Deborah Feldman

Sharon and my Mother-in-Law—Suad Amiry

Jerusalem—Yotam Ottolenghi and Sami Tamimi (Cookery Book)

Mornings in Jenin—Susan Abulhawa

ACKNOWLEDGEMENTS

Thank you to our friends and neighbours for enriching our lives in Jerusalem and Palestine. You made our time there a joy and a learning curve in equal measure. I want to name you all, but you know who you are.

This book was written for family and friends so that we could share the amazing time we had in Jerusalem. Just as the book was finished, it was awarded non-fiction book of the year by The Scottish Association of Writers (SAW), and I dared to have a little ambition for its future and who might read it. So thank you to SAW for pushing me forward to publication.

Peter Lawrence (www.peterlawrence.uk), the British watercolourist, has been a family friend for decades, and I was thrilled when he agreed to paint the beautiful cityscape of Jerusalem for the cover. Thank you, Peter.

Thanks too to Jacky Donovan, my editor, for guiding me through the minefield of publishing. It's a whole new world to explore. Jacky, your interest in the subject, professionalism and support are invaluable. Thank you to all at Ant Press for showing me the way forward and for providing a clear path through the whole publishing process and beyond.

My writing time wouldn't be possible without the love and support of my husband, Chris, who has insisted on breaks for fun, food and fresh air when I have locked myself away. There have always been wine and treats in the fridge, and for that I am thankful.

Liberty and Morgan, you are in our hearts wherever we travel, and although you have spread your wings, we hope that you will always come home to roost. Amber, you are with us, always…